The Main Idea

The Main Idea
Reading to Learn

SECOND EDITION

Myrna Bigman Skidell
Sidney Graves Becker
Nassau Community College

ALLYN AND BACON
Boston   London   Toronto   Sydney   Tokyo   Singapore

Vice President, Humanities: Joseph Opiela
Editorial Assistant: Rebecca Ritchey
Marketing Manager: Lisa Kimball
Production Administrator: Rowena Dores
Editorial-Production Service: Sydney Baily-Gould, Saxon House Productions
Cover Administrator: Jennifer Hart
Composition Buyer: Linda Cox
Manufacturing Buyer: Suzanne Lareau

Library of Congress Cataloging-in-Publication Data

Skidell, Myrna Bigman
    The main idea : reading to learn / Myrna Bigman Skidell, Sidney
Graves Becker. — 2nd ed.
      p. cm.
    ISBN 0-205-28322-5 (pbk.)
    1. Reading (Higher education)—United States—Handbooks, manuals,
etc. 2. Developmental reading—United States—Handbooks, manuals,
etc. 3. Reading comprehension—United States—Handbooks, manuals,
etc. 4. College readers. I. Becker, Sidney Graves.
II. Title.
LB2395.3.S55   1999
428.4'071'1—dc21   98-15220
                                                CIP

Credits

Page 11. "Gloomy Outlook," from *NEA TODAY*, November 1993. Copyright © 1993, The
    Washington Post. Reprinted with permission. Page 23.
Page 12. "Give 'Em More," from *NEA TODAY*, November 1993. Copyright © 1993, by The
    National Education Association of the United States. Reprinted by permission. Page 23.

Credits continued on page 449, which constitutes an extension of the copyright page.

Printed in the United States of America

10 9 8 7 6 5 4 3 2 1   01 00 99 98

Contents

PART FOUR   Critical Reading

PART FIVE **Vocabulary**   **259**

12   *Applying Vocabulary Strategies*   *259*

Preface to the Instructor

The Main Idea: Reading to Learn, Second Edition, continues to provide a concise, clear plan designed to help developmental students to more successfully handle the demands of college reading. It is based on our combined knowledge of theory and many years of experience in the fields of reading and learning disabilities. Because the first edition of the book has been used by instructors across the country, as well as in our college, we have been able to keep what works best and to revise other content to most effectively meet the needs of developmental students.

The second edition continues to address the developmental reader's need for direct instruction in basic reading behaviors (which we call *strategies*) that are essential to the acquisition of knowledge in the content areas. *The Main Idea,* Second Edition, is more user friendly than the first edition because it has clearer explanations about and more examples of reading strategies. It also has new reading selections that were field-tested with our students and found to be interesting. Based on the comments of instructors who are using the first edition and our own continuing field testing of it, we have shortened some areas, such as previewing, and expanded others, such as organizing information. Specific instruction remains clear, brief, and consistent in all parts of the book. Learners are provided with opportunities to evaluate their use of the strategies. Metacognitive aspects of learning (selecting strategies appropriate to the task and evaluating their effectiveness) continue to be emphasized.

Unique Features of the Second Edition

- Reading is approached as a holistic, meaning-making task, with the reader as the center of the process. The lessons and accompanying activities are constructed to enable students to understand their reading behaviors and to respond appropriately to text-related questions.
- The language of instruction is concise and comprehensible. It is a dialogue that respects the student as a capable learner. In many sections, more explanation and examples have been added to help the student understand the use of strategic behaviors.
- The text even more strongly approximates a natural reading/writing/thinking process. Students are continually asked to think and write about what they read individually and with their peers.
- Strategic behaviors are contextualized. Students are frequently reminded to build on previous strategies to acquire more complex strategies. Additional activities have been added throughout the book that require application of strategies to college text and real-world materials.
- Direct skill instruction has been made even clearer and regrouped to provide more user-friendly clusters of strategies that we still call game plans. These reorganized and refined groups enable students to better understand what they are doing and, more important, why they are using the game plans.
- Many of the short reading selections have been changed, and many of the longer selections (many more than are found in most developmental texts) have been replaced with material from college texts so that students have numerous opportunities to work with materials that are found in content area courses.
- The critical reading section has been expanded and rewritten to better help the student understand and apply these valuable strategies to college-level materials.

We have written this book to bring out the best in pedagogy. We believe that instructors bring many unique traits to the teaching/learning process. Students have individualized needs and learning styles as well. There is enough variety of experience in the text to enable each instructor to effect the all-important match between teaching and learning styles. Thus, the entire text need not be covered over the course of a semester by the entire class.

Overview and Organization of Second Edition

The second edition of *The Main Idea* is organized to take advantage of what research has determined to be a proficient reader's process and what the users of the text have told us worked well and what needed revision. Thus, instruction is based on an interactive reading model in which reading becomes the tool that students use to understand and organize information that must be learned in college. The emphasis is on learning to learn and learning to respond to information in a variety of ways.

Because users agreed with our basic organization of the book into six main parts, they remain. However, there are now a total of thirteen chapters because we have moved "Five Methods to Learn New Words" to Appendix A. This allows instructors to use it when they think appropriate in the course or to assign individual work in it to those students who seem to need such practice. "Applying Vocabulary Strategies" now comes after instruction on reading college text material, as all the applications are from college texts.

Parts 1, 2, and 3 include the strategies and game plans students need to understand and interpret information **before, during,** and **after** they read. The explanations and examples of organizing information in Part 3, "After You Read," have been clarified and expanded. In addition, there are extensive new readings and more textbook excerpts to be used during application of the strategies. Part 4 focuses on critical reading and thinking. This very important aspect of preparing students to read successfully in college is extensively revised, based on reviewers' suggestions to include more instruction and practice in making inferences and in critical reading of college texts. In Part 5, students have the opportunity to practice applying vocabulary strategies to text from specific academic disciplines. This chapter can be used in this sequence or assigned periodically during the semester. Part 6 consists of themed reading about intergenerational relationships around the world. Four of the readings have been replaced with two selections about family issues from textbooks and two current intergenerational biographic selections. These readings offer instructors limitless opportunities to expand their students' social views and reading/writing/thinking proficiencies. There are now three appendices. Appendix A now contains the "Five Methods to Learn New Words." Appendix B, "Game Plan Review," which is very useful as a reference, and Appendix C, "Test-Taking Strategies," which students find particularly helpful, have been expanded and revised to match the changes in the text.

We have worked continuously to improve *The Main Idea* since it was first published. We have listened carefully to the comments, criticisms, and suggestions from our colleagues and our students. We think that this second edition will be a more useful and enjoyable book for you to use and that it will encourage your students to engage in the wonderful act of reading to learn.

Acknowledgments

We greatly appreciate the encouragement that we have received from our colleagues and students during the revision process. Nassau Community College always provides us with a laboratory in which to develop and test our materials. Dr. Sean Fanelli, the college president, and Dr. Jack Ostling, Vice President for Academic Affairs, as always were interested in and supportive of our work. All our colleagues in the Department of Reading and Basic Education were helpful. In particular, we are grateful to Carol Hunt, Barbara Levy, Margaret Shaw, Christine Berg, and James Farley.

We thank the following colleagues who reviewed the first edition after using it for their incisive commentary. The quality of this edition was greatly enhanced by the suggestions of Alison O. Lee, Merritt College; Hope Lieberman, Cincinnati State Technical and Community College; and Patricia Panitz, Cape Cod Community College.

Preface to the Student

We have written the second edition of this book to help you cope with the many reading demands of your college courses. We have made changes in the book based on the thoughtful comments of students taking a developmental reading course and on the useful suggestions of the instructors teaching those courses. We want you to use this book to improve your reading and study skills. We hope that the game plans that we have developed and revised will help you understand and remember what you read and study.

Reading is not a subject like history or psychology. It is a tool that will help you learn important information in any college course. This book shows you how to use this tool to your best advantage to become a better reader and thus a better student.

The Main Idea, Second Edition, is divided into six main parts, thirteen chapters, and three appendices. The first three parts deal with strategies to use **before, during,** and **after** you read. Each chapter explains the strategy you will learn, tells you why you should use it, and most important, explains how to use it. There are enough practice activities provided with each strategy so that you will feel as comfortable when you use it as you do your actual reading assignments in other courses.

Part 4, "Critical Reading," will help you develop your critical reading, thinking, and writing skills. Chapter 9 includes newspaper and magazine articles so that you will be able to analyze what you read daily. In this part of the book, you will also learn how to apply critical reading and writing strategies to your college texts.

Part 5 guides you in applying vocabulary strategies to actual college text material. If you are unsure of how to determine the meaning of a word, you can always refer to Appendix A, "Five Methods to Learn New Words."

Part 6, "Reading Selections," focuses on relationships between and among generations, which we call intergenerational relationships. We added four new selections to expand the variety of readings to include actual college text material and biographic selections, which our students particularly like to read. Reading and thinking about these selections will give you an opportunity to practice all the strategies that you have mastered in the text.

Appendix A contains strategies and opportunities to practice figuring out the meaning of unfamiliar words. It also includes methods that you can use to remember new and difficult vocabulary. Appendix B is a reference guide and summary of all the strategies that you have learned and used in this book. Appendix C consists of test-taking strategies that you will be able to use to successfully prepare for exams.

This book does not have a magic formula to improve your reading. However, if you use it, do the assignments, and apply the strategies to your other course work, you will most certainly become a better reader and as a result a more successful student. We hope that you will enjoy this book and benefit from the work that you do to improve your reading.

Questions

1. What do you expect from this course?

   _____

   _____

   _____

   _____

2. How might this book help you?

   _____

   _____

   _____

   _____

The Main Idea

PART ONE

BEFORE YOU READ

CHAPTER

1

Getting Started

Let us be honest. When you are given a reading assignment, what is the first thing you do? If you are like most students, you probably look at the title and then begin to read the first sentence of the first paragraph. Do you have a game plan (or a group of strategies) to help you understand what the reading will be about? Probably not.

Most students either have never heard of prereading strategies or do not know how important they are. These strategies take extra time, which most students do not think they have. Once you understand the strategies, however, they take just a few worthwhile moments that can save you valuable rereading time.

In this chapter, you will learn two prereading strategies:

1. Developing a mind-set
2. Previewing

When you have mastered these strategies, you will be able to understand and remember important information more easily.

Developing a Mind-Set

Think for a minute about the word *dog*. If you have one, you probably have positive feelings toward these animals and know a great deal about them. If, however, you were ever bitten by a dog, you might have negative feelings and not know, or want to know, much about dogs. These are two different mind-sets about a single subject.

We all have different mind-sets about different things or subjects depending on what we know or do not know about them.

When given a reading assignment, most successful readers think about what they already know about the topic or subject. Although you may not realize it, just looking at the title of a book, a textbook chapter, or a single reading selection will trigger something already in your mind about the subject.

In this section, you learn two ways to pinpoint what you already know, do not know, or might want to know about the subject or topic of a reading assignment.

Freewriting

You may be familiar with **freewriting** from your English classes. It means the same thing in reading. When you freewrite, you just write whatever comes to your mind about a subject. When you freewrite, you do not have to worry about organization, grammar, or spelling. All you have to do is write what you think about the subject.

Practice 1

*Below are some topics for you to **freewrite** about. Think about what you know, do not know, believe, or think about each topic and write whatever comes to your mind. It might seem strange at first. Do not worry. Just write!*

Example: *Reading*
I'll have to do it. Might not like it much. Never was too good but guess I'll learn. I wish that there was an easy way to do it. But I would like to get better. This course should be fine.

1. Friends: 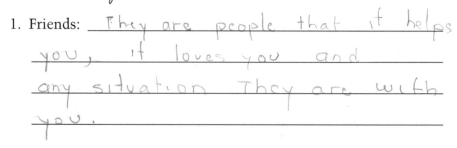 They are people that it helps you, it loves you and any situation They are with you.

2. Mathematics: _It is a signature very important. It has a many sections how aritmetic, algebra Geometry and-others._

3. Good moods, bad moods: _They are feelings. Good moods depending of your life's stile that you have it. They are parts our emotions_

Listing

If you do not feel comfortable freewriting, you can also develop a mind-set about the subject by making a **list** of everything you know, do not know, or might like to know. You **do not** have to **both freewrite and make a list.** Either one will give you a mind-set about the topic.

Practice 2

*Now **list** three things that you know or do not know about each topic.*

Example: *Reading*
1. *Must do*
2. *I'm going to learn*
3. *I think I like this course*

Money

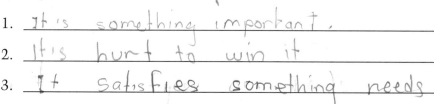

1. _It is something important._
2. _It is hurt to win it_
3. _It satisfies something needs_

AIDS

1. _It is expression._
2. _It is mean something it help_
3. _It is maybe other thing_

U.S. government

1. _It has a president._
2. _It has a group of Senators_
3. _It is Democratic._

College

1. _It is a high education's level_
2. _A few people go to college_
3. _It is too expensive in U.S._

Music

1. _It is Universal Language._
2. _There are many kind_
3. _It is a form of expression_

---

*Remember: **Freewriting** or **listing** what you know or do not know about a topic develops your mind-set for the reading.*

Previewing

What Is Previewing?

Previewing means to look over (or view) something beforehand. For example, if you are invited to preview a movie, you will see it before everyone else does. The word part *pre* means before, and the word *view* means to look at or see. When you preview reading material, you look it over quickly to get a general idea of what it is about before you actually read the text carefully.

Books are not written to confuse you. Each book is organized so that you can see how the topics and the information about the topics work together to help you understand the material.

Previewing gives you a quick idea of how hard or easy an assignment will be. When you preview, you begin to think about what you already know or may need to know about the subject. Previewing provides you with the big picture of what you will learn.

Previewing College Textbooks

All college textbooks have a great deal in common. They are published in an organized way with similar features, and each feature has a purpose. In most courses you will have at least one required textbook. As soon as you get it, you should preview it by using the following game plan:

The Title Page

Read the **title page** of any college textbook. Ask yourself: *What does the title tell me about this book? What do I think I can learn from this book?*

By reading the title page, you can tell what the subject of the book is and determine whether the book will be useful for you. The title page also tells you who wrote the book, who published the book, and what edition of the book you have. This is important because when there is more than one edition of a book, you will probably want the most recent one because that edition will contain the latest information about your subject.

Practice 3

Look at the titles below. What do you think the books will be about? Write your answer next to each title.

1. *Mathematics for Today:* ___I think this book___
   ___it's about numbers___

2. *The Art of Chinese Cooking:* ___This is a___
   ___book about cooking's recipes___

3. *First Impression–Best Impression:* ___I think___
   ___this book is about Personal's relationships___

4. *Out on a Limb:* _____

_____

_____

The Copyright Date

Turn over the title page. You will see the word *copyright* followed by a date. **Copyright** means that no person except the author may publish any of the information contained in the book without the author's and the publisher's permission. The most important thing about the copyright date is that it gives you a sense of how current the information is. If there is more than one date listed, you know when the book was first published, the dates of later editions, and the year in which the edition you have was published. Once you read these dates, you should be able to answer these questions:

1. When was the book first published?
2. Am I reading the most recent edition? If so, when was this edition published?

Look at any textbook that you have with you. Can you answer the above questions?

The Foreword or Preface

Find a book with a foreword (not all books have one) and read that section. The **foreword** is written by someone other than the author of the book. It tells you why this is an important book and gives you a little information about the author. Once you have read a foreword, you should be able to answer the question: *What does someone other than the author think is important about this book?*

The **preface,** written by the author of the book, tells you the author's reasons for writing the book and what he or she thinks is the main content of the book. It also includes a list of individuals who helped the author with the book (you may not have to read that part). Reading the preface helps you answer these questions:

1. Why did the author write the book?
2. What does the author say are the main ideas of the book?

Use one of your textbooks to answer the questions above.

The Introduction

The **introduction,** usually written by the author, tells you about the subject of the book, how it is organized, and what you might expect to learn when you read the book. If there is no preface, the author may also tell you the purpose of the book. After reading the introduction, you should be able to answer these questions:

1. What is the book about?
2. How is the book organized?
3. How can the book help me?

Read the introduction to one of your textbooks. Can you answer the above three questions?

The Table of Contents

The **table of contents** shows you how the text is organized. It lists the topics and subtopics that a book covers, indicates on what pages the different information can be found, and shows how the topics are related to each other. After looking through the table of contents of this or any other textbook, ask yourself:

1. *What topics and subtopics are covered?* The **topic** is the main subject of an article, a textbook chapter, or a whole textbook. A **subtopic** is a part of the main topic that is covered separately so that you are better able to understand the main topic. For example, the main topic, as well as the title, of Chapter 1 in this book is "Getting Started." The subtopics of this same chapter are "Developing a Mind-Set," "Previewing," and "Setting a Purpose for Reading." All the subtopics relate to the main topic because they are the steps that you need to take before you read.

2. *Do I generally know something about these topics, or will this information be mostly new learning?* Answer the above questions by looking at the table of contents of one of your textbooks.

The Index

The **index** is a guide to the information in the book. It lists, in alphabetical order, the topics and the people written about in the book. It is a handy reference when you are studying or writing papers. Not every book has an index.

Special Features

Glossary. The **glossary** is a mini dictionary that defines important words in the book. It is really helpful when you are studying. Again, check one of your texts and answer the question, *Does this book have a glossary?*

Appendix. This is additional information at the end of a book. The book is really complete without the **appendix,** but the author has added material that is related to the text. An appendix may contain charts, graphs, tables, or other visual aids that help you better understand the text.

Lastly, look for relationships among the parts of the book. This means that you should spend a few minutes thinking about how the book is organized and how you can use it to your best advantage. Ask yourself, *How can I make the best use of this book?*

Practice 4

*Now practice **previewing** this book that you are reading,* The Main Idea. *Reread the section "Previewing College Textbooks" to answer the following questions about the book.*

1. What is the title?

   The Main Idea Reading To
   Learn.

2. What does the title mean to you?

   That I going to learn how
   to read and Learn

3. When and where was this book published?

4. According to the authors, what will this book help you learn?

5. What are four main topics covered in this book?

a. _____

b. _____

c. _____

d. _____

6. Where in the book did you find this information?

_____

7. Does this book have an index? _____

A glossary? _____

8. What do you think you will learn from reading and using this book?

_____

_____

As you may have figured out by now, you can use these questions to preview any college textbook. Practice previewing another college textbook.

Review: Previewing a College Textbook

- Read the **title page:** *What do I think this book is about?*
- Check the **copyright date:** *Am I reading the most recent edition? When was it first published?*
- Read the **foreword** and/or **preface:** *What is important about this book?*
- Read the **introduction:** *How is this book organized?*
- Check the **table of contents:** *What topics and subtopics are covered in the book? Will this be mostly new to me?*
- Look for an **index, glossary,** or **appendix.**

Previewing Textbook Chapters

Previewing Visual Aids

Before you read a selection or a chapter, it is a good idea to "read" any pictures, illustrations, tables, graphs, or maps that are a part of the text. These are called **visual aids.** They are a clear, condensed presentation of important information that is written about in the text. Visual aids help you learn about the text before you actually read it. Knowing about the content of the text before you read makes understanding it easier.

To learn as much as you can from the visual presentation of information, you should read and ask questions. Use the following guidelines:

1. Read the title or caption (short explanation).
   Ask: *What is the topic?*
   Ask: *What does the visual aid show about the topic?*

2. Read the labels (headings of tables or graphs).
   Ask: *What do the vertical columns and horizontal rows represent?*
   Ask: *If there are numbers, are they in hundreds, thousands, or millions?*
   Ask: *If there is a legend (an explanatory caption), what does it explain?*

3. Think of general questions.
   Ask: *If I had to write one sentence to explain the visual aid, what would I write?*
   Ask: *If there are numbers in the visual aid, what do they represent or mean? What are the highest and lowest numbers or rates of increase or decrease? What appears to be the average number or rate? Is there a percent of increase or decrease? If so, what is it?*

"Read" the following **visual aids** and answer the questions about them.

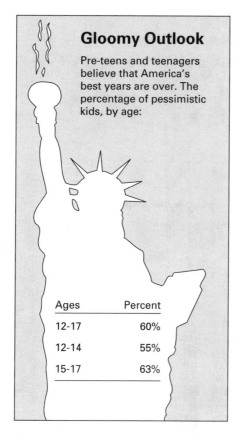

Gloomy Outlook

Pre-teens and teenagers believe that America's best years are over. The percentage of pessimistic kids, by age:

Ages	Percent
12-17	60%
12-14	55%
15-17	63%

Figure 1.1
Source: NEA TODAY, November 1993.

1. What is the title of this visual aid?

_____

2. What is the topic?

_____

_____

3. What percentage of all American teenagers believe that the country's best years are over?

_____

4. Do older or younger teenagers feel more pessimistic about the future of America?

_____

5. What would you expect to read about in the selection related to this figure?

_____

_____

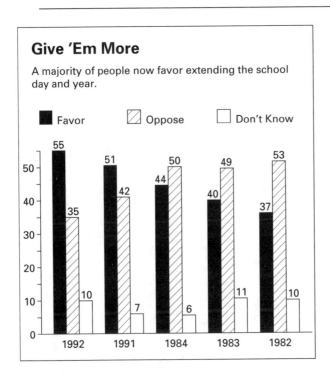

Figure 1.2
Source: NEA TODAY, November 1993.

1. What do the title and the caption tell you is the topic of the graph?

_____

_____

2. What do the title and the caption tell you about the topic?

_____

_____

_____

_____

3. What question do you think individuals were asked who participated in this survey?

_____

_____

4. What three responses could be given to the question asked?

_____

_____

_____

5. What do the numbers on the vertical column represent?

_____

6. List the years in which this question was asked.

_____

7. What trend (movement in a certain direction) can be seen in this graph?

_____

_____

_____

8. In what year was opposition to the extended school year at its peak?

_____

9. In what year did most people begin to favor the extended school day and year?

_____

10. What do you think could be the cause of the change in people's response to this question?

_____

_____

_____

_____

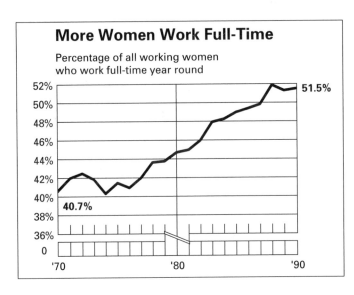

Figure 1.3
Source: USA TODAY, March 11, 1992.

1. What is the topic of this chart?

_____

_____

2. What does the chart tell you about the topic?

_____

_____

_____

3. What do the numbers in the vertical column represent?

   _____

4. What do the numbers in the horizontal row represent?

   _____

   _____

5. Write one sentence that explains this chart.

   _____

   _____

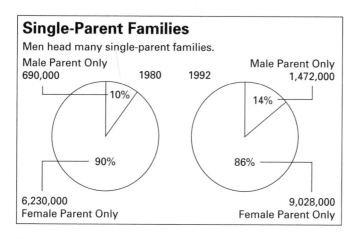

Figure 1.4
Source: NEA TODAY, November 1993.

1. What does the caption under the title of this pie graph tell you about single-parent families?

   _____

   _____

2. What percentage of single-parent families were headed by a male in 1980? _____ in 1992? _____ What is the percentage of increase? _____

3. What percentage of single-parent families were headed by a woman in 1980? _____ in 1992? _____ What is the percentage of decrease? _____

4. How many single-parent families were there in 1980? _____ in 1992? _____ How many more single-parent families were there in 1992 than in 1980? _____

5. Write one sentence that explains this pie graph.

_____

_____

_____

6. Would you predict that the number of single-parent families would increase or decrease by the year 2000?

_____

Why?

_____

_____

_____

Practice 6

*After you examine the next two **visual aids**, work with a group of your classmates to do the three exercises below.*

1. Create two specific questions about each one.

2. Create two thinking questions about each one. Do not ask what the topic is or what it is about. Use the information in the visual aid to challenge your classmates.

3. Exchange questions with another group and answer their questions.

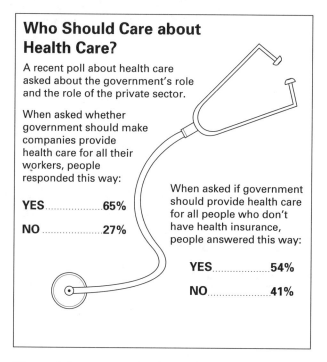

Who Should Care about Health Care?

A recent poll about health care asked about the government's role and the role of the private sector.

When asked whether government should make companies provide health care for all their workers, people responded this way:

YES................**65%**

NO **27%**

When asked if government should provide health care for all people who don't have health insurance, people answered this way:

YES................**54%**

NO..................**41%**

Figure 1.5
Source: NEA TODAY, November 1993.

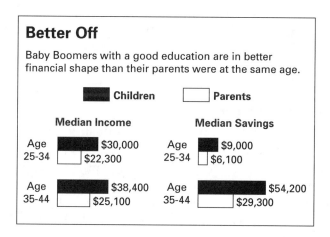

Better Off

Baby Boomers with a good education are in better financial shape than their parents were at the same age.

■ **Children**   □ **Parents**

Median Income

Age 25-34 $30,000
            $22,300

Age 35-44 $38,400
            $25,100

Median Savings

Age 25-34 $9,000
            $6,100

Age 35-44 $54,200
            $29,300

Figure 1.6
Source: NEA TODAY, November 1993.

2

Getting Started with Reading Selections

Sometimes you are given a selection to read that is not in your textbook but has important information that is related to your course work. Most successful readers skim or scan the selection to get an overview of the main points before actually reading it. If you take a few minutes to apply the following **preview strategy,** you will get the "big picture" of the information in the reading.

- Read the title.
- Read the headings, if there are any; some readings will have headings and others will not.
- Read the introduction. This will probably be the first paragraph; it might not be called the introduction.
- Read the first sentence of each paragraph. In a well-organized reading, the first sentence of each paragraph tells you what the paragraph will be about. This part of your preview strategy is extremely important if the reading does not have headings.
- Read the last paragraph. This usually ties the reading together or is a summary of the selection.

Ask yourself the following questions:

1. What is this selection about?
2. What can I expect to learn from it?

Some students find it helpful to highlight their preview. Others do not. Use the preview strategy in a way that will help you to understand the reading.

Practice 1

*Preview the following reading selection. Be sure to develop a mind-set about it either by **freewriting** or by **listing** any information that comes to mind from the title.*

1. Freewrite or list about the title "Lost in a Vitamin Maze?"

2. Answer the following preview questions about "Lost in a Vitamin Maze?"

   a. What is this selection about?

   b. What kind of information do you think this article gives you?

   c. How did the headings help your preview?

   d. How did the mind-set (the information) that you already had about vitamins help your preview?

Lost in a Vitamin Maze?

Multivitamins, natural vitamins, chelated minerals, stress-reducing supplements, "animal packs" (prepackaged megadoses)—a stroll down the aisle of your local drugstore is like a trip to an unfriendly planet. Although Americans spend more than $6.6 million a day on vitamins and minerals, with 40 percent of us taking some sort of supplement, according to Food and Drug Administration (FDA) surveys, most of us don't have a clue as to what we're getting. 1

"For too long, health officials have failed to view vitamin supplements seriously and to offer adequate guidance, so it's not surprising that so many consumers end up buying the wrong ones," says Bonnie Liebman, director of nutrition for the Center for Science in the Public Interest, a Washington, D.C., consumer advocacy group. 2

Even all the right vitamins in all the right doses don't add up to a sure thing, nutritionally speaking. But once you sort the myths from the facts and consider the promise vitamin supplementation holds for disease prevention, it is likely you'll conclude that vitamins don't hurt and may help more than we now know. 3

The myths

Among the most common misconceptions about vitamin supplements is that they will give you a quick energy boost. Vitamins and minerals can oil the body's engine, but only calories provide the fuel that generates energy. And contrary to what many people believe, supplements have never been shown to relieve emotional stress or to counteract its physical effects. "This idea is a gross misinterpretation of the evidence demonstrating that your vitamin needs may increase when you suffer an extreme physical trauma, such as major surgery," says Liebman. Claims that certain kinds of nutrients can increase virility, control thyroid functioning or improve athletic prowess are, to date, simply not backed by any solid scientific evidence. 4

The facts

For the vast majority of Americans, the fact that vitamin supplements prevent such malnutrition-related diseases as scurvy, beriberi and rickets is almost irrelevant. But supplements do counter several first-world health problems. Iron deficiency is common among women with heavy menstrual periods and can usually be counteracted with an iron supple- 5 ment of 18 mg or more a day (the main drawback of taking iron is that it often causes constipation, so users should be diligent about eating high-fiber foods). The evidence that calcium supplements (800 to 1,200 mg a day) are a good way to reduce the likelihood of osteoporosis is generally well accepted, too.

And even those nutritionists with a strong antisupplement bias, who believe we get all the vitamins and minerals we need from food, agree that certain groups of people run the risk of being deficient in certain nutrients if they don't supplement: Women on oral contraceptives need vitamins B6 and folic acid; smokers should take vitamin C; women who are pregnant or breastfeeding need to up their intake of the whole spectrum of vitamins and minerals; and people who diet rigorously (eating fewer than 1,500 calories a day) should also take a multivitamin. 6

The promise

The future of vitamins, many researchers believe, lies in the study of supplements as disease-fighting antioxidants—in particular, vitamins E and C, and beta carotene (from which vitamin A is derived). Although the findings are still preliminary, studies show that vitamin supplementation can lower one's risk of developing heart disease, cancer, and cataracts, and that it may even retard aging. The thinking is that antioxidants steel the body against disease-promoting and age-accelerating "free radicals" in our cells. 7

The best strategy

Consider the facts as well as the theories about vitamins and minerals, and it's clear that the risks in taking supplements are extremely low, the potential rewards high. But bear in mind that to reap the benefits of vitamins and minerals, you must commit. "You have to take supplements consistently for years—for life, really—to maximize the potential benefit," says Jeffrey Blumberg, Ph.D., associate director of the U.S. Department of Agriculture Human Nutrition Research Center on Aging at Tufts University in Boston. "And in the doses we're talking about, there's no risk of toxicity." 8

Until recently, nutritionists were concerned that in advising the public to take vitamins regularly they risked sending the message that diet wasn't so important. That attitude is beginning to change. "I don't think people are incapable of handling two messages at once—one, to eat a well-balanced diet and two, to supplement," says Dr. Blumberg. 9

Here, then, is what experts in favor of supplementing   10
generally recommend. Each day, along with eating a healthy
diet, take:

- a multivitamin/mineral that provides 100 percent of the   11
  RDAs
- 100 to 400 mg of vitamin E, 500 micrograms of beta carotene for additional antioxidant benefits, keeping in mind
  that taking any higher doses of these supplements is un-
  likely to confer any additional benefit and could be harmful.

—Janis Graham

Practice 2

Preview the following reading selection. Develop a mind-set about it either by freewriting or by listing any information that comes to mind from the title.

1. Freewrite or list about the title "Spread the Mood."

   The title it give me the idea
   about I can spread my
   good feeling.

2. Answer the following preview questions about "Spread the Mood."

   a. What is this selection about?

   It's about the mood

   b. What kind of information do you expect to learn?

   I expect it tells something
   about the feelings

c. Explain how the absence of headings helped or hindered your preview.

_____

_____

_____

Spread the Mood

Something about being around Andrew always puts Sarah in a good mood. One gray Sunday morning, for example, she was battling the blues when, quite by accident, she bumped into him on the sidewalk. Over an impromptu brunch, he raised his Bloody Mary glass and, with typical theatrical flourish, toasted the richness of life. "I can't bear it," he declared. "Let's buy something." 1

Although the last thing Sarah needed was another pair of blue jeans, she found herself being swept along in search of the nearest Gap. Later, when she was alone and as Andrew's happy influence gave way to the sobriety of Sunday night, Sarah thought to herself, Why did I buy these? I can't even fit them into my closet. But those mundane thoughts were quickly supplanted by the realization that, thanks to Andrew, never had such a banal transaction brought her such pleasure. 2

Andrew's uncanny ability to raise the spirits of those around him typifies a psychological phenomenon we all recognize from our personal experience, but which human-behavior experts have only recently begun to comprehend: Emotions, like colds and flus, are contagious. Researchers are also finding that while we can all be both transmitters and receivers, some people, such as Andrew, have a natural tendency to beam their moods, while others—women in particular—may be more susceptible to catching emotions. 3

Although the study of mood contagion is relatively new, interest in the "group mind" and the "madness" of crowds dates back to the late 1800s. We know, for instance, that in the wake of the Black Plague, frantic dancing manias swept through Europe; that in Malaysia, entire communities have fallen prey to contagious depression; that in East Africa, hysterical laughter and crying once overcame portions of the population; and that in the New Guinea highlands there have been mass expressions of anger, giddiness and sexual acting out. Yet whether it's in a primitive culture or a modern-day 4 society, the purpose of mood contagion appears to be the same: to bring kindred spirits together while subtly separating those who are not compatible.

Now, thanks in part to computers and other technological advances, researchers are finding scientific substantiation for their observations, and "the whole study of contagion and emotions is exploding," says Elaine Hatfield, Ph.D., a University of Hawaii psychologist. For example, researchers now know that the transmission of moods occurs via split-second mimicry, when one person unconsciously imitates the facial expressions, posture and tone of voice of another. It's through the mimicry that the person comes to feel as her model feels. "It's totally unconscious, and it's amazing how fast it happens," says Dr. Hatfield. Even the lightning-quick Muhammad Ali needed a minimum of 190 milliseconds to see a flash of light and an additional 40 milliseconds to throw a punch in response to the light. Yet studies have shown it takes college students only 21 milliseconds to synchronize their movements. Hatfield first noticed the unconscious interplay of moods during her therapy sessions. "A client might be saying that everything was going well, while I was picking up anger, anxiety or some other mood that contradicted what he or she was telling me," she says. "I also noticed that if a client was depressed, it was hard for me to work with that person because I would lose energy and get depressed myself. Certainly what I was experiencing was a paler version of the client's emotion, but mood contagion is really quite powerful." 5

So powerful, in fact, that psychologists say understanding how moods are passed from one person to another might help explain how a mediocre baseball team can suddenly come from behind to win the championship, or why creative energy at the office inexplicably increases when a new boss is brought in or why a weaker army is able to defeat a seemingly more powerful fighting force. It might even serve as an accurate predictor of long-term compatibility in relationships. 6

Emotional rapport—whether people feel awkward or comfortable together—depends in large measure on how well orchestrated their physical movements are according to Frank Bernieri, Ph.D., a psychologist at Oregon State University in Corvallis. "It's not a reactive thing, like watching well-matched tennis players; it's more of a togetherness, an anticipatory thing, like dancing," he says. "When things click, you don't have to think about where you are going or what you are doing. It happens simultaneously and in unison." 7

Researchers agree that there is no way, short of keeping your distance, to inoculate yourself against someone else's 8 moods, and the more intimate you are with a person, the harder it is to shield yourself. However, Chris Hsee, a Yale University graduate student who conducted moods contagion experiments with Hatfield, believes Bernieri is taking the best approach. "If you can somehow convince yourself that the other person's mood has nothing to do with you, then you are less likely to be vulnerable," he says.

Just who is more likely to pass along emotions and who   9
is more apt to pick up somebody else's moods is still open to question. Evidence suggests, however, that the more emotionally expressive and charismatic a person is, the more likely she is to be a mood transmitter, whereas highly sensitive people who sweat easily, whose hearts flutter, and whose stomachs churn are more likely to be swayed by the moods of others. "A television evangelist, for example, is a 'high synchronizer,'" Bernieri says. "You can see the audience swaying to his rhythms and picking up on his emotions." Women, however, tend to be more accurate perceivers of nonverbal communication, which may make them more vulnerable to other people's moods.

The advantage to those who are sensitive to another's   10
moods is that these nonverbal clues don't lie. So the next time your boyfriend or husband tells you everything is terrific—but you're feeling worse and worse about the relationship—trust your emotions rather than his words. You've probably just caught his real mood.

—Jennifer Kaylin

Questions about the Preview Selections

1. Now that you have previewed both selections, which one do you think is easier to read?

   Lost in a vitamin Maze?

   Why?

   The language used it is more

   easy.

2. How did your preview help you make up your mind?

   It let me got an idea of the

Practice 3

Preview the following selection. **Freewrite** or **list** any information that you have about the topic of the reading. There is space at the end of the selection to write down the new information that you learned from your previews.

1. Freewrite or list about the title "Death and Justice."

_____

_____

_____

_____

Death and Justice

Last December a man named Robert Lee Willie, who   1
had been convicted of raping and murdering an 18-year-old
woman, was executed in a Louisiana state prison. In a statement issued several minutes before his death, Mr. Willie
said: "Killing people is wrong. . . . It makes no difference
whether it's citizens, countries, or governments. Killing is
wrong." Two weeks later in South Carolina, an admitted
killer named Joseph Carl Shaw was put to death for murdering two teenagers. In an appeal to the governor for clemency,
Mr. Shaw wrote: "Killing was wrong when I did it. Killing is
wrong when you do it. I hope you have the courage and the
moral strength to stop the killing."

It is a curiosity of modern life that we find ourselves   2
being lectured on morality by cold-blooded killers. Mr. Willie
previously had been convicted of aggravated rape, aggravated
kidnapping, and the murders of a Louisiana deputy and a man
from Missouri. Mr. Shaw committed another murder a week
before the two for which he was executed, and admitted mu-
tilating the body of a 14-year-old girl he killed. I can't help
wondering what prompted these murderers to speak out
against killing as they entered the death-house door. Did

their newfound reverence for life stem from the realization that they were about to lose their own?

Life is indeed precious, and I believe the death penalty helps to affirm this fact. Had the death penalty been a real possibility in the minds of these murderers, they might well have stayed their hand. They might have shown moral awareness before their victims died, and not after. Consider the tragic death of Rosa Velez, who happened to be home when a man named Luis Vera burglarized her apartment in Brooklyn. "Yeah, I shot her," Vera admitted. "She knew me, and I knew I wouldn't go to the chair." 3

During my 22 years in public service, I have heard the pros and cons of capital punishment expressed with special intensity. As a district leader, councilman, congressman, and mayor, I have represented constituencies generally thought of as liberal. Because I support the death penalty for heinous crimes of murder, I have sometimes been the subject of emotional and outraged attacks by voters who find my position reprehensible or worse. I have listened to their ideas. I have weighed their objections carefully. I still support the death penalty. The reasons I maintain my position can be best understood by examining the arguments most frequently heard in opposition. 4

(1) *The death penalty is "barbaric."* Sometimes opponents of capital punishment horrify with tales of lingering death on the gallows, of faulty electric chairs, or of agony in the gas chamber. Partly in response to such protests, several states such as North Carolina and Texas switched to death by lethal injection. The condemned person is put to death painlessly, without ropes, voltage, bullets, or gas. Did this answer the objections of death penalty opponents? Of course not. On June 22, 1984, *The New York Times* published an editorial that sarcastically attacked the new "hygienic" method of death by injection, and stated that "execution can never be made humane through science." So it's not the method that really troubles opponents. It's the death itself they consider barbaric. 5

Admittedly, capital punishment is not a pleasant topic. However, one does not have to like the death penalty in order to support it any more than one must like radical surgery, radiation, or chemotherapy in order to find necessary these attempts at curing cancer. Ultimately we may learn how to cure cancer with a simple pill. Unfortunately, that day has not yet arrived. Today we are faced with the choice of letting the cancer spread or trying to cure it with the methods available, methods that one day will almost certainly be considered barbaric. But to give up and do nothing would be far 6 more barbaric and would certainly delay the discovery of an eventual cure. The analogy between cancer and murder is imperfect, because murder is not the "disease" we are trying to cure. The disease is injustice. We may not like the death penalty, but it must be available to punish crimes of cold-blooded murder, cases in which any other form of punishment would be inadequate and, therefore, unjust. If we create a society in which injustice is not tolerated, incidents of murder—the most flagrant form of injustice—will diminish.

(2) *No other major democracy uses the death penalty.* 7
No other major democracy—in fact, few other countries of any description—is plagued by a murder rate such as that in the United States. Fewer and fewer Americans can remember the days when unlocked doors were the norm and murder was a rare and terrible offense. In America the murder rate climbed 122 percent between 1963 and 1980. During that same period, the murder rate in New York City increased by almost 400 percent, and the statistics are even worse in many other cities. A study at M.I.T. showed that based on 1970 homicide rates a person who lived in a large American city ran a greater risk of being murdered than an American soldier in World War II ran of being killed in combat. It is not surprising that the laws of each country differ according to differing conditions and traditions. If other countries had our murder problem, the cry for capital punishment would be just as loud there as it is here. And I dare say that any other major democracy where 75 percent of the people supported the death penalty would soon enact it into law.

(3) *An innocent person might be executed by mistake.* 8
Consider the work of Adam Bedau, one of the most implacable foes of capital punishment in this country. According to Mr. Bedau, it is "false sentimentality to argue that the death penalty should be abolished because of the abstract possibility that an innocent person might be executed." He cites a study of the 7,000 executions in this country from 1893 to 1971, and concludes that the record fails to show that such cases occur. The main point, however, is this. If government functioned only when the possibility of error didn't exist, government wouldn't function at all. Human life deserves special protection, and one of the best ways to guarantee that protection is to assure that convicted murderers do not kill again. Only the death penalty can accomplish this end. In a recent case in New Jersey, a man named Richard Biegenwald was freed from prison after serving 18 years for murder; since his release he has been convicted of committing four murders. A prisoner named Lemuel Smith, who, while serving four life sentences for murder (plus two life sentences for kid-

napping and robbery) in New York's Green Haven Prison, lured a woman corrections officer into the chaplain's office and strangled her. He then mutilated and dismembered her body. An additional life sentence for Smith is meaningless. Because New York has no death penalty statute, Smith has effectively been given a license to kill.

But the problem of multiple murder is not confined to the nation's penitentiaries. In 1981, 91 police officers were killed in the line of duty in this country. Seven percent of those arrested in the cases that have been solved had a previous arrest for murder. In New York City in 1976 and 1977, 85 persons arrested for homicide had a previous arrest for murder. Six of these individuals had two previous arrests for murder, and one had four previous murder arrests. During those two years the New York police were arresting for murder persons with a previous arrest for murder on the average of one every 8.5 days. This is not surprising when we learn that in 1975, for example, the median time served in Massachusetts for homicide was less than two-and-a-half years. In 1976 a study sponsored by the Twentieth Century Fund found the average time served in the United States for first degree murder is ten years. The median time served may be considerably lower. 9

(4) *Capital punishment cheapens the value of human life.* On the contrary, it can be easily demonstrated that the death penalty strengthens the value of human life. If the penalty for rape were lowered, clearly it would signal a lessened regard for the victims' suffering, humiliation, and personal integrity. It would cheapen their horrible experience, and expose them to an increased danger of recurrence. When we lower the penalty for murder, it signals a lessened regard for the value of the victim's life. Some critics of capital punishment, such as columnist Jimmy Breslin, have suggested that a life sentence is actually a harsher penalty for murder than death. This is sophistic nonsense. A few killers may decide not to appeal a death sentence, but the overwhelming majority make every effort to stay alive. It is by exacting the highest penalty for the taking of human life that we affirm the highest value of human life. 10

(5) *The death penalty is applied in a discriminatory manner.* This factor no longer seems to be the problem it once was. The appeals process for a condemned prisoner is lengthy and painstaking. Every effort is made to see that the verdict and sentence were fairly arrived at. However, assertions of discrimination are not an argument for ending the death penalty but for extending it. It is not justice to exclude everyone from the penalty of the law if a few are found to be so favored. Justice requires that the law be applied equally to all. 11

(6) *Thou Shalt Not Kill.* The Bible is our greatest source 12
of moral inspiration. Opponents of the death penalty frequently cite the sixth of the Ten Commandments in an attempt to prove that capital punishment is divinely proscribed.
In the original Hebrew, however, the Sixth Commandment
reads, "Thou Shall Not Commit Murder," and the Torah specifies capital punishment for a variety of offenses. The biblical
viewpoint has been upheld by philosophers throughout history. The greatest thinkers of the 19th century—Kant, Locke,
Hobbes, Rousseau, Montesquieu, and Mill—agreed that natural law properly authorizes the sovereign to take life in order
to vindicate justice. Only Jeremy Bentham was ambivalent.
Washington, Jefferson, and Franklin endorsed it. Abraham
Lincoln authorized executions for deserters in wartime.
Alexis de Tocqueville, who expressed profound respect for
American institutions, believed that the death penalty was in-
dispensable to the support of social order. The United States
Constitution, widely admired as one of the seminal achievements in the history of humanity, condemns cruel and inhu-
man punishment, but does not condemn capital punishment.

(7) *The death penalty is state-sanctioned murder.* This 13
is the defense with which Messrs. Willie and Shaw hoped to
soften the resolve of those who sentenced them to death. By
saying in effect, "You're no better than I am," the murderer
seeks to bring his accusers down to his own level. It is also a
popular argument among opponents of capital punishment,
but a transparently false one. Simply put, the state has rights
that the private individual does not. In a democracy, those
rights are given to the state by the electorate. The execution
of a lawfully condemned killer is no more an act of murder
than is legal imprisonment an act of kidnapping. If an individual forces a neighbor to pay him money under a threat of
punishment, it's called extortion. If the state does it, it's
called taxation. Rights and responsibilities surrendered by
the individual are what give the state its power to govern.
This contract is the foundation of civilization itself.

Everyone wants his or her rights, and will defend them 14
zealously. Not everyone, however, wants responsibilities, especially the painful responsibilities that come with law
enforcement. Twenty-one years ago a woman named Kitty
Genovese was assaulted and murdered on a street in New
York. Dozens of neighbors heard her cries for help but did
nothing to assist her. They didn't even call the police. In such
a climate the criminal understandably grows bolder. In the
presence of moral cowardice, he lectures us on our supposed
failings and tries to equate his crimes with our quest for
justice.

The death of anyone—even a convicted killer—diminishes us all. But we are diminished even more by a justice system that fails to function. It is an illusion to let ourselves believe that doing away with capital punishment removes the murderer's deed from our conscience. The rights of society are paramount. When we protect guilty lives, we give up innocent lives in exchange. When opponents of capital punishment say to the state: "I will not let you kill in my name," they are also saying to murderers: "You can kill in your *own* name as long as I have an excuse for not getting involved." 15

It is hard to imagine anything worse than being murdered while neighbors do nothing. But something worse exists. When those neighbors shrink back from justly punishing the murderer, the victim dies twice. 16

—Edward Koch

What did you learn from your preview of "Death and Justice"?

I learned some reason why
capital punishment is unfair.

Practice 4

Preview the following selection. **Freewrite** *or* **list** *any information that you already know about the topic of the reading. There is space at the end of the selection to write down the new information that you learned from your previews.*

1. Freewrite or list about the title "I'm Listening as Hard as I Can."

I'm Listening as Hard as I Can

At the age of twelve I won the swimming award at the Lions Camp for Crippled Children. When my name echoed over the PA system the girl in the wheelchair next to me grabbed the box speaker of my hearing aid and shouted, "You won!" My ear quaking, I took the cue. I stood up straight— the only physically unencumbered child in a sea of braces and canes—affixed a pained but brave grin to my face, then limped all the way to the stage. 1

Later, after the spotlight had dimmed, I was overcome with remorse, but not because I'd played the crippled heroine. The truth was that I was ashamed of my handicap. I wanted to have something more visibly wrong with me. I wanted to be in the same league as the girl who'd lost her right leg in a car accident; her artificial leg attracted a bevy of awestruck campers. I, on the other hand, wore an unwieldy box hearing aid buckled to my body like a dog halter. It attracted no one. Deafness wasn't, in my eyes, a blue-ribbon handicap. Mixed in with my envy, though, was an overwhelming sense of guilt; at camp I was free to splash in the swimming pool, while most of the other children were stranded at the shallow end, where lifeguards floated them in lazy circles. But seventeen years of living in the "normal" world has diminished my guilt considerably, and I've learned that every handicap has its own particular hell. 2

I'm something of an anomaly in the deaf world. Unlike most deaf people, who were either born deaf or went deaf in infancy, I lost my hearing in chunks over a period of twelve years. Fortunately I learned to speak before my loss grew too profound, and that ability freed me from the most severe problem facing the deaf—the terrible difficulty of making themselves understood. My opinion of deafness was just as biased as that of a person who can hear. I had never met a deaf child in my life, and I didn't know how to sign. I imagined deaf people to be like creatures from beyond: animal-like because their language was so physical, threatening because they were unable to express themselves with sophistication—that is, through speech. I *could* make myself understood, and because I had a talent for lipreading it was easy for me to pass in the wider world. And for most of my life that is exactly what I did—like a black woman playing white, I passed for something other than what I was. But in doing so I was avoiding some very painful facts. And for many years I was inhibited not only by my deafness but my own idea of what it meant to be deaf. 3

My problems all started when my mother, seven months pregnant with me, developed a serious kidney infec- 4 tion. Her doctors pumped her full of antibiotics. Two months later I was born, with nothing to suggest that I was anything more or less than a normal child. For years nobody knew that the antibiotics had played havoc with my fetal nervous system. I grew up bright, happy, and energetic.

But by the time I was ten I knew, if nobody else did, that 5 something somewhere had gone wrong. The people around me had gradually developed fuzzy profiles, and their speech had taken on a blurred and foreign character. But I was such a secure and happy child that it didn't enter my mind to question my new perspective or mention the changes to anyone else. Finally, my behavior became noticeably erratic—I would make nonsensical replies to ordinary questions or simply fail to reply at all. My teachers, deciding that I was neither a particularly creative child nor an especially troublesome one, looked for a physical cause. They found two: I wasn't quite as blind as a bat, but I was almost as deaf as a doornail.

My parents took me to Wilford Hall Air Force Hospital 6 in San Antonio, where I was examined form ear to ear. My tonsils were removed and studied, ice water was injected into my inner ear, and I underwent a series of inexplicable and at times painful exploratory tests. I would forever after associate deafness with kind attention and unusual punishment. Finally a verdict was delivered: "Congenital interference has resulted in a neural disorder for which there is no known medical or surgical treatment." My hearing loss was severe and would grow progressively worse.

I was fitted with my first hearing aid and sent back home 7 to resume my childhood. I never did. I had just turned twelve, and my body was undergoing enormous changes. I had baby fat, baby breasts, hairy legs, and thick pink cat-eye glasses. My hearing aid was about the size of a small transistor radio and rode in a white linen pouch that hit exactly at breast level. It was not a welcome addition to my pubescent woe.

As a vain child trapped in a monster's body, I was fran- 8 tic for a way to survive the next few years. Glimpsing my reflection in mirrors became such agony that I acquired a habit of brushing my teeth and hair with my eyes closed. Everything I did was geared to making my body more inhabitable, but I only succeeded in making it less so. I kept my glasses in my pocket and developed an unbecoming squint: I devised a smile that hid two broken front teeth, but it looked disturbingly like the grin of a piranha; I kept my arms folded over my would-be breasts. But the hearing aid was a different story. There was no way to disguise it. I could tuck it under my blouse, but then all I could hear was the static of cotton. Besides, whenever I took a step the box bounced around like a third breast. So I resigned myself: A monster I was, a monster I would be.

I became more withdrawn, more suspicious of other people's intentions. I imagined that I was being deliberately excluded from schoolyard talk because the other children didn't make much of an effort to involve me—they simply didn't have the time or patience to repeat snatches of gossip ten times and slowly. Conversation always reached the point of ridiculousness before I could understand something as simple as "The movie starts at five." (The groovy shark's alive? The moving stars that thrive?) I didn't make it to many movies. I cultivated a lofty sense of superiority, and I was often brutal with people who offered the "wrong" kind of help at the "wrong" time. Right after my thirteenth birthday some well-meaning neighbors took me to a revivalist faith healing. I already had doubts about exuberant religions, and the knee-deep hysteria of the preacher simply confirmed them. He bounded to my side and put his hands on my head. "O Lord," he cried, "heal this poor little lamb!" 9

I leaped up as if transported and shouted, "I can walk!" 10

For the first few years my parents were as bewildered as I was. Nothing had prepared them for a handicapped child on the brink of adolescence. They sensed a whole other world of problems, but in those early stages I still seemed so normal that they just couldn't see me in a school for the deaf. They felt that although such schools were there to help, they also served to isolate. I have always been grateful for their decision. Because of it, I had to contend with public schools, and in doing so I developed two methods of survival: I learned to read not just lips but the whole person, and learned the habit of clear speech by taking every speech and drama course I could. 11

That is not to say my adolescent years were easygoing— they were misery. The lack of sound cast a pall on everything. Life seemed less fun than it had been before. I didn't associate that lack of fun with the lack of sound. I didn't begin to make the connection between the failings of my body and the failings of the world until I was well out of college. I simply did not admit to myself that deafness caused certain problems—or even that I was deaf. 12

From the time I was twelve until I was twenty-four, the loss of my hearing was erratic. I would lose a decibel or two of sound and then my hearing would stabilize. A week or a year later there would be another slip and then I'd have to adjust all over again. I never knew when I would hit bottom. I remember going to bed one night still being able to make out 13 the reassuring purr of the refrigerator and the late-night conversation of my parents, then waking the next morning to nothing—even my own voice was gone. These fits and starts continued until my hearing finally dropped to the last rung of amplifiable sound. I was a college student at the time, and whenever anyone asked about my hearing aid, I admitted to being only slightly hard of hearing.

My professors were frequently alarmed by my almost maniacal intensity in class. I was petrified that I'd have to ask for special privileges just to achieve marginal understanding. My pride was in flames. I became increasingly bitter and isolated. I was terrified of being marked a deaf woman, a label that made me sound dumb and cowlike, enveloped in a protective silence that denied me my complexity. I did everything I could to hide my handicap. I wore my hair long and never wore earrings, thus keeping attention away from my ears and their riders. I monopolized conversations so that I wouldn't slip up and reveal what I was or wasn't hearing; I took on a disdainful air at large parties, hoping that no one would ask me something I couldn't instantly reply to. I lied about the extent of my deafness so I could avoid the stigma of being thought "different" in a pathetic way.   14

It was not surprising that in my senior year I suffered a nervous collapse and spent three days in the hospital crying like a baby. When I stopped crying I knew it was time to face a few things—I had to start asking for help when I needed it because I couldn't handle my deafness alone, and I had to quit being ashamed of my handicap so I could begin to live with its consequences and discover what (if any) were its rewards.   15

When I began telling people that I was *really* deaf, I did so with grim determination. Some were afraid to talk to me at any length, fearing perhaps that they were talking into a void; others assumed that I was somehow an unsullied innocent and always inquired in carefully enunciated sentences; "Dooooooooo youuuuuuuuuu driiiinnk liquor?" But most people were surprisingly sympathetic—they wanted to know the best way to be understood, they took great pains to talk directly to my face, and they didn't insult me by using only words of one syllable.   16

It was, in part, that gentle acceptance that made me more curious about my own deafness. Always before it had been an affliction to wrestle with as one would with angels, but when I finally accepted it as an inevitable part of my life, I relaxed enough to do some exploring. I would take off my hearing aid and go through a day, a night, an hour or two—as long as I could take it—in absolute silence. I felt as if I were   17 indulging in a secret vice because I was perceiving the world in a new way—stripped of sound.

Of course I had always known that sound is vibration, 18 but I didn't know, until I stopped straining to hear, how truly sound is a refinement of feeling. Conversations at parties might elude me, but I seldom fail to pick up on moods. I enjoy watching people talk. When I am too far away to read lips I try reading postures and imagining conversations. Sometimes, to everyone's horror, I respond to things better left unsaid when I'm trying to find out what's going on around me. I want to see, touch, taste, and smell everything within reach; I especially have to curb a tendency to judge things by their smell—not just potato salad but people as well—a habit that seems to some people entirely too barbaric for comfort. I am not claiming that my other senses stepped up their work to compensate for the loss, but the absence of one does allow me to concentrate on the others. Deafness has left me acutely aware of both the duplicity that language is capable of and the many expressions the body cannot hide.

Nine years ago I spent the summer at the University of 19 Texas's experimental Shakespeare workshop at Winedale, and I went back each year for eight years, first as a student and then as a staff associate. Off and on for the last four years I have written and performed for Esther's Follies, a cabaret theater group in Austin. Some people think it's odd that, as deaf as I am, I've spent so much of my life working in the theater, but I find it to be a natural consequence of my particular circumstance. The loss of sound has enhanced my fascination with language and the way meaning is conveyed. I love to perform. Exactly the same processes occur onstage as off—except that onstage, once I've memorized the script, I know what everybody is saying as they say it. I am delighted to be so immediately in the know. It has provided a direct way to keep in touch with the rest of the world despite imposed isolation.

Silence is not empty; it is simply more sobering than 20 sound. At times I prefer the sobriety. I can still "hear" without a hearing aid—that is, I can discern noise, but I can't tell you where it's coming from or if it is laughter or a faulty drain. When there are many people talking together I hear a strange music, a distant rumbling in my consciousness. But when I take off my hearing aid at night and lie in bed surrounded by my fate, I wonder, "What is this—a foul subtraction or a blessing in disguise?" For despite my fears there is a kind of peace in the silence—albeit an uneasy one. There is, after all, less to distract me from my thoughts.

But I know what I've lost. The process of becoming deaf   21
has at times been frightening, akin perhaps to dying, and
early in life it took away my happy confidence in the image
of a world where things always work right. When I first came
back from the Lions Camp that summer I cursed heaven and
earth for doing such terrible wrong to me and to my friends.
My grandmother tried to comfort me by promising, "Honey,
God's got something special planned for you."

But I thought, "Yes. He plans to make me deaf."   22

—Terry Gallaway

What did you learn from your preview of "I'm Listening as Hard
as I Can"?

I was learned about a person
that may be had a
big sickness,

Review: Previewing a Reading Selection

Read:

- Title
- Headings, if any
- Introduction (first paragraph)
- First sentence of each paragraph
- Last paragraph

Ask yourself:

1. What is the main topic of this selection?
2. What can I learn from it?

Questions about Previewing

1. Why should you preview any reading assignment?

   _____

   _____

   _____

2. How can previewing help you understand your reading assignments?

   _____

   _____

   _____

3. What can you learn by reading the introduction to a textbook chapter?

   _____

   _____

   _____

4. What is the purpose of the table of contents besides telling you what pages the different chapters are on?

   _____

   _____

   _____

5. Why should you freewrite or list before you preview?

   _____

   _____

   _____

   _____

3

Setting a Reading Purpose: Developing Questions

There is always a reason why you are given a reading assignment. Sometimes you need to remember specific facts, as in a science course. At other times you need to understand ideas, as in a psychology course. Sometimes you need to read to develop your own ideas, as in a literature course.

To get the most out of your reading, it is a good idea to have a **purpose** for what you will be doing. You should first determine why the assignment was given and then ask yourself what you can learn from the material. Good readers have a specific strategy to help them learn, understand, and remember information. These readers ask questions about the material before they read to set a purpose or to give them a reason to read the assignment. One proven **prereading game plan** that good readers use is to **develop questions** from their preview. By developing meaningful questions, you focus your reading and have a purpose other than the fact that your teacher gave you the assignment.

Developing Questions When There Are Headings

Let us take a look at a selection that you have already previewed, "Lost in a Vitamin Maze?" on pages 20 to 22. Because this selection has main headings, it is easy to develop questions to set a reading purpose.

The game plan for developing meaningful questions when a reading has main headings is simply to turn the headings into questions. Then, your purpose for reading is to answer the questions.

Here are some questions that you might ask to make "Lost in a Vitamin Maze?" more meaningful.

Heading	Question
1. Lost in a Vitamin Maze?	1. What is a vitamin maze?
2. The myths	2. What are myths? What are vitamin myths?
3. The facts	3. What are some facts about vitamins?
4. The promise	4. What do vitamins promise?
5. The best strategy	5. What is the strategy? What is it for? How is it used? Why is it best?

Practice 1

Reread the selection "Lost in a Vitamin Maze?" to answer the questions. Write your answers here.

1. The many kinds of vitamins are in a drugstore that people can buy. and many times, we don't have a clue as to what we're buying

2. They are common misconceptions about vitamin supplements. they will give us a quick energy, increase virility, control Thyroid functioning, e

3. _____

4. _____

_____

_____

_____

_____

5. _____

_____

_____

_____

Practice 2

*Following is a selection from a sociology textbook. The exercises will help you practice the **prereading game plan** that you have been learning in this chapter.*

1. Freewrite or list about the title of the selection "What Indian Cultures Developed in the Americas?" Write about any information you might have that is triggered by the title.

   _____

   _____

   _____

   _____

2. Preview the selection.

3. Develop questions to set your purpose for reading.

   Heading   *Question*

   a. _____   a. _____

   _____   _____

b. _____   b. _____

c. _____   c. _____

d. _____   d. _____

e. _____   e. _____

4. Read the selection to answer the questions you developed in question 3.

a. _____

b. _____

_____

_____

_____

c. _____

_____

_____

_____

d. _____

_____

_____

_____

e. _____

_____

_____

_____

What Indian Cultures Developed in the Americas?

After thousands of years, many Indian cultures began to emerge throughout the Americas. In North America, most tribes lived in harmony with the land, respecting each other's territory. In Central and South America, however, a few groups conquered neighboring tribes. Eventually, these Indians extended their rule over a vast region. They also developed complex ways of life that differed greatly from the Indian cultures of North America. 1

Early Civilizations in the Americas

As time passed, some Indian groups developed highly advanced cultures called **civilizations.** Most civilizations have 2 several basic characteristics. (1) A division of labor usually exists. That is, people with different skills do different jobs. (2) Civilizations often demonstrate intellectual achievements, such as a system of writing or a calendar. (3) Many civilizations have complicated forms of group living, such as cities. (4) Almost all civilizations use metals, such as copper, bronze, or iron.

The first civilizations in the Americas flourished in Central and South America. Among the earliest were those of the Mayas (MY-uhs), the Aztecs, and the Incas. 3

The Mayas

The civilization of the Mayas began in the rain forests of Central America. It lasted from about 200 A.D. to 1200 A.D. The Mayan people lived by farming, growing such crops as corn, pumpkins, and chili peppers. They built religious centers where beautiful stone temples stood on the flat of stone pyramids. 4

At such centers Mayan scholars studied the movements of the sun, moon, and planets across the sky. They also developed a system of writing and a system of mathematics. Using this knowledge, the Mayas worked out a calendar to keep track of the changing seasons. As late as the 1400's, the Mayan calendar was more accurate than the one used by the people of Europe. 5

For many years the Mayan culture was the most highly developed Indian culture in the ancient Americas. However, some time around 800 A.D., it began to decline. By the time the Spanish explorers found the Mayas in the early 1500's, the lush jungle had overgrown many of their religious centers. The Mayas had forgotten their mathematics and their knowledge of the heavens. The reason for the decline of the Mayan civilization remains a mystery. 6

The Aztecs

The Aztecs lived in the region that is now called Mexico. There they farmed the land and mined gold and silver. In the 1300's Aztec warriors conquered and enslaved several other Indian civilizations. In this way the Aztecs built a great empire. The Aztecs used some of their wealth to build a beautiful capital city called Tenochtitlan (tay-nohch-tee-TLAHN). This magnificent city rose from islands that floated in a saltwater lake. Those who saw Tenochtitlan for the first time called it a city of wonders—a jewel set in a silver lake. The only routes into the city were three wide, raised roads, broken here and there by drawbridges. Within the city large stucco, or plaster, houses gleamed in the brilliant sun. Flower gardens covered the rooftops and filled the courtyards. 7

More than 100,000 people lived in Tenochtitlan. The 8
first Spanish explorers reported that the place looked like a
series of castles with great towers and temples of stone. Some
of the soldiers described it as "a thing in a dream." Early in
the 1500's, however, these same Spaniards seized Tenochtitlan. Aided by enemies of the Aztecs, they destroyed the capital and brought Aztec civilization to an end.

The Incas

The Incas organized and ruled a great empire centered in 9
what is now Peru. Like the Aztecs, the Incas had a complex
culture. They worshiped the sun as the greatest of all gods
and required everyone within their empire to do the same. In
honor of the sun god, the Incas fashioned many gold orna-
ments. Gold, they said, was "the sweat of the gods."

The Incas were skilled farmers and builders. Gardens 10
grew inside magnificent stone cities perched high in the
Andes Mountains. One of these cities was the Incan capital
of Cuzco (KOOS-koh), which still stands today.

To connect their cities, the Incas built an excellent sys- 11
tem of roads. Running along these roads, messengers could
travel quickly from one part of the Incan Empire to another.
Farmers could also easily transport goods to market on the
backs of animals, such as the llama (LAH-muh) and alpaca
(al-PA-kuh). These roads served as a valuable link until the
1500's. At this time Spanish soldiers marched down the roads
to conquer the civilization that had built them.

North American Indians

Unlike the Indians of South America, few North Amer- 12
ican tribes belonged to large empires, such as those of the
Aztecs or the Incas. Instead each tribe lived independently.
Each had its own territory, its own special customs, and often
its own language. Those Indians who lived in similar environments did, however, tend to develop similar cultures.

A region in which most tribes share the same culture is 13
known as a **cultural area**.

The Indians Shared Some Beliefs

Despite their cultural variety, the American Indians held 14
some of the same beliefs. Every Indian group had its own
name. These names all reflected the deep pride that the Indians had in themselves and their culture. They called themselves such names as "the ancient ones," "the people," or "the
genuine ones." The Indians also had a respect for the land and

all aspects of nature. "I live in good relation to the earth, to all that is beautiful," declared one ancient Indian song.

On the other side of the Atlantic, people in Europe were 15 developing another set of ideas and beliefs. They knew nothing of the peoples or cultures in the Americas. Eventually, however, certain events would take place in Europe that would lead Europeans westward. They would bring guns and other technological developments unknown to the Indians. Such things would help the Europeans to take over the land that the Indians so valued.

—Leonard C. Wood, Ralph C. Gabriel, and Edward L. Biller

Developing Questions When There Are No Headings

It is a little more difficult to develop questions for your pre-reading game plan when a selection has no headings. Here is how one of our students set her reading purpose for the following selection, "Garbage Overboard." This selection has no headings. Her game plan was to turn the title and the first sentence of each paragraph into questions. As you practice doing this, it will become easier. You will be amazed at how quickly questions come to mind as you preview.

Practice 3

1. Freewrite or list about the title "Garbage Overboard."

_____

_____

_____

_____

2. Preview the selection.

3. Here are three questions that our student developed.
   a. *What does garbage overboard mean?*

b. *Why was dumping forbidden?*

c. *What are antidumping rules?*

Develop three of your own questions from your preview of "Garbage Overboard."

a. _____

_____

b. _____

_____

c. _____

_____

4. Read the selection. There is space provided for the answers to your questions at the end.

Garbage Overboard

Kelly Milan says he first noticed the dumping while the Crown Odyssey sailed off the coast of Europe last year. Milan, a trombonist in the cruise ship's orchestra, would walk on deck during breaks and see plastic garbage bags shooting into the sea from the ship's stern. 1

As the Crown Odyssey sailed across the Atlantic, through the Caribbean, and into the Pacific, Milan says he observed 14 instances of dumping, each involving about 50 garbage bags. It always occurred at night, while passengers dined, he says. 2

A sign on the ship warned that such dumping was forbidden and gave the telephone number of the Center for Marine Conservation, a Washington, D.C., environmental group. So Milan called it, joining a growing number of cruise-line employees, passengers, and environmental organizations that have reported cruise ships for dumping garbage into the sea. 3

In the past two and a half years, the Center for Marine Conservation says it has received 22 dumping complaints against 14 cruise lines. The Coast Guard's Miami office says it receives about two complaints a month. 4

"We've seen cruise ships throwing plastic over the side," says Lt. Donna Kuebler, a marine environmental protection officer with the Coast Guard, which enforces antidumping rules in U.S. waters. "It's often not a cruise line's policy to do this, but, rather, the action of one guy on the ship who is overworked. The guy should incinerate all the trash, but he wants to go to bed early and he throws it overboard."

International conventions to establish a pollution-control treaty were held in 1973 and 1978. But it wasn't until 1987 that the United States joined more than 30 other countries in agreeing to abide by Marine Pollution Annex V, which, among other things, forbids discarding plastics anywhere in the ocean. To enforce rules against dumping near American shores, Congress passed the Marine Plastic Pollution Research and Control Act that same year.

Why so much concern about plastics? Because environmentalists estimate that one million birds and 100,000 marine mammals and sea turtles die each year from ingesting plastic products or becoming entangled in them.

And last year, at the marine conservation organization's annual international beach cleanup, volunteers gathered more than 1,800 tons of garbage—including items from 15 cruise lines. Among the plastic debris collected were cups, shampoo bottles, cocktail stirrers, and cologne bottles—all with cruise-ship logos.

"The fact that something is found in the ocean doesn't mean the cruise line is responsible," says John T. Estes, president of the International Council of Cruise Lines, which represents 18 operators. "We have a problem with taking the garbage to off-loading places on land and then the off-loading companies dump it in the water." The Coast Guard adds that some ports, particularly those in less developed nations, cannot accommodate the huge garbage loads of cruise ships. On a seven-day cruise, a medium-size ship (about 1,000 passengers) might accumulate 222,000 coffee cups, 72,000 soda cans, 40,000 beer cans and bottles, and 11,000 wine bottles.

But environmentalists say that if there is a problem with off-loading companies, it's that their prices are too high, providing an incentive to dump at sea. In any event, the environmentalists have assembled a collection of eyewitness accounts of cruise-line violations.

For example, Al Levett, a passenger aboard the Regal Princess, which is operated by Princess Cruises, saw 20 to 30 plastic garbage bags being dropped over the side as the ship headed for Port Everglades, Florida, after a one-week cruise to the Caribbean and Mexico last October. "It seemed so pointless," recalls Levett. "We were only a few hours from port."

Levett says he reported the incident to an officer on the ship but was told that all garbage is incinerated. When Levett reached port in Florida he called the Coast Guard. 12

An employee of another cruise line reported that above five times each week plastics and other debris are dumped overboard from his ship. "This includes milk containers, cooking-oil jugs, plastic bags of various types and sizes, beer and soda cans, and other forms of refuse," the employee wrote in a letter to the Center for Marine Conservation. 13

Few complaints are as carefully documented as that of Milan, who worked on the Crown Odyssey from July through mid-December 1992. He made a videotape of the garbage bags bobbing in the ship's wake, and he plotted each instance of dumping on a map. Another musician on board, Kent Sangster, also witnessed dumping. "The sheer quantity of the stuff that's thrown overboard gets you mad," Sangster says. 14

Coast Guard officials in Washington say they have begun an investigation of the case and add that they have the power not only to assess a penalty of up to $25,000 but also to turn the case over to federal prosecutors, which could result in a fine of up to $500,000. That's a new stance for the Coast Guard. The Crown Odyssey, like most cruise ships, is registered abroad, and in the past the agency usually referred dumping cases to the State Department, which was responsible for pursuing the matter with a foreign government. 15

Jim Naik, president of Royal Cruise Line, which operates the Crown Odyssey, says company policy forbids the dumping of plastics. "We have a very strict policy, and we're very conscious about a clean environment," says Naik. "If a person dumps plastics overboard, the captain should fire him on the spot." 16

Says Peter Ratcliffe, chief operating officer of Princess Cruises: "We're very sensitive to all these environmental issues, and we spend a lot of money to avoid dumping garbage in the sea. On the Regal Princess, we have an incinerator on board, so there's no reason for garbage to be dumped overboard." 17

Other types of ships, including recreational boats and fishing vessels, generate and dump their share of garbage and are not blameless. But that may not be much solace for cruise-ship passengers. "I spend a lot of money to pay for a cruise," says Levett, "and I would have thought twice about spending the money if I had known that this practice was going on." 18

—Gary Stoller

Look back at Practice 3, question 3.

1. Write your answers to our student's preview questions about "Garbage Overboard" here.

   a. _____

   _____

   _____

   _____

   b. _____

   _____

   _____

   _____

   c. _____

   _____

   _____

   _____

   _____

2. Write your answers to your own preview questions about "Garbage Overboard" here.

   a. _____

   _____

   _____

   _____

   _____

   b. _____

   _____

c. _____

_____

_____

_____

_____

Review: Developing Questions Before You Read

By **developing questions** before you read, you will be able to focus on the most important information in the text.

To develop prereading questions from **a reading selection:**

- When there are main headings, turn the headings into questions.
- When there are no main headings, turn the first sentence of each paragraph into a question.

Questions about Developing Questions

1. How does previewing help you develop questions to set your purpose for reading?

_____

_____

_____

_____

PART TWO

CHAPTER

4

Locating the Main Idea

In Part 1, you developed a prereading game plan to preview and set a purpose for the reading of different kinds of college text material. This chapter and the two that follow focus on **strategies to help you while you read**—that connect you with a writer's ideas. To do this, you will learn how to:

1. Find the main idea of paragraphs and the controlling idea of an entire reading selection.
2. Find important details.
3. Become an active reader by writing while you read to remember important information.

Readers and writers have important responsibilities to each other. The writer of a textbook should present information so that the reader will understand it. The reader, in turn, is responsible for understanding and remembering the important information that the writer has presented. In this chapter and the following two, you develop a **reading game plan** to become involved with text material.

Questions

1. What strategies will you learn in this chapter?

_____

_____

_____

2. What is a writer's responsibility?

_____

_____

3. Why is a reader/writer connection important?

_____

_____

_____

The Main Idea

The writer of a text builds his or her information around a central point. This central point is the **main idea.** It is the most important message that the writer wants to convey to the reader. All the other information in the paragraph relates to the main idea.

To find the main idea, you have to do two things, which make up the **main idea strategy.** First, you have to find the **topic**—what the text is mainly about. After you discover the topic, or subject of the reading, you need to find out what the writer is saying about that topic. The most significant statement that the writer is making about the topic is the main idea.

The strategy for finding the topic and the main idea is to ask yourself two questions:

1. What or who is this text mainly about? (*Topic*)
2. What is the writer saying about the topic? (*Main Idea*)

Finding Topics or Subjects

You get a sense of the **topic** when you preview. Very often, the title of a reading selection gives you the **topic** or **subject** of the text. After previewing a reading selection or a textbook chapter, ask yourself, *What is this mainly about?*

In Chapter 1, you previewed a selection titled "Lost in a Vitamin Maze?" If you ask yourself what it is mainly about, you will probably say that it has something to do with vitamins. You might also ask yourself what vitamins have to do with being lost in a maze. In any case, you realize that the topic of the reading selection is vitamins. Once you find the topic, or what the selection is mainly about, you have completed the first step in your main idea strategy.

Practice 1

Find the **topics** *in the following paragraphs. Remember to ask yourself:* What is this mainly about? *There is <u>extra space</u> because you will be doing more work with these paragraphs later on.*

Example:

Travel is a part of our way of life. People commute to jobs that are a considerable distance from their homes. Some students even travel many miles to school. Stores and businesses are clustered in central locations.

—Robert K. Gerver and Richard J. Sgroi

What is this mainly about?

Was your answer to the question "travel"? Travel is the correct answer because travel is what the paragraph is mainly about. Even though many examples of why people travel are given, they all relate to the topic, which is travel. Each example makes some point about travel or traveling.

1. Under some conditions, Social Security pays benefits to family members of disabled workers. Social Security can also act as a life insurance policy. If an eligible worker dies, benefits are paid to the surviving family members.

—Robert K. Gerver and Richard J. Sgroi

What is this mainly about?

_____

_____

_____

_____

_____

_____

2. There is some interesting scientific research being done to determine whether the hormones in which our brains are immersed in the womb determine whether or not we will have a male or female outlook on life. The research is controversial and the answer to the question, "Are men and women's brains different?" is still not clear.

—Myrna B. Skidell

What is this mainly about?

_____

_____

_____

_____

_____

_____

3. Stress can make you miserable. On a continuous basis it can cause ulcers or heart attacks, and it can make you a victim of chronic back pain. A person might be able to avoid stress-related disorders by dealing with stress as it occurs.

—Myrna B. Skidell

What is this mainly about?

_____

_____

_____

_____

_____

_____

_____

4. Your brain is divided into two hemispheres, right and left. They are connected by a bundle of nerve fibers called the *corpus collosum.* It operates like a telephone cable sending thousands of words a minute back and forth, keeping the two hemispheres in constant communication.

—R. Fenker with R. Mullins

What is this mainly about?

_____

_____

_____

_____

_____

_____

_____

5. Industry has generally opposed legislation designed to clean up the environment. Industry opponents have argued that compli-

ance with pollution standards will increase costs of production. Thus, if strip miners must heal the scars inflicted by their giant scoops, or steel mills must reduce the smoke from their stacks, or chemical plants must filter their wastes, or automobile manufacturers must purify the gases contained in exhaust, new and often costly technology will be needed. Small, inefficient concerns sometimes warn that they cannot afford to make extensive changes and therefore stringent pollution control standards will force them out of business.

—James E. Anderson et al.

What is this mainly about?

_____

_____

_____

_____

_____

_____

_____

_____

Were you able to find the topics of each of the practice paragraphs?

_____

If not, why not?

_____

_____

_____

Finding Stated Main Ideas in Paragraphs

After you have figured out the topic of a paragraph, the next part of your **main idea strategy** is to determine the most important information that the writer is saying about the topic. You can do this by asking yourself, *What is the writer saying about the topic?* Another way to do this is to ask yourself, *What is the main idea?*

Practice 2

Reread practice paragraphs 1 through 5 on pages 55 through 58. You have already found the topics. Now, find the **main idea** *in each paragraph by asking,* What is the writer saying about each topic? *Write your answers under each topic in the extra space provided below each paragraph. You will still have room to work with the practice paragraphs later on.*

Example: Look back at the example on page 55. The topic of the paragraph was travel. To find the main idea, ask yourself, *What is the writer saying about travel?*

The answer: *Travel is a part of our way of life.*

This is the main idea of the paragraph because the writer is giving you a specific (or particular) point of information about the topic "travel."

There is a definite relationship between the topic and the main idea in any paragraph. The *topic* is the subject of the paragraph (what the paragraph is about). The *main idea* tells the most important thing about the topic. Thus, you can find the topic and the main idea by asking yourself only two questions:

1. What or who is this paragraph mainly about? (*Topic*)
2. What is the most important idea about the topic? (*Main Idea*)

In all the practice paragraphs, the main idea was stated. The writer told the reader what the main idea was. Both the topic and the main idea in each of the practice paragraphs were in the same sentence. These sentences are called **topic sentences,** and they can be found at the beginning, in the middle, or at the end of a paragraph. Take a moment to look at the practice paragraphs on pages 55 through 58 once again. *Underline the topic sentence in each paragraph.*

Now compare the topic sentence in each paragraph with the main idea that you wrote. Chances are that the main ideas that you wrote are the same as the topic sentences. As you continue with the practice exercises, it is a good idea to write the main idea in your own words rather than copying it directly from the text. You are the one who needs to understand what the writer has to say, and you will remember it more easily if you write it in your own words.

Practice 3

In each of the following numbered paragraphs:

1. Find the **topic,**
2. Underline the **topic sentence,** and
3. Write the **main idea** in your own words.

We have left more space than you need because you will be doing more work with these paragraphs later on.

Example:

Social Scientists are interested in how people live. They are interested in what is happening to cities today. Some new cities have been planned with the help of social scientists. <u>It is possible that social scientists will have much to do with the planning of new cities in the future.</u>

—Frederick M. King et al.

Topic: *Social Scientists*

Main Idea: *Social Scientists might help plan future cities.*

1. People like the convenience of packaged foods, but they are sometimes doubtful about the nutritional value. They are especially concerned about the *additives,* with little or no food value, which many processed foods contain. Examples of additives are caramel color, artificial flavors, propionate, citrate, and nitrite. Additives improve the flavor, appearance, color, or texture of a food product; or they help keep the product from spoiling.

—Stanley L. Weinberg

Topic: _____

Main Idea: _____

_____

_____

_____

_____

_____

_____

2. A substantial breakfast helps balance your daily diet. Experiments at the University of Iowa showed that students who ate adequate breakfasts were more alert, did better work, and maintained better health generally. Those who went to class without breakfast tended to get overly hungry, and they made up the missing calories by nibbling and overeating the rest of the day.

—Stanley L. Weinberg

Topic: _____

Main Idea: _____

_____

_____

_____

_____

_____

_____

3. *Individualism* is a dominant theme in American culture. Most of us believe that a person's primary obligation is to him- or her-

self, not to parents, grandparents, brothers and sisters, aunts and uncles. We maintain ties with relatives, but our own interests come first. Indeed, we consider an adult who devotes his or her life to caring for a parent somewhat foolish. We spend a great deal of time and effort on *self*-improvement, through jogging or adult education or psychotherapy. We are judged—and we judge others—by individual effort and personal achievement.

—M. Bassis, R. Gelles, and A. Levine

Topic: _____

Main Idea: _____

_____

_____

_____

_____

_____

_____

_____

4. Social and political subjects received much attention from writers in the 1930's. For example, Richard Wright's *Native Son*, published in 1940, told a story of racial tensions. Wright was one of the nation's great African-American authors. *Native Son* quickly became a best seller. Sinclair Lewis wrote about the dangers of fascism. Ernest Hemingway's *For Whom the Bell Tolls* dealt with the futility of war.

—Harold H. Eibling, Carlton L. Jackson, and Vito Perrone

Topic: _____

Main Idea: _____

_____

_____

_____

_____

_____

_____

_____

5. If your loan application is turned down, you are protected by the _Fair Credit Reporting Act._ The lending institution must give you the reason, in writing. If the loan has been denied because of a poor credit rating, the lending institution must give you the name of the credit reporting agency that supplied your credit history. You are entitled to see a copy of your credit rating free of charge if you have been denied credit. You can get a copy of your credit history for a fee if you haven't been denied credit.

—Robert K. Gerver and Richard J. Sgroi

Topic: _____

Main Idea: _____

_____

_____

_____

_____

_____

_____

_____

Finding Unstated Main Ideas in Paragraphs

The main idea is not always stated (or written). Sometimes you have to _infer_ (decide from the information given) what the main idea is. You make inferences in your daily life and, with a good strategy, will probably not have much difficulty doing the same thing with text.

For example, if you were going out on a blind date and were told that your date has a good sense of humor, you would most likely infer that you would have fun. You will have made an inference based on the information that your date has a good sense of humor.

To find an **unstated** (inferred or implied) **main idea** in a paragraph, you need to look at the information that the writer has given and figure out the main idea based on this information. The game plan, or strategy, is the same one that you used for finding **stated main ideas**, but you have to think about all the information given, not just the topic sentence.

Practice 4

*Read the following paragraphs. Find the **unstated main ideas** by asking yourself the following questions:*

1. Who or what is the paragraph mainly about?
2. Based on the information given, what is the **main idea?**

There are extra lines because you will do more work with these paragraphs later on.

Example:

> I once heard an engineer who spoke to all sorts of community groups about his corporation's engineering projects. Unfortunately, he spoke the same way to graduate engineering students as he did to retirees who had no previous experience in the field. You can imagine how well his highly technical speeches went over with the retirees.
>
> —Joan Detz

Topic: *An engineer's speech.*

Main Idea: *The speech was not appropriate for his audience.*

Explanation: *The writer does not state the main idea, but gives examples that lead the reader to infer that the engineer should not give the same speech to graduate students as he does to retirees. Examples given are:*

1. The writer used the word unfortunately to signal you that the engineer gave the same speech to both experienced and nonexperienced people. The word unfortunately implies something negative.

2. The last sentence of the paragraph is sarcastic or mocking. It implies that the retirees did not enjoy the speech.

3. If you ask what the writer is saying about the topic, you will come to the conclusion that the engineer's speech was not appropriate for his audience.

1. People used to feel safe and comfortable in their own homes. Family activities, going out with friends, or dining in a restaurant used to provide excitement. Things are different now. These days, when people read about violence in the newspaper or see it on television, they just hope that it doesn't come into their own lives either inside or outside their homes.

— Myrna B. Skidell

Topic: _____

Unstated Main Idea: _____

_____

_____

_____

_____

_____

_____

2. Being thin or even skinny is one of the demands that many women believe society makes on them. Consider the woman who desperately strives to lose weight. If she loses weight, she

might find it easier to get a job, meet a man, and escape social ridicule. However, should we not consider how she is sacrificing her body for approval and how difficult it may be for her to maintain her new status. Is this feminism?

—Myrna B. Skidell

Topic: _____

Unstated Main Idea: _____

_____

_____

_____

_____

_____

_____

3. Our bodies react to our own deceit, even to a single incident of lying, particularly if we feel conflicted and guilty about it. These clues provide important nonverbal information to others in relationships. The last time I told an outright lie, I reflexively turned my face away while speaking, knowing that my expression might "give me away." Similarly, I rely on my reading of other people's bodies to detect deception, as we all do: I register what is popularly called "body language." I note obvious incongruities (a client in my psychotherapy practice says she's not angry, but she looks angry). I pick up subtle ones (my husband says he is paying attention, but I sense he's distracted). When a person's words tell me one thing and my automatic "knowing" intuits something different, I put more trust in what my body registers than in the words I hear.

—Harriet Lerner

Topic: _____

Unstated Main Idea: _____

_____

_____

_____

_____

_____

_____

_____

4. Babies quickly progress from lying there looking at the world for the first time to speaking and comprehending a complex system such as language and the emotions that go along with it, all within one year. A day-old breast-fed baby can identify his or her mother by her smell. Before the age of six months, a baby can distinguish objects by size, shape, and color and may actually recognize not only some of the different words spoken to him or her but also foreign languages. Babies make all the sounds found in all languages, but quickly stop making those sounds not found in the language or languages not spoken to them. By five months, babies may also be able to count.

—Sidney G. Becker

Topic: _____

Unstated Main Idea: _____

_____

_____

_____

_____

_____

_____

5. The Kennedys are a famous American family that has been involved in politics and marked by tragedy. One son, John F.

Kennedy, became President of the United States. Robert Kennedy was a Senator, who later became Attorney General in his brother's administration. Edward Kennedy has been a Senator for many years. Joseph Kennedy, the father, had great ambitions for his children. He and his wife, Rose, instilled toughness and determination in all of their children. Many people have considered the Kennedys the closest thing to American royalty. The dynasty, however, has been the victim of a series of tragedies. First, there was the assassination of John. Then Robert was also assassinated. Finally, there was a scandal involving Edward in the death of a young woman. Americans watched in horror as one after another tragedy befell this high-profile political family. As each young man assumed a political role, he seemed to become more vulnerable to the reactions of an increasingly violent and critical society.

—Myrna B. Skidell

Topic: _____

Unstated Main Idea: _____

_____

_____

_____

_____

_____

_____

_____

Finding Details in Paragraphs

Writers have much more information to give you than just main ideas. Writers support their main, or controlling, ideas by giving facts, examples, proof, and/or explanations. The kinds of support that writers give to main ideas are called **details.** You will find details easily if you ask yourself the question, *How does the writer support the main, or controlling, idea?*

Practice 5

Read the following paragraphs. Ask yourself these three questions:

1. What or who is this paragraph about? (**Topic**)
2. What is the writer saying about the topic? (**Main Idea**)
3. How does the writer support the main idea? (**Details**)

*These questions give you a complete **reading game plan** for finding the **topic**, the **main idea**, and the **details** of a paragraph. Go back to the practice paragraphs on pages 55 to 58, pages 60 to 63, and pages 64 to 68. You have already found the topics and main ideas. Now find two details for each paragraph and write them in the extra space left under the main ideas.*

Example:

> While there have been some studies over the years suggesting a role for the moon in the extremes of human behavior, the results have been muddy, as well as inconsistent. For instance, researchers in Cincinnati found that in 1969, some types of crime (rape, domestic abuse, robbery) increased during the full moon, but others (murder) didn't. A subsequent, more thorough study analyzed crimes committed in the same part of the country over a two-year period, tracking nearly 109,000 calls to police and fire departments. No lunar pattern emerged. And researchers have analyzed 37 studies that collected data on hospital admissions, psychiatric disturbances, crisis calls, and homicides and other crimes. Their conclusion: The moon played no roles.
>
> —*Health Magazine*

1. What is this about? (Topic) *The moon's effect on extreme human behavior.*

2. What about the moon's effect on human behavior? (Main Idea) *Studies have not proven whether or not there is an effect.*

3. How does the writer support the main idea? (Details) *In this paragraph, the writer gives examples of studies done. These are:*

   a. Cincinnati study in 1969 showed that some crimes increased, but others didn't.

b. *109,000 calls to police and fire departments were tracked over two years and showed no lunar pattern.*

c. *37 studies were analyzed and the conclusion was that the moon played no role.*

1. There is evidence that grades are often the only recognition female students receive in the math classroom. Several studies document that in high school and college, boys get significantly more attention from both male and female math teachers. Boys are spoken to more, called on more and receive more corrective feedback, social interaction, individual instruction, praise and encouragement. There is one form of attention bestowed more frequently on girls: In one study of ten high school geometry classes, girls received 84 percent of the discouraging comments.

—Le Anne Schreiber

What is this about? (*Topic*)

_____

What about it? (*Main Idea*)

_____

_____

_____

How is the main idea supported? (*Details*)

a. _____

_____

_____

b. _____

_____

_____

2. A fundamental reason for both the historic and contemporary success of snappers is that they are among the most reproductively vigorous of turtles. Mating occurs from April through

November. When ready to lay, which she may do once a year in northern areas, sometimes twice a year in warm climates, a female leaves the water and scoops out a depression. In it she may deposit 90 or more eggs, though more typically there are 20 to 40 in each clutch. The eggs have thin, somewhat flexible shells. They are spherical and about an inch in diameter. After laying them, the female covers and smooths over the nest, to roughly camouflage or protect it, and then she leaves the site. With the sun providing incubating heat, hatchlings usually begin to emerge from the shells 55 to 90 days later.

—Bil Gilbert

Who or what is this about? (Topic)

_____

What about it? (Main Idea)

_____

_____

_____

How is the main idea supported? (Details)

a. _____

_____

_____

b. _____

_____

_____

3. For the hundred years that it has been around, chiropractic has not been accepted as medicine by the American Medical Association. Recent studies, however, have shown that for certain kinds of back pain, chiropractic care may be more appropriate than traditional medical care. Many people still believe that chiropractors are "quacks" and have no place in American mainstream medicine. However, the National Institute of Health is not only studying chiropractic, but other forms of nontraditional

medicine as well. Also, many health insurance plans now reimburse for chiropractic care. Only recently has it gained reluctant acceptance by traditional medical practitioners.

—Sidney G. Becker

Who or what is this about? (Topic)

_____

What about it? (Main Idea)

_____

_____

_____

How is the main idea supported? (Details)

a. _____

_____

_____

b. _____

_____

_____

4. However one chooses to assess mathematical achievement, the differences in performance that exist between American boys and girls are minuscule compared with the differences that exist between American and foreign students. In a study made public by the Educational Testing Service last year, American 9-year-old students ranked ninth out of 10 industrialized nations in math and 13-year-olds ranked thirteenth out of 15 industrialized nations. Firm evidence of foreign superiority is seldom followed, however, by government funding for biological research into its causes. Calls for curriculum reform are more likely.

—Le Anne Schreiber

What is the topic?

_____

What is the main idea?

_____

_____

_____

What are the details?

a. _____

_____

_____

b. _____

_____

_____

5. The Sioux would come up the river toward the big lake, and they would steal the ponies of the Ojibwe people who lived along the banks of the river. The Ojibwe would follow, ten or twenty or a hundred, down the shores of the river, down a narrow trail that fell breathlessly toward the water. There would be a great battle, and many Ojibwe and many Sioux would fall, and there would be blood staining the snow along the narrow path, and blood running red down the river too. There were many battles along this trail, and there was so much blood that the Ojibwe people called the little path Ka-beck-a-nung, "the Trail of War."

—Charles P. Pierce

Topic:

_____

Main Idea:

_____

_____

_____

Details:

a. _____

b. _____

_____

_____

_____

_____

Finding Controlling Ideas in Longer Selections

Paragraphs have only one main idea. Most of the time, how-ever, you will be reading text that consists of more than one para-graph. For example, you may be assigned an entire article or chapter to read at one time. Your **main idea strategy** will be very helpful, but you will have more than one main idea to deal with in this type of reading. Because all the main ideas in longer selections relate to the topic, it will be necessary for you to use all the main ideas from the selection to determine the **controlling idea.** The controlling idea in this case is the overall idea that the writer wants you to understand about the entire reading.

The **reading game plan** to use with longer selections is to:

1. Find the topic of the selection (often this is stated in the title).
2. Number each paragraph.
3. Find the main idea of each paragraph.
4. Find the details of each paragraph.
5. Use the main ideas from each paragraph to determine the controlling idea of the entire selection or chapter.

Practice 6

*Read the following selections, which will give you practice in using the **reading game plan** for finding the **controlling idea** in longer readings. Be sure to look over the examples first. Then:*

1. *Find the topic.*
2. *Find the main idea of each paragraph.*
3. *Find the details of each paragraph.*
4. *Determine the controlling idea of the selection and write it in your own words.*

Examples:

American Families Today

(*Paragraph 1*)   The idea of two parents, 2.2 children, Dad with the only job, and Mom in the kitchen is no longer the norm for the American family. In fact, this pattern held true for only 7 percent of American families in the mid-1980s, down from 60 percent in the 1950s (Hodgkinson, 1985).

Topic of Paragraph 1: *Change in American families*

Main Idea of Paragraph 1: *Most American families no longer consist of Mom and Dad and 2.2 children, with only Dad working outside the home.*

Details in Paragraph 1:

1. *The old pattern was true of only 7 percent of families in the 1980s.*

2. *The old pattern was true of 60 percent of families in the 1950s.*

(*Paragraph 2*)   Many students today have only one or no sibling, or they may be part of **blended families** (parents, children, and stepchildren merged into families through re-marriages), with stepbrothers or stepsisters who move in and out of their lives. Some students may live with an aunt, with grandparents, with one parent, in foster or adoptive homes, or with an older brother or sister.

Topic of Paragraph 2: *Make-up of families today*

Main Idea of Paragraph 2: *Many students live in blended families.*

Details in Paragraph 2:

1. *Many students have one or no siblings.*

2. *Many students have stepbrothers or stepsisters.*

3. *Some students live with one parent, foster or adoptive parents, or older siblings.*

(*Paragraph 3*)   Many middle-class couples are waiting longer to have children and are providing more material advantages. Children in these homes may have more "things," but they may also have less time with their parents. Of course, not all students are middle-class. About one-quarter of all children under 18 live with one parent, usually their mother, and almost half of these families have incomes below the poverty level (U.S. Bureau of the Census, 1990). Students are likely to be alone or unsupervised much of the day. The growing number of these latchkey children has prompted many schools to offer before- and after-school programs.

—Anita E. Woolfolk

Topic of Paragraph 3: *Supervision of children in the home*

Main Idea of Paragraph 3: *Children in middle-class and poor families both have less parent supervision.*

Details in Paragraph 3:

1. *Although middle-class parents may wait longer to have children to give them more "things," the children may have less parental supervision.*

2. *Children living in poor families are likely to be latchkey kids (at home without adults at times).*

3. *As a result, many schools have before- and after-school programs.*

Topic of selection: *The American family today*

Controlling idea of selection: *Today the American family is often a blended family in which the adults have less time to spend with their children.*

Selection 1:

The Purpose of a Resume

[*Paragraph 1*] Before proceeding with the resume preparation process, it is important to have a thorough understanding of what this document is intended to accomplish. Unfortunately, many employment candidates have a somewhat narrow understanding of the role of the resume, and therefore, end up with something that is inappropriate, at best.

Topic of Paragraph 1: _____

Main Idea of Paragraph 1:

_____

_____

_____

Details in Paragraph 1:

1. _____

_____

_____

2. _____

_____

_____

[*Paragraph 2*]   The primary purpose of the resume is to serve as a tool in helping you secure an employment interview. It must, therefore convince a prospective employer that you are an outstanding candidate, who has something of value to contribute to the organization, and that it will be well worth his or her time to grant you a personal interview. The key word here is value. The resume must convey that somehow the company's performance and profitability will be enhanced by hiring you.

Topic of Paragraph 2: _____

Main Idea of Paragraph 2:

_____

_____

_____

Details in Paragraph 2:

1. _____

_____

_____

2. _____

_____

_____

[*Paragraph 3*]   Therefore, the resume should emphasize your major contributions and accomplishments. It must not simply state the names of past employers and list the job titles of past positions that you have held. These factors alone cannot be expected to convince an employer of your merit. Instead, your resume must convince the employer that you are someone who will bring improvements and make worthwhile contributions through the solution of major problems and issues confronting the organization. Only past accomplishments will serve to make the sale.

—Richard H. Beatty

Topic of Paragraph 3: _____

Main Idea of Paragraph 3:

_____

_____

_____

Details in Paragraph 3:

1. _____

_____

_____

2. _____

_____

_____

Topic of Selection: _____

_____

Controlling Idea of Selection:

_____

_____

_____

Selection 2:

Cardiovascular Fitness

[*Paragraph 1*]   Some think diving is relatively non-physical. But although the activity of diving is not high tempo, it is done in the heavy medium of water, requiring strength, and is done for extensive periods, requiring stamina. Just as with skiing, it is a good idea to prepare yourself for "the season."

Topic of Paragraph 1: _____

Main Idea of Paragraph 1:

_____

_____

_____

Details in Paragraph 1:

1. _____

_____

_____

2. _____

_____

_____

[*Paragraph 2*]   For diving, it is recommended that the first thing you do is get a medical checkup. After determining that you are in good health, do a little "tuning up" by exercising your heart and lungs. Common aerobic exercises include jogging, cycling, swimming, aerobic dance, and sports in which cardiovascular activity is sustained.

Topic of Paragraph 2: _____

Main Idea of Paragraph 2:

_____

_____

Details in Paragraph 2:

1. _____

_____

_____

2. _____

_____

_____

[*Paragraph 3*]   Cardiovascular fitness also means increased circulation. This helps keep divers warmer longer, helps them stay alert, which is important in problem solving, and also means less work for the lungs in getting oxygen into the blood, which allows the diver to consume less tank air.

—*Open Water Diver's Manual*

Topic of Paragraph 3: _____

Main Idea of Paragraph 3:

_____

_____

_____

Details in Paragraph 3:

1. _____

_____

_____

2. _____

_____

_____

Topic of Selection: _____

_____

Controlling Idea of Selection:

_____

_____

_____

Selection 3:

Gypsies

[*Paragraph 1*]   Gypsies do not go to school? Not very often—
and not for very long. They feel that formal education is not
germane to their way of life and that the American school
system would tend to "de-Gypsyize" their youngsters. Both
claims are at least partially true, and the subject will be dis-
cussed in a later section.

Topic of Paragraph 1: _____

Main Idea of Paragraph 1:

_____

_____

_____

Details in Paragraph 1:

1. _____

_____

_____

2. _____

_____

_____

[*Paragraph 2*]   Gypsies neither read nor write? True. A large portion of them are functionally illiterate. They cannot even read or write in their own language, Romany, for it is a spoken rather than a written tongue. The literacy situation is improving, but so far progress has been slow. In spite of their self-imposed linguistic handicap, however, Gypsies have made a remarkable adaptation to their environment.

Topic of Paragraph 2: _____

Main Idea of Paragraph 2:

_____

_____

_____

Details in Paragraph 2:

1. _____

_____

_____

2. _____

_____

_____

[*Paragraph 3*]   Gypsies do not pay taxes? Some observers would reply: "Not if they can help it." And it is true that many Gypsies do not pay property taxes because they have no taxable property. They often prefer to rent rather than to buy a dwelling place. Also, many Gypsies work irregularly, and have low-paying jobs, so that their income taxes would be negligible. A fair number are on welfare. On the other hand, at least some Gypsies are moving into white-collar occupations, and their tax payments are commensurate with those of other white-collar workers.

—William Kephart and William Zellner

Topic of Paragraph 3: _____

Main Idea of Paragraph 3:

_____

_____

_____

Details in Paragraph 3:

1. _____

_____

_____

2. _____

_____

_____

Topic of Selection: _____

Controlling Idea of Selection:

_____

_____

_____

Selection 4:

Are You Sick of Those Phony Sweepstakes?

[*Paragraph 1*]   Next time you get a phone call or a promotion in the mail that sounds fishy, don't get angry—get even! Consumer fraud has become so widespread that the National Consumers League had decided to take action. Now there's a toll-free number for people to call when they suspect someone has tried to defraud them.

Topic of Paragraph 1: _____

Main Idea of Paragraph 1:

_____

_____

_____

Details in Paragraph 1:

1. _____

_____

_____

2. _____

_____

_____

[*Paragraph 2*]   What constitutes fraud? Often, it's an offer of a "free" prize or vacation or what looks like a check for a large sum of money that you can only redeem by calling an expensive 900 number and then there turns out to be no prize after all! Don't fall for it.

Topic of Paragraph 2: _____

Main Idea of Paragraph 2:

_____

_____

_____

Details in Paragraph 2:

1. _____

_____

_____

2. _____

_____

_____

[*Paragraph 3*]   From 10:00 a.m. to 4:00 p.m. E.S.T. Monday through Friday, you can call (800) 786-7060 and report the name and phone number of the company that you suspect of fraud: the information will be pooled among local and national law enforcers and make catching the crooks easier. Take the law into your own hands!

—Claudia Bowe

Topic of Paragraph 3: _____

Main Idea of Paragraph 3:

_____

_____

_____

Details in Paragraph 3:

1. _____

_____

_____

2. _____

_____

_____

Topic of Selection: _____

Controlling Idea of Selection:

_____

_____

_____

Selection 5:

Latinos

[*Paragraph 1*]   Latino is a category made up of many separate cultural and racial subgroups bound together by a common language, Spanish (although even language patterns vary by country of origin). In 1989, about 21 million Spanish-speaking people were officially recorded as residing in the United States, and several million others are believed to have entered without official documents. Because of their generally younger ages and high birthrates, it is likely that Spanish-speaking Americans will soon outnumber African-Americans as the single largest minority group.

Topic of Paragraph 1: _____

Main Idea of Paragraph 1:

_____

_____

_____

Details in Paragraph 1:

1. _____

_____

_____

2. _____

_____

_____

[*Paragraph 2*]   In 1989, the four major ethnic subdivisions within the Spanish speaking population were Mexican Americans; Puerto Ricans; Cubans; and people from Central and South American countries, particularly the Dominican Republic, Colombia, and El Salvador. . . . The remainder were from other Spanish-speaking nations. . . . Differences within the Spanish-speaking minority are striking, especially in terms of education and income. Each ethnic group has its own immigration history, cultural patterns, and its own internal diversity.

Topic of Paragraph 2: _____

Main Idea of Paragraph 2:

_____

_____

_____

Details in Paragraph 2:

1. _____

_____

_____

2. _____

_____

_____

[Paragraph 3]   There is a stratification system within the Latino population based not only on indicators of socioeconomic status of Spanish-speaking Americans, but within the stratification system of the wider society and within the hierarchy of the Latino subculture. These divisions reduce the likelihood of the development of shared interests necessary to build a unified Latino power base.

—Beth Hess, Elizabeth W. Markson, and Peter J. Stein

Topic of Paragraph 3: _____

Main Idea of Paragraph 3:

_____

_____

_____

Details in Paragraph 3:

1. _____

_____

_____

2. _____

_____

_____

Topic of Selection: _____

Controlling Idea of Selection:

_____

_____

_____

Review: Main Idea

To find the **main idea** of a paragraph, ask yourself three questions:

1. What is this text mainly about? (*Topic*)
2. What is the most important point about the topic? (*Main Idea*)
3. How is the main idea supported or explained? (*Details*)

Remember: *Writers do not always state the main idea. In this case, look at the details and make an inference about the main idea based on the information given.*

To find the **controlling idea** of a longer reading selection, ask yourself:

• What is the main point of all the main ideas?

State the main ideas and the controlling idea in your own words so that you will remember them easily.

Questions about Finding the Main Idea

*Write the answers to the following questions based on what you have learned about choosing **main ideas** from paragraphs and longer selections.*

1. In your own words, describe the reading game plan that you would use to find the main idea of any paragraph.

_____

_____

_____

_____

2. What is the difference between finding a stated main idea and a main idea that is inferred (not stated)?

_____

_____

_____

_____

3. Why is it necessary to find the main idea?

_____

_____

_____

_____

4. What is the relationship between main ideas and details?

_____

_____

_____

_____

5. Describe the reading game plan that you would use to find the controlling idea of a long reading selection?

_____

_____

_____

_____

6. Based on the controlling idea in the practice selection about Gypsies on pages 81 to 82, why would you like or not like to be a Gypsy? Base your answer on the information provided in the selection. Write your answer here.

_____

_____

_____

_____

_____

_____

_____

_____

_____

_____

CHAPTER

5

Writing to Read and Remember

It is a good idea to read with a pencil in your hand so that you can mark important information for later study while you use your **main idea strategies.** In your **reading game plan,** two effective strategies to emphasize important text information are:

1. Marking main ideas, important details, and signal words.
2. Annotating text. This means making notes in the margin that might explain, clarify, or question something from the text.

You must remember to answer your preview questions, which helps you focus on important text information.

Marking Important Information

The purpose of **marking** your text is to provide a review of the most important information. Many students mark their texts by underlining and highlighting. When they do this, they generally underline or highlight so much of the reading material that they lose sight of the most important information. They become overwhelmed at exam time because they think that they have to memorize everything.

To get the most out of your text marking (either by underlining or by highlighting—not both), it is necessary to use your **main idea strategy questions.** Ask yourself:

1. What is the topic? Mark it!
2. What is the main idea? Mark it!
3. What are the most important details? Mark them!

By marking the answers to these questions, you extract the most important information to study. However, you must mark only the words that answer the questions. If the main idea is not stated, jot your inference down in the margin.

The second kind of information that you should mark is **signal words.** They are called signal words because they let you know that the writer is about to make an important point. These words indicate that the writer is going to explain differences between ideas, cause and effect, additional points, and conclusions or is going to summarize the selection.

The following examples of signal words will be most helpful. You will become familiar with more on your own.

To Show Similarities and Differences

like	on the other hand	but
similar to	different from	although

To Show Cause and Effect

because	due to	therefore
the reasons why	happens	results of

To Show Order

first, second, etc.	next	finally
then	after that	

To Summarize

finally	in summary	at last
in conclusion	last of all	therefore

Practice 1

Read the following short selections. **Mark** *the text by underlining or highlighting* only *the most important information and the* **signal words.** *Reread only the underlined or highlighted material. You should have a summary of the most important information to study later.*

Example: "Choosing a Wet Suit"

A <u>good fit</u> is one of the <u>most important</u> considerations when choosing a wet suit. If the <u>suit</u> is <u>too loose</u> it will <u>allow water</u> to <u>circulate inside</u> it, <u>cooling</u> the <u>body.</u> If it is <u>too tight</u> it can <u>restrict circulation</u> and <u>movement,</u> can <u>cause pressure spots,</u> and can <u>make</u> a <u>diver exert excess energy</u> while fighting against its tight fit.

The suit should be <u>snug without binding or pinching,</u> and it should <u>not have gaps</u> or <u>sags under the arms or at</u> the <u>crotch.</u> The <u>neck, wrist, waist,</u> and <u>ankle openings</u> should <u>be tight enough</u> to <u>prevent water from sloshing in,</u> but <u>loose enough</u> to <u>allow comfort</u> and free <u>blood circulation.</u>

<u>Though</u> they are <u>more expensive</u> than off the rack suits, a <u>custom</u> fitted <u>suit</u> is <u>ideal.</u> Having a <u>suit</u> which conforms to your body <u>cuts</u> down on <u>sags</u> and <u>gaps,</u> assuring <u>less water exchange</u> and <u>therefore less heat loss</u> and <u>greater comfort.</u>

—Open Water Diver's Manual

What should you know when buying a wet suit? Write the most important information here.

_____

_____

_____

_____

_____

_____

_____

Selection 1:

Language

If the truth be told, all languages are a little crazy. As Walt Whitman might proclaim, they contradict themselves. That's because language is invented, not discovered, by boys and girls and men and women, not computers. As such, language reflects the creativity and fearful asymmetry of the human race, which, of course, isn't really a race at all. That's why *six, seven, eight,* and *nine* change to *sixty, seventy, eighty,* and *ninety,* but *two, three, four,* and *five* do not become *twoty, threety, fourty,* and *fivety.* That's why we can turn lights off and on but not out and in. That's why we wear a pair of pants but, except on very cold days, never a pair of shirts. That's why we can open up the floor, climb the walls, raise the roof, pick up the house, and bring down the house.

Still, you have to marvel at the unique lunacy of the English language, in which your house can simultaneously burn up and burn down, in which your alarm clock goes off by going on, in which you are inoculated for measles by being inoculated against measles, and in which you first chop a tree down—and then you chop it up.

—Richard Lederer

*Reminder: Did you underline or highlight **only** the main ideas, details, and signal words? Were you efficient?*

From your text marking (underlining or highlighting), answer the following questions:

1. Why are all languages a little crazy?

   _____

   _____

2. Why do we wear a pair of pants but not a pair of shirts?

   _____

   _____

3. How do you add up a column of figures?

   _____

   _____

4. What do you do after you chop down a tree?

   _____

   _____

Selection 2:

Managers

In the early 1900s most managers came from wealthy families. Today's executives come from a wider range of socio-economic classes. The reason? Education. The greater availability of education has made it possible for people from all backgrounds to qualify for jobs in large organizations. This opportunity, together with the stress on science in higher education, has increased upward mobility.

This is not to say that you must go to a prestigious school, come from a big city, be willing to move, or work for a large corporation in order to succeed. Today there are opportunities at all managerial levels for all kinds of people.

—Theo Haimann, William G. Scott, and Patrick E. Connor

From your highlighting or underlining, can you give the reason why executives today are different from those in the 1900s?

_____

_____

_____

_____

Selection 3:

Computers

To many people, computers are mysterious and incomprehensible. Therein lies a danger. We are likely to feel either that these modern electronic creations are capable of doing almost anything or that they are totally beyond our amateur grasp. Do you face a problem? Feed it into the computer and let the computer solve it. But the danger is in overestimating the machine.

Never forget that computers are not human. They cannot think, they cannot originate new ideas, they cannot be creative. Only a human being can perform these functions.

Computers are helpful, obedient, faithful servants. They are merely tools to assist the researcher in doing what is either tedious routine or tiresome repetition. They will do menial tasks. But that is the end of their genius. Use them, let them save you hours of slow plodding with pen and pencil. But do not be disappointed or dismayed if you realize that the work of thinking, planning, and critically creating is still a domain where you must work alone to gather flashes of insight.

—Paul Leedy

1. What is the topic?

_____

_____

2. What are the main ideas?

_____

_____

_____

_____

_____

_____

3. What is the controlling idea of the selection?

_____

_____

_____

_____

Annotating Text

A good strategy to help make important information easier to review and remember is called **annotation.** When you annotate, you make notes directly on the text and in the margin as well. For example, if you have a question about something that you are reading, jot it down in the margin. You might want to jot down any additional information you might have about the topic or some comment that will help you better understand the material. You can also use symbols (e.g., stars, checks) or mark the text in any way that will help you to remember what you have read. Annotation, combined with text marking (underlining or highlighting), helps to make important information easy to review and remember.

Practice 2:

In the following selections:

1. *Use your preview strategy.*
2. *Use your main idea strategies.*
3. *Annotate and underline important information. (Unlike the example below, you will need to write your notes in the margins.)*
4. *Then, answer the questions at the end of both selections. You will need to read **both** selections to answer the questions.*

Example: Notice how one student annotated the following short selection about democracy.

American Democracy

The <u>political system</u> of the United States is <u>based</u> on
not sure this is true!
the ideal of <u>democracy</u>—<u>rule by</u> the <u>people</u>. As presented

in classrooms, textbooks and philosophical writings, the
is the ideal practiced?
<u>democratic ideal stresses</u> the following points:

- *The importance of the* (individual.) Political institu-

tions exist in order to help the individual live a fuller life.

The <u>individual</u> has "<u>inalienable rights</u>," which are speci-

fied in the <u>Declaration of Independence</u> as the <u>right</u> to <u>life</u>,

<u>liberty</u>, and the <u>pursuit of happiness</u>. These <u>rights existed</u>

<u>before</u> the <u>state</u>, and it is the <u>state's duty</u> to <u>uphold</u> them
justice? fair trial?
on <u>behalf of</u> the <u>individual</u>. At the <u>same time</u>, the <u>Consti-

tution</u> is <u>designed</u> to <u>protect individuals</u> from unnecessary
—look this up—
interference, or (tyranny) <u>by</u> the <u>state</u>.

- *Consent of the governed.* Government gets its authority from the people. In small communities the people themselves may exercise authority through direct democracy. But in large political systems, like our state and national governments, the populace entrusts authority to elected representatives, *in what is called representative democracy.* The balance between direct and representative democracy may vary, but some form of participation in the democratic process is the duty of every citizen.

  electoral college ex. of this

- *Majority rule and minority rights.* Elections are won and laws passed in accordance with the will of the majority, but this does not mean that minorities can be neglected or oppressed. Their rights—to vote, to be heard, to dissent—must be protected and upheld no less vigorously than those of the majority.

  sometimes more impt.

- *Equality of opportunity.* The Declaration of Independence proclaims that "all men are created equal." Obviously, some people are more intelligent, more creative, or more ambitious than others. In this sense, all people are not created equal. But in a democracy all individuals have the same freedom and rights, and should have the same opportunities. The question of how to achieve equality of opportunity has been the subject of much controversy in recent decades, as blacks, women, and others have

  and women

  but don't always

  African-Americans

<u>challenged</u> the <u>privileges</u> traditionally <u>granted</u> to <u>white males</u>. <u>Programs</u> designed to <u>assist minorities</u> have <u>provoked mixed reactions</u>.

—M. Bassis, R. Gelles, and A. Levine

How did the underlining and annotation help the student understand the text information?

_____

_____

_____

_____

Selection 1:

Types of Warranties

Industry today has the technology to create everything from lipstick to lasers. Some products are manufactured with more care than others. For instance, how long should a television last? You would probably like it to last forever. Modern technology might be able to produce a television that would last a very, very long time. However, the cost of inventing and producing such a set would be high. Instead, television makers manufacture sets that will probably last a limited amount of time. This is called **planned obsolescence.** 1

You should not expect goods to last forever, but you do have a right to expect them to last a reasonable amount of time. If a television you bought last week stopped working, you would certainly return it. But what if the set was two years old when it stopped working? Would you still be entitled to have the set repaired free of charge? What if you accidentally dropped a brand new television set while carrying it home? Should the manufacturer pay for necessary repairs? 2

A good way to answer these questions is to think about the manufacturer's guarantee, or _warranty_, of the product. All products are sold with a warranty. A warranty is a guarantee of a product's performance. Warranties protect consumers against defective products. There are four types of warranties. 3

- **Implied warranty.** This is an unwritten guarantee that a product will do what it is supposed to do. *Every* product carries this type of warranty. A light bulb must provide light; a pencil must write. 4

- **Express warranty.** This is a written guarantee covering specific conditions of the warranty. It lists the specific parts that are guaranteed, the length of the warranty, and any labor charges for warranty repairs. 5

- **Full warranty.** This is a written guarantee covering repairs or replacement of the entire product or certain parts of the product for the specified time. 6

- **Limited warranty.** This written guarantee covers only certain parts of the product for specified lengths of time. If a limited warranty covers only parts, the customer is required to return the product to the factory for repair and pay for handling fees and labor costs. 7

You should always find out what type of warranty a major purchase has. It often may be wise to pay a little more for a product and receive a better warranty. That way, you are protected if anything goes wrong with the product. 8

Indeed, you should always be careful when you shop, especially when you are making major purchases. The Latin phrase **caveat emptor** (let the buyer beware) has become a battle cry for consumers. You can be a careful shopper by comparing prices and warranties when possible. You should also notice the conditions of the sale. Know what your rights as a consumer are—and are not. 9

—Robert K. Gerver and Richard J. Sgroi

Selection 2:

Illiterate? Who, U.S.?

Undoubtedly the most alarming educational information to come to light in the 1980s was the number of adult Americans who cannot read or write. Most Americans associate illiteracy with Third World nations and previous generations. Unfortunately, they are wrong. The United States ranks an embarrassing forty-ninth among the 158 members of the United Nations in literacy. According to conservative estimates, 25 million Americans cannot read at all. About 45 million more read at a level well below that necessary to function adequately in our society, and that number is growing by 2 million a year (Zuckerman, 1989). All told, a third 1 of the adult population cannot read the poison warnings on a can of Drano, understand a letter from their child's teacher, or interpret a "help wanted" ad or a notice from the gas and electric company.

The majority of illiterate adults in the United States today are white and native-born. However, the problem is proportionately greater for minority groups. Forty-four percent of black and 56 percent of Hispanic adults are functionally or marginally illiterate, compared to 16 percent of white adults. Figures for young people indicate illiteracy is increasing, not declining. Some 15 percent of recent graduates of urban high schools cannot read at a sixth-grade level, a million teenagers read at only a third grade level. Forty-four percent of young blacks and 56 percent of young Hispanics are functionally illiterate, despite years in school (Levin, 1986).

Illiteracy is expensive, for individuals and for societies. The Senate Select Committee on Equal Educational Opportunity estimates the unrealized earning potential forfeited by men ages twenty-five to thirty-four who have less than high school-level skills at $237 billion. Half of the heads of households classified below the federal poverty line cannot read an eighth-grade book; more than a third of mothers on welfare are functionally illiterate. So are 60 percent of the adult prison population and 84 percent of juveniles who come before the courts. Businesses have difficulty filling such entry level jobs as clerk, bank teller, and paralegal. A major insurance firm reports that 70 percent of dictated letters must be retyped "at least once," because secretaries cannot spell and punctuate correctly. The military also pays a price for illiteracy. The navy has stated that 30 percent of new recruits are "a danger to themselves and costly to equipment" because they cannot read or understand simple instructions.

The human costs of illiteracy are difficult to grasp for those of us who take reading for granted. Illiterates cannot read notices from the IRS, welfare offices, or a housing bureau, and so do not know what rights they have or what deadlines and requirements they must meet to obtain them. For the most part, they do not vote. As a result they are "half-citizens," whose rights exist on paper they cannot read. Illiterates lack freedom of choice in our print society. They cannot help their children with homework and often do not visit the school for fear of embarrassing their child or themselves.

—M. Bassis, R. Gelles, and A. Levine

Questions about the Selections

1. Which selection was easier to underline and annotate?

   _____

2. Why was it easier?

   _____

   _____

   _____

3. How did the annotation strategies help you?

   _____

   _____

   _____

4. Were your preview questions answered?

   _____

   If not, why?

   _____

   _____

Review: Writing to Read and Remember

- **Mark** the text by underlining or highlighting **only** main ideas, supporting details, and signal words.
- **Annotate** in the margins. Jot down comments, questions, and additional information about the reading.
- Answer your **preview questions.**

Questions about Writing to Read and Remember

1. How will underlining or highlighting help you understand information?

_____

_____

_____

2. What is the purpose of text annotation?

_____

_____

_____

3. Describe the game plan that you would use while reading a selection titled "How the West Was Won."

_____

_____

_____

4. Decide whether it would be easier to study a reading selection that has headings, subheadings, and questions than one which has just the title and text without headings. Support your answer with information from the chapters you have previously worked on.

_____

_____

_____

_____

6

Using Game Plans with Longer Selections

In this chapter, you practice using your **prereading** and **reading game plans** on three longer selections. Two selections are parts of textbook chapters. The third selection is an essay. For this selection, you need to review the **preview strategy** for a reading without headings (see Chapter 2).

For each selection, you need to do the following:

1. Preview.
2. Develop three preview questions.
3. Find the main ideas and details. Underline or highlight them.
4. Mark the text by underlining or highlighting signal words.
5. Annotate in the margins.
6. Answer your own preview questions.
7. Answer the questions at the end of each selection.

Practice 1

Take a look at the reading selection "Early Settlers in the Americas," which follows. It is an excerpt from a textbook chapter.

104

Write your preview questions here:

_____

_____

_____

_____

_____

Answer your preview questions here if possible:

_____

_____

_____

_____

_____

_____

_____

_____

Early Settlers in the Americas

In 1492 the world as Columbus knew it was Europe, North Africa, and parts of Asia. Columbus knew nothing about the western hemisphere and the people living there. Yet, in this hemisphere lived people with many different languages and cultures. And they were spread from Alaska to the tip of South America. 1

The first settlers in the Americas left no written records. What little we know today about them we owe mostly to the work of *archaeologists*. Archaeologists are social scientists who study the remains of people who lived long ago to find 2 out when and how they lived. Archaeologists have learned much about the first Americans. But many questions about man's arrival and early settlement in the western hemisphere remain unanswered.

Why do archaeologists study the remains 3
of ancient people?

The Arrival of the First Americans

When They Came. A method called radiocarbon dat- 4
ing is often used to find out the age of certain remains of ancient peoples. Scientists measure the amount of carbon left in things that once were alive, such as bones or hair. In this way, scientists can tell how old such objects are. Radiocarbon dating has shown that man has been in the Americas 11,000 or 12,000 years.

But no one is quite sure when people first came to the 5
Americas. There is some evidence that man was living here at least 25,000 years ago. And a few scholars believe it possible that the first people reached the Americas between 40,000 and 70,000 years ago. It may have taken that long for early man to spread out over the two continents.

According to radiocarbon dating, how long have people 6
lived in the Americas?

Where They Came From. The first people to settle in 7
the Americas were probably hunters from northeastern Asia. Studies show that four times in the distant past, much of the northern part of the earth was covered with huge sheets of ice. The ice was formed of water taken mostly from the oceans. So the oceans held less water than they do now, and much of the earth that is covered by water today was dry land. In those times a wide strip of land, called a land bridge, connected Asia with what is now Alaska. Hunters, it is believed, followed animal herds that were their food supply across the land bridge into North America. And during a period of thousands of years, they settled in many parts of the Americas.

For the most part, the routes of the early Americans 8
have gone. But scientists know that the ice sheets moved and changed over the years. Sometimes there were ice-free paths open to the south. The animals followed these paths in search of food. And since these early people were hunters, they would have tracked the animals. Thus the animals very likely chose the routes which man followed through Alaska and Canada to the rest of the Americas.

Early Cultures in the Americas

Geography and Culture.   To a social scientist, culture 10
means the way a group of people live. Culture is made up of
the kinds of houses the people build, the tools they make, the
way they act, and even the way they think. The early people
living in the Americas developed many different cultures. In
North America alone, early man developed at least five major
cultures. Several of these were like the early cultures of Middle and South America.

The lives of the early Americans and the cultures they 11
developed were greatly affected by the *environment,* or geo-
graphic setting, in which they lived. South of the ice sheet,
there were many different kinds of weather, plant life, and
animal life. As groups moved south, they often changed their
ways of living, or culture, to suit a new environment.

Why did the early people who moved within the 12
Americas often develop new cultures?

—Harold H. Eibling, Carlton L. Jackson, and Vito Perrone

Practice 2

*Use your **preview strategy** for reading the textbook chapter
without headings, "Smoking—A Slow Suicide," which follows.
Then, after reading the selection, answer the questions that follow it.*

Write your preview questions here:

_____

_____

_____

_____

_____

Answer your preview questions here, if possible:

_____

_____

_____

_____

_____

_____

_____

_____

_____

_____

_____

Smoking—A Slow Suicide

Smoking is one of the biggest health hazards today. The scientific evidence of the dangers of smoking is tremendous. In 1979 Joseph Califano, then Secretary of the Department of Health, Education, and Welfare, wrote: "Smoking is the largest preventable cause of death in America." In 1979, over 55 million American men and women smoked 615 billion cigarettes; and worldwide consumption was about 3 trillion each year. Since then regular cigarette smoking by adults has dropped slightly from 40 percent to about 33 percent. Whereas the percentage of adult male smokers decreased from 50 to 38 percent between 1964 and 1978, the percentage of adult female smokers remained the same at 30 percent.

Projections by the World Conference on Smoking and Health sponsored by the World Health Organization (WHO) show that even if present consumption rates of cigarettes stay steady—and all data indicate a continued increase—the annual number of premature deaths caused by tobacco will rise from about 3 million worldwide in the 1990s to 10 million by the year 2025. Over half a billion people alive today, including 200 million currently under the age of 20, will die from tobacco-induced disease, and half of these will be in middle age.

The WHO Conference said that the tobacco companies   3
have targeted for expansion Third World countries, countries in Eastern Europe, Thailand, and other Far Eastern Countries. Also targeted are women and girls, and young boys.

Smoking among children has increased dramatically.   4
Since 1968, the number of girls between the ages of 12 and 14 who smoke has increased eightfold. Six million children between the ages of 13 and 19 are regular smokers. Smoking among blacks exceeds that by whites. However, on a positive note, about 30 million Americans have become ex-smokers since massive educational warnings were issued by the federal government.

More deaths and physical suffering are related to ciga-   5
rette smoking than to any other single cause: over 228,700 deaths (and rising) each year from cancer, over 325,000 deaths from cardiovascular disease, and more than 50,000 deaths from chronic lung diseases. Compare these figures with the number of people who died in the following wars (combat and noncombat fatalities): World War I (from 1917–1918), 116,708; World War II (from 1941–1946), 407,316; Korean War (from 1950–1953), 54,246; and the Vietnam conflict (from 1964–1973), 58,151. The cigarette industry's own research over a ten-year period (1964–1974), which cost over $15 million, confirmed the fatal dangers of smoking cigarettes. In a one-year period, a one-pack-a-day smoker inhales 50,000 to 70,000 puffs which contain over 2,000 chemical compounds, many of which are known carcinogens. A president of the American Cancer Society, Dr. Robert V. P. Hutter, said that many tobacco product ingredients, such as flavoring additives, are kept secret even from the government.

The cost of smoking-related diseases is staggering.   6
Health care in the United States costs over $280 billion each year. Smoking accounts for approximately $53 billion per year. A great deal of this cost is paid by nonsmokers and smokers through ever-increasing health insurance premiums, disability payments, and other programs. It doesn't seem fair that nonsmokers have to pay one penny for self-induced smokers' diseases.

The longer a person smokes, the greater is his or her risk   7
of dying. A person who smokes two packs a day has a death rate two times higher than a nonsmoker. The earlier a person

starts smoking, the higher is his or her risk of death. Smokers who inhale have higher mortality rates than smokers who do not.

If a smoker stops smoking, his or her mortality rate 8 decreases progressively as the number of nonsmoking years increase. Those who have stopped for fifteen years have mortality rates similar to those who never smoked, with the exception of smokers who stopped after the age of 65. Persons who smoke cigars and pipes also have an increased risk of death. Life expectancy is eight to nine years shorter for a two-pack-a-day smoker of age 30 to 35 than it is for a nonsmoker, and those who smoke cigarettes with higher contents of "tar" and nicotine have a much higher death rate. Overall, the greatest mortality is seen in the 45 to 55 age groups. Hence, death from smoking is premature death!

—Charles B. Simone, M.D.

1. According to the WHO, what will happen to the number of premature deaths caused by tobacco in the future?

2. Why will this happen?

3. What did the cigarette industry's own research show over a ten-year period?

Questions about the Textbook Chapters

Compare the two textbook chapters that you just read by answering the following questions.

1. Which chapter was easier to work with? Why?

   _____

   _____

   _____

2. Which strategy did you find most helpful? Explain.

   _____

   _____

   _____

3. How did the writer of the history chapter help you focus on the most important information?

   _____

   _____

   _____

3. What was different about the way each chapter was organized?

   _____

   _____

   _____

   _____

   _____

   _____

_____

_____

_____

_____

_____

_____

_____

_____

Practice 3

*Preview the following selection. Begin by using the **listing** or **freewriting** skills you first learned in Chapter 1.*

Freewrite or list here:

_____

_____

_____

_____

_____

Write your preview questions here:

_____

_____

_____

_____

_____

Culture Clash: Foreign Parents, American Child Rearing

Sophisticated New Yorkers don't slow down at the sight of a headless chicken on the steps of the Bronx courthouse. They pretend not to notice when a taxi driver crosses himself passing a church. And they have learned to live with dense accents, impolite shopkeepers, loud music and the strong smell of curry. 1

But there are limits to how far New Yorkers are willing to go in the name of cultural sensitivity. That limit was recently tested in three cases involving children and their foreign parents. 2

In April a Russian couple left their 4-year-old daughter home alone and went out dancing. Last May a Danish tourist left her 14-month-old daughter outside a restaurant while she ate inside. This month a Russian émigré left her 7-year-old son to play in a park while she went to work. 3

The parents all told the police they were only doing what is the norm back home. Their lawyers claimed theirs were not criminal cases but incidents of cultural differences and that understanding, not punishment, was required. New Yorkers were unmoved. Here, they answered, we call that kind of behavior child endangerment. And it's illegal. 4

Perhaps American children are spoiled (studies certainly show that). Perhaps their parents are overprotective, even paranoid. But when a child's welfare is in jeopardy, they quickly respond. New York City in particular turns into a small town and reacts with a vengeance against parents who behave badly. In each of the three New York cases the parents were arrested and their children placed in foster care. 5

Whether the defense of cultural differences is legitimate or not, it is irrelevant, social workers say. Yet today more and more parents are claiming such differences when faced with accusations of child neglect or abuse. 6

Different Strokes

New York City is not atypical. In Lincoln, Neb., Iraqi-born parents were charged with child abuse after they married their teen-age daughters (13 and 14) to grown men. The parents said they were following tradition. In Miami, Jorge Arévalo, a Peruvian, had to prove to social workers that he was a fit father after a woman in a parking lot complained that he had grabbed his screaming 5-year-old by the neck. 7

"It's amazing the things we don't know about this country," Mr. Arévalo said, "I learned that in this country anybody can call the police if they see you pulling your son's ear." 8

Social workers say Americans also beat their children, send them to bed hungry or cleanse them in religious rites that are frightening and sometimes dangerous. But foreign-born parents pose a tougher challenge because they can plead ignorance or cultural differences, a highly charged term in these politically correct times.

Social workers are trained to be sensitive to these idiosyncrasies, but not permissive. A child who is found to be at risk is put in foster care while the parents are investigated, regardless of their claims, said Dr. Marceline Watler, director of community education with the Administration for Children's Services.

"Cultural differences are beautiful, but they have nothing to do with the law," she said. "We can't possibly have a set of laws for Americans, a set of laws for immigrants and then a set of laws for tourists."

Mrs. Watler often encounters parents who simply do not understand what abuse is. They say they should be able to rear their children as they were reared, she said. They also invoke their new American rights. They ask: Isn't this the land of the free? Why is the Government meddling in my private affairs? Social workers must explain the difference between discipline and punishment, and that hitting, in public or private, is unacceptable.

Children Dominate

But sociologists argue that cultural differences are real and should be considered when applying the law. Child protective agencies, they say, sometimes rigidly react to immigrants and tourists who are not necessarily abusive.

Julia Wrigley, a professor of sociology at the graduate center of the City University of New York and the author of *Other People's Children* (Basic Books, 1995), found that foreigners are often surprised at how sheltered American children are. Preoccupied with their children's emotional and intellectual development, American are overly attentive.

"Our children dominate the household, the dinner table chatter," Mrs. Wrigley said. "But people from other cultures don't encourage high-demand children. Their children tend to be much more independent. Those from Western countries especially, are not accustomed to what they see as our paranoia with children."

In many places in Europe, children go out to play by themselves, she said, because of a basic trust among adults, however naïve, that nobody would want to harm a child. They also live in societies that are safer, more community oriented than America. People new to this country should adapt, Mrs. Wrigley said, but separating a mother from a child for a small cultural transgression is extreme.

Social workers agree that education, not punishment, is 17 the best way to adapt to America's attitudes. But if a child's life is at stake, emergency measures are required, Mrs. Watler said. The parents will have to learn the hard way.

—Mirta Ojito

Write the answers to your preview questions here, if possible.

_____

_____

_____

_____

_____

_____

_____

_____

Essay Question

The writer presents two viewpoints about some foreign parents' treatment of their children in America. Explain the two views and tell which one you agree with and why.

_____

_____

_____

PART THREE

CHAPTER

7

Organizing Information

Once you have carefully read, marked, and annotated the most important information in a text, you are ready to complete your **game plan for effective reading.** By using the **strategies** you learned in Part 1, "Before You Read," and Part 2,"While You Read," you identified the information that you must now organize in a meaningful way.

The organization of information is vital to successful studying, participating in class discussions, and performing well on tests. Also, the organizing process helps you to see the relationship among the facts, ideas, and concepts that make up the text.

The strategies that you learned to use in the **prereading** ("Before You Read") and **reading** ("While You Read") helped you comprehend written information. Now you are going to learn how to organize the information so that you can remember it and use it to your advantage. The three **postreading strategies** that you will learn to help you organize information from the text are:

1. Outlining
2. Mapping
3. Summarizing

The two main advantages of organizing information are that you have all of the key material at your fingertips in an easy to understand format and that you do not have to reread the entire text when you need to study to prepare for a class or a test.

Questions

1. What strategies will you learn to use to organize information?

_____

_____

_____

2. Why is organizing the information that you have read important?

_____

_____

_____

Outlining

Outlining is a method that condenses or shortens a great deal of material into manageable units and helps you keep track of the main ideas and important details.

An outline organizes information by relating main ideas and details to the topic of the text. An outline also helps you identify the controlling ideas of a long reading and provides you with a study guide that should be used to prepare for class discussions and tests.

However, outlining is time-consuming. Therefore, it is most useful when you need to study complex or difficult material. When you outline, beware of including too many details, as many students do. If you choose to outline as an information organizer, be sure to include only main ideas, major details, and a few examples that are essential to your understanding of the main ideas.

There is no need to write complete sentences in an outline. Key words and short phrases will do. As you make an outline, be sure to keep its purpose in mind—to condense information so that you can remember it.

The following sequence demonstrates an outline's structure:

Outlining

I. Helps students organize information

    A. Shows relationship of Main Ideas to Controlling Idea in longer selections

    B. Shows relationship of Details to Main Ideas

II. Helps students prepare for class and tests

    A. Condenses large amounts of information

        1. Groups important ideas and details together

            a. Makes remembering easier

            b. Makes material clearer and more meaningful

        2. Eliminates rereading of entire text before class or test

As you will see in the practice exercise that follows, you must use the **game plans** that you learned in the previous chapters before you make an outline. The **outlining strategy** is to:

1. Use the previewing, main idea, and marking and annotation strategies.
2. Think and decide what the topic is. This becomes the title of the outline.
3. Think and decide which main ideas and details are important.
4. Make the main ideas the major headings (roman numerals).
5. List the details under the main ideas.

Practice 1

Example: On the next page is a brief textbook selection and an **outline** of it. The selection is marked and annotated so that you can see how the outline is developed from the strategies used **while reading.** You will notice that the topic becomes the title, the important main ideas become the roman numerals, the most important details related to the main idea become the capital letters, and minor details related to important details become arabic numbers. When you make your outline, you must think carefully to decide (1) which main ideas and details are important enough to include and (2) how the information is related. You will also see that words of the selection have been paraphrased (stated in the reader's own words), which lets the reader check his or her understanding and helps him or her remember the content.

Topic

Gender Differences in Aggression

Main Idea

Most researchers agree that greater <u>physical aggression</u> in <u>males</u> is one of the most <u>consistent</u> and <u>significant differences</u> observed <u>in</u> comparative <u>studies</u> of <u>gender</u>. And these *differences are consistent across cultures* <u>differences</u> have been <u>found</u> in virtually <u>every culture</u> where aggressive behavior has been studied. Such an observation is hardly surprising. We need only <u>consider the number</u> *example* <u>ber of men in prison for violent crimes compared to the</u> <u>number of women.</u>

Main Idea

   <u>Greater aggression</u> can usually be <u>observed</u> in <u>boys</u> from the time they are <u>2 to 2½</u> years old. They are <u>more</u> *example* <u>likely</u> than girls <u>to engage</u> in <u>mock fighting</u> and rough-and-tumble play and to <u>have aggressive fantasies</u> (Maccoby & Jacklin, 1974). *word of caution* (But) <u>females can be aggressive</u>, too. They may be even <u>more likely</u> than males <u>to use *indirect*</u> forms *examples* of <u>aggression</u>, such as <u>gossip, spreading rumors</u>, and <u>rejecting, ignoring</u>, or <u>avoiding the target of aggression</u> (Bjorkquist et al., 1992).

—Samuel E. Wood & Ellen Green Wood

Gender Differences in Aggression

I. Greater physical aggression in males is consistent research finding

   A. True across cultures that are studied

   B. Example: greater number of males in prison for violent crimes

II. Greater aggression observed by two years

    A. Boys more apt to include mock fighting, pushing, and rough stuff in play activities

    B. Girls' aggressive behavior mostly *indirect*

        1. Gossip, ignoring

        2. Avoidance of person they want to hurt

Now it's your turn. Refer to the selection about American democracy on pages 97 to 99 to complete the following outline. Use the annotated and underlined material.

American Democracy

I. Political system of United States based on rule by the people

    A. Importance of the individual

        1. _____

           _____

           _____

           _____

        2. Inalienable rights

           a. _____*life*_____

           b. _____*liberty*_____

           c. _____*pursuit of happiness*_____

        3. These rights are protected by the state

           a. _____*constitution*_____

           b. _____*tyranny*_____

    B. Consent of the governed

        1. Government gets power from _____*people*_____

           _____

           _____

2. Direct democracy is _used in small communities_

3. Representative democracy is _used in large political systems_

4. Participation is _a duty for every citizen_

C. Majority rule and minority rights

   1. Majority determines winners of elections
     and _laws passed_

   2. Minorities must have _right to vote, to be heard to dissent must be protected_

D. Equality of opportunity means that _all men and women are created equal_

   1. Achieving equality of opportunity is controversial
     because _African Americans challenge privileges granted to whites_

   2. _Programs that assist minorities provoke mixed reactions_

How did annotating and underlining help you complete the outline?

Very helpful easier to understand once outline is done.

Practice 2

In each of the following selections:

1. **Annotate** and **underline** the main ideas and important details.
2. Make an **outline** that shows the main ideas and important details.

Selection 1:

A Nation of Beepers

There are 15 million pagers in use today. That number ₁ could easily be 50 million by 2000. "Beepers" are used, for example, in many shopping malls: Restaurants that take no reservations lend pagers so you need not wait around for 45 minutes. One-hour eyeglass laboratories beep you when your specs are ready. The mall's babysitting service will alert you if your child demands that you return.

Add other convenient uses, such as the ability to reach ₂ a delayed delivery-truck, and you can see how rapidly the use of pagers will grow. Fortunately, you won't hear all these gadgets scream in a crowd: The term "beeper" is nearly obsolete. New pagers play a soft musical tone or vibrate gently against you body to announce a message.

They're also getting cheaper. In most parts of the coun- ₃ try you can lease a basic pager for $10 to $15 a month. For $25 and up, you can have an "alphanumeric" pager that prints a message like, "Go to John's at 4:00," not just a phone number to call. All paging rates are about half what they were two years ago and could fall more because of heavy competition in this wide-open business.

—*Kiplinger's Personal Finance Magazine*

Some numerals and letters have been put in to help you start your outline and serve as a guide. Cross them out and use more space for your outline entries if you need to.

Outline

I. _frequent use of Beepers_

   A. _to inform_

   B. _emergencies_

II. _working useage_

   A. _alert for whatever reason_

   B. _noise isn't loudmusic / vibrate_

III. _cost_

   A. _varies depending on what the beeper does_

   B. _some pagers print messages the bussiness is widespread so there is losts of rompetion_

Selection 2:

Gender Stereotyping—Who Wins? Who Loses?

A majority of the people on the planet are female, yet around the world women are vastly underrepresented in positions of power. Gender stereotypes define males as decisive, aggressive, unemotional, logical, and ambitious. These qualities are perceived by many men and women alike as precisely the "right stuff" for leaders, decision makers, and power people at all levels of society. But women, too, can be strong, bold, and decisive leaders—like former British Prime Minister Margaret Thatcher, Golda Meir of Israel, and Indira Ghandi of India. Yet in 1995, only 8 of the 100 U.S. senators and 48 of the 435 members of the House of Representatives were women.

Today, 99 percent of men and 98 percent of women say that women should receive equal pay for equal work (Newport, 1993). Yet the average female worker in the United States is paid only 77 cents for every dollar paid to a male worker (Famighetti, 1994). And women are more likely to hold low-paying, low-status jobs. 2

—Samuel E. Wood and Ellen Green Wood

I. Effects of Gender Stereotyping _____

    A. _____

        1. _____

        2. _____

    B. _____

        1. _____

        2. _____

        3. _____

II. _____

    A. _____

    B. _____

Selection 3:

Risk Factors for Becoming an Alcoholic

We have known for some time that one's risk for becoming an alcoholic increased three to four times if members of one's family were alcoholics. Researchers have discovered that this increased risk, which exists across cultures, may result from both environmental and genetic factors. 1

Environmental risk factors include a number of psychological and emotional traits that are learned by being in a 2 family with one or more alcoholic members. Examples of environmental risk factors, which occur in children of alcoholic parents, include difficulties in showing trust, overdependency in relationships, and exaggerated reaction to events out of their control. When faced with these and other problems, children of alcoholic parents may turn to alcohol and abuse it as did their parents.

Genetic risk factors, which are inherited predispositions that increase the potential for alcoholism, have been identified by Robert Cloninger (1987) and his associates. They report that children of alcoholic parents, even when adopted by nonalcoholics, are three or four times more likely to become alcoholics than children born to nonalcoholics. 3

It is important to remember that not every child of an alcoholic parent becomes an alcoholic. Thus, other environmental variables, such as support in childhood, quality of home life, and successful coping with stress, apparently decrease the risk of alcoholism. 4

—Rod Plotnik

Outline

_____

_____

_____

_____

_____

_____

_____

_____

_____

_____

_____

_____

Selection 4:

A Function of Education: Socialization

Because it transmits the values, skills, and knowledge of a culture to a society's new members, including the young and immigrants, education perpetuates culture. Students learn from their teachers and peers to behave in socially acceptable ways, so the educational process also acts as a type of social control. In fact, attending school gives many students their first opportunity to develop loyalties outside the family, something they will later do in the world of work. In this way, they learn how to behave in secondary groups after spending their early years in primary groups. 1

At home, children are treated according to their personal needs and tastes and according to their personal relationships with other members of the family. In school, however, children are treated and evaluated by their performance rather than according to their personal characteristics. The schools use a grading system based on standardized criteria, and students learn that their performance in school is being assessed and will have consequences for their future educational and work careers. In general, they learn to see their academic success or failure as a product of their own abilities, rather than as a consequence of luck or some ascribed social trait. Schools theoretically treat and evaluate all students according to standards that are applied to everyone in the same way, but in fact students of different genders, classes, and ethnic groups are often treated less objectively. 2

—John R. Conklin

Outline

_____

_____

_____

_____

_____

_____

_____

_____

_____

_____

_____

Selection 5:

Frederick Douglass

Frederick Douglass (1817–95), a leading advocate of civil   1
rights for both blacks and women, was the son of a slave and
an unidentified white man. Although born into slavery, Douglass learned how to read and write. Once he escaped to the
North (where 250,000 free blacks lived), he became a well-
known orator and journalist. He spoke to abolitionist groups
about his experiences as a slave and included these experiences in his autobiography, _Narrative of the Life of Frederick
Douglass._ His life was also romanticized in song.

In 1847 he started a newspaper, _The North Star,_ in   2
Rochester, New York, and it quickly became a powerful
voice against slavery. Douglass was a strong abolitionist,
who urged President Abraham Lincoln to emancipate the
slaves and helped recruit black soldiers for the Union forces
in the Civil War. His home in Rochester, New York, was a
station along the Underground Railroad. Douglass was also a
firm believer in women's suffrage, and he attended the
Seneca Falls Convention (the first women's rights convention) in 1848. He was a close friend of John Brown, whose raid
at Harpers Ferry was a pivotal moment in the antislavery
movement. After the Civil War, Douglass was appointed to
several minor federal posts, including that of minister to
Haiti from 1889 to 1891. He was considered the greatest
black leader of his time. When he died in 1895, five states
adopted resolutions of regret, and two U.S. senators and one
Supreme Court justice were among honorary pallbearers.

—Karen O'Connor and Larry J. Sabato

Outline

_____

_____

_____

_____

_____

_____

_____

_____

_____

_____

_____

_____

_____

_____

_____

_____

_____

Review: Outlining

- Use the **previewing** and **main idea** strategies.
- Use the **text marking** and **annotating** strategies.
- Think and include the major main ideas and details in the **outline.**
- Show the relationship of important **details** to **main ideas** and **main ideas** to the **controlling idea** by using roman numerals, capital letters, and arabic numbers.

Questions about Outlining

1. How does outlining help you organize information?

_____

_____

_____

2. How do you show that details are related to main ideas in an outline?

_____

_____

_____

Mapping

Another method of condensing text to make it easier to remember is to make what we call a **map** of the information. Maps let you "see" the main ideas of the information in the text. They also help you organize the information by showing details related to main ideas. In addition, making a map helps you remember what you have read because you must paraphrase, or write in your own words, the material that you have read. When you can clearly paraphrase the writer's words, you are much more likely to remember the information.

Following is a sample of a **mapping structure.**

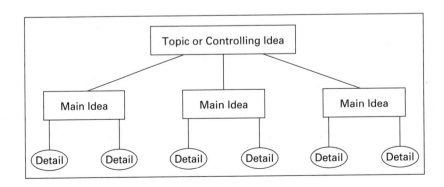

You can design your maps to fit your own needs. You do not need to write complete sentences in your maps. Key words or short phrases will do. The idea is for the map to trigger your memory about important information that you need to remember.

Practice 3

*For each of the following selections, make a **map** that shows the **topic** or the **controlling idea, main ideas,** and **details.** Remember to use the previewing, main idea, annotating, and marking strategies as you read the selections. Study the example below before you begin and try mapping a selection you have already read, "Choosing a Wet Suit," in the space provided.*

Example: Here is a **map** of the selection "Purpose of a Resume," from Chapter 4. You can "see" the main ideas and details related to the controlling idea.

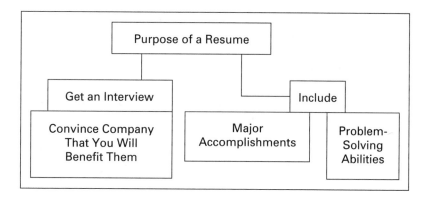

You can see that the lines drawn from the title (the topic) are connected to the two main ideas and that the boxes under the second main idea contain details about it. Maps can be made to show these important pieces of information about any selection.

Here is the beginning of a map of the selection "Choosing a Wet Suit," on page 93. Check to see how the underlined information is used. Then complete the map on a separate piece of paper and answer the question that follows.

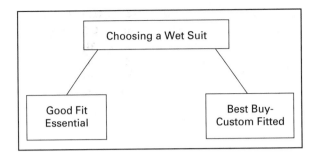

```
┌─────────────────────────────────────────────┐
│            ┌──────────────────┐              │
│            │ Choosing a Wet Suit │           │
│            └──────────────────┘              │
│          /                      \            │
│  ┌──────────────┐        ┌──────────────┐    │
│  │  Good Fit    │        │  Best Buy-   │    │
│  │  Essential   │        │ Custom Fitted│    │
│  └──────────────┘        └──────────────┘    │
└─────────────────────────────────────────────┘
```

How were you able to use the annotated and underlined material to help you make the map?

_____

_____

_____

_____

_____

Selection 1:

Heartening Health News

Here's a welcome reprieve from ominous health reports: Two new studies suggest a couple of painless ways to ward off heart disease. 1

In one, researchers from the British Heart Foundation claim that taking a walk before eating high-fat meals may speed your body's ability to rid itself of triglycerides, which are the fats that can cause heart disease. 2

They studied a group of male and female volunteers in their twenties for a four-day period. Some days, the group took a brisk two-hour walk before sitting down to a breakfast consisting of fatty cereals, chocolate, buns and cream. Other days, the group simply rested before the hearty repast. 3

The concentration of triglycerides was lower on the walking days than it was on the rest days. The researchers were so enthused by the results, they're already working on their next experiment: determining the effect of post-meal walking on triglyceride levels. 4

Another study, by the Centers for Disease Control and Prevention in Atlanta, also offers some clear-cut advice: 5

cheer up. The CDC researchers found that mildly to moderately depressed people are more prone to heart disease.

Over a period of 12 years, researchers followed 2,832 adult volunteers, 11 percent of whom claimed to be down in the dumps. At the end of the study, those who had complained of depression were more likely to have become ill or died from heart disease than those who hadn't complained at all. 6

The moral of the story? Keep your spirits up and take walks for a healthy heart. 7

—C. J. Vimont

Make your map here:

Selection 2:

Alternative Medicine

Long a staple in many cultures, alternative medicine is the choice of a growing number of American health care consumers. One out of three American adults has tried some type of "unconventional" medical treatment, the *New England Journal of Medicine* reported earlier this year. And the number of visits to providers of unconventional therapy was found to be greater than the number of visits to all primary care physicians nationwide. 1

What's behind this growing revolution in health care? A number of factors, including skyrocketing costs for conventional treatment, a desire for a more holistic approach to treatment, and a need to find long-range solutions to many chronic conditions, such as back pain, sinusitis and headache. 2

While there's no single recognized system of classification for alternative medicine, the majority of therapies can be divided into four general categories. 3

Treatment with physical forces and devices. Practitioners include chiropractors, body works practitioners, and acupuncturists. 4

Spiritual and psychological therapies. Practitioners include those who use mental imagery techniques and hypnosis as well as psychics, mystics, and others who engage in paranormal health remedies. 5

Nutritional therapies. Treatments include herbal, vitamin, and mineral dietary supplements, and specific regimens, such as a macrobiotic diet. 6

Drug and biologic treatment. Practitioners, including homeopathic physicians, prescribe treatments including drugs, chemicals, and serums. 7

Most experts from both traditional and alternative medicine agree that nontraditional treatment should be viewed as a complement to conventional medical treatment, rather than a replacement for it. This is particularly true in emergency situations, such as those involving broken bones, chest pains, high fevers, or excessive bleeding. 8

Today, alternative medical therapy is used primarily by people with chronic health problems that don't respond to conventional medical treatment and by those who use it as a method of preventive health care. 9

—*NEA Today*

Make your map here:

Selection 3:

Mayan Culture

In the isthmus of Central America, the Mayans built a brilliant civilization a thousand years before Columbus. Giant temples for their gods and pyramids for the dead suggest the importance of religious beliefs. Furthermore, the Mayan notion of an afterlife, of spirits that existed beyond the realm of sight and sound and touch, was a powerful idea that took the thoughts of men and women away from the day-to-day gathering of food. The building of temples required an army of workers. Cities sprang up around these construction projects, and people were fed by food growers in the hinterland. Specialization of work encouraged trade, and prosperity fostered art and science. A thousand years before the Spaniards came, the Mayans had a civilization equal to any in the world. Among its achievements were the development of paper, the invention of the numerical concept of zero, and the use of a solar calendar.

—Norman K. Risjord

Make your map here:

Selection 4:

Depression

For our early ancestors, depression was a beneficial state 1
when they had to put up with a period of harsh conditions in
their environment. When things got rough, they really had to
withdraw to retrench. Our early ancestors who got depressed
and just sat around during very frustrating times were more
likely to conserve their resources and energy. In doing so,
they increased their chances for survival until better times
came along. We probably see an indication of this primitive
emotional residue in ourselves on a cold, overcast, wintry
Saturday when, for no reason we can put our finger on, we
find it difficult to do anything besides snacking, napping, and
moping around the house. The common depression you and
I often experience may last from several hours to several
days. We feel miserable, but with time and some positive experience our depression lifts.

In the relatively affluent society we live in today, de- 2
pression and withdrawal have no apparent survival benefits.
For most of us, conditions are not so physically harsh and demanding as they were for our early ancestors. So this psychological "hibernation" mechanism of depression, evolved

by our ancestors for successfully waiting out harsh periods in the environment, does nothing for us. Our frustrations today do not come from the environment but from the action of other people. Patients that therapists see today because they have a long-term depression have a history of being frequently frustrated.

—Manuel J. Smith

Make your map here:

Selection 5:

Profit

The *profit* principle is another basic characteristic of the capitalist system. A capitalist economy provides more opportunity for profit than any other economy because it guarantees three freedoms that are not commonly found in other systems—freedom of trade and occupation, freedom of property and freedom of contract.

When the capitalist system is described as a profit system, it is frequently forgotten that the other side of the transaction is equally important—capitalism is also a *loss* system. Although it is true that never have so many made so much profit as under capitalism, it is equally true that in no other system have so many lost so much. In American economic development, bankruptcies and failures were very common in the early stages of the mining, railroading, and automotive industries. In the computer industry the Radio Corporation of America, a giant company, tried in vain to get a permanent place in the business. After making computers for two decades, RCA finally decided to close down computer production. In a typical year about four out of ten corporations report net losses. Of ten business firms started in an average year, five close down within two years and eight within ten years—lack of success being the main reason.

—William Ebenstein and Edwin Fogelman

Make your map here:

Review: Mapping

- Use the **previewing** and **main idea strategies.**
- Use the **underlining** and **annotating strategies.**
- Make a **map** to show the main ideas and important details related to the topic in a short selection or the controlling idea in a long selection.

Questions about Mapping

1. How did the strategies you learned in the previous chapters help you with mapping?

_____

_____

_____

_____

_____

2. Which method, outlining or mapping, helps you understand and remember what you have read better?

_____

Why?

_____

_____

_____

Summarizing

A **summary** is a short or condensed version of the information you have read. It is written in your own words in complete sentences. When you summarize, you are making sure that you understand and remember the most important information in the text.

A good summary can be written by first using the strategies you have already learned to understand and organize information. Writing a summary forces you to review the author's controlling idea, main ideas, and important details. In a summary, you restate or paraphrase this important information in your own words. If you can easily write an accurate summary, you probably have a very good understanding of the material you have read. If you have difficulty writing a summary, you probably need to reread and reapply the strategies you have learned.

Writing a summary can be easy if you take the following steps:

1. Use your previewing, marking, and annotating strategies.
2. Think and decide on the controlling idea of the selection.
3. Make a map or outline of the selection.
4. Write a first sentence that paraphrases the controlling idea of the text.
5. Write more sentences to restate the main ideas and, if necessary, important details that are essential to making the controlling idea clearly understood. Use the headings on your outline or map to do this.

Practice 4

Use the five steps listed in this section to help you write two **summaries**—*a summary of one of the articles that you outlined and a summary of one of the articles that you mapped.*

Example: Here is a **summary** of the selection "Gender Differences in Aggression," which was annotated and outlined in this chapter on page 120. As you read the summary, notice that the controlling idea is in the first sentence of the summary and that the main ideas and details are **paraphrased** (rewritten in your own words) in the same order they were found in the selection. It is important to keep the same sequence or order of ideas in your summary as found in the article so that events or related ideas do not become confused.

You also should notice that the summary can be written from either the marked and annotated text or the outline. Most students say that it is easier to use the outline or map to write the summary, but you should try it both ways to see which is most helpful to you.

Gender Differences in Aggression

Researchers state that males show greater physical aggression than females in almost every culture in which aggressive behavior has been studied. This is demonstrated in our culture where far more men than women are in prison for violent crimes. By age two boys are more aggressive than girls, which they show by pretend fighting and aggressive fantasies. Females do show aggression, but it is usually indirect (gossip, rejecting and avoiding).

—Samuel E. Wood and Ellen Green Wood

Go back and reread this summary and note that the first sentence not only states the main idea of the selection but combines supporting details found in the second and third sentences. Combining a main idea with supporting details in one sentence is a good idea because it helps you see related ideas and lets you keep the summary short. Sentence two of the summary is a detail that helps prove the first sentence. Now, reread the third sentence of the summary and you will see that it combines the second main idea with important, specific examples. The last sentence of the summary explains the second main idea by telling how girls' aggressive behavior is different from boys'.

1. Write a summary of one of the articles that you outlined.

_____

_____

_____

_____

_____

_____

_____

_____

_____

_____

_____

2. Write a summary of one of the articles that you mapped.

_____

_____

_____

_____

_____

_____

_____

_____

_____

_____

_____

Questions about Summarizing

1. How did the other strategies you have learned help you write the summary?

_____

_____

_____

_____

2. Did you find it easier to write a summary using an outline or a map? _____ Explain what features of the outline or map made your summary writing easier.

_____

_____

_____

_____

_____

Practice 5

As you read the following selections:

1. Apply the **annotating** and **marking strategies.**
2. Identify the **controlling idea.**
3. Make a **map** or **outline** of the selection.
4. Write a **summary** of the selection.

Selection 1:

Women and Karate

Rosalind Wiseman, one of five female American "tang soo do" black belts, enjoys bucking the stereotype that women are not meant to be involved in hand-to-hand combat. She is one of the 900,000 more women who study martial arts in the 1990's than did in the 1980's. Wiseman's presence was condoned in the dojo when the Pan American Union of Karate-Do Organizations gave women permission to compete in their tournaments in the mid-1980's. Now, women make up approximately thirty percent of all martial artists in the United States. [1]

The mental and spiritual challenges of Karate are an adjunct to the calesthenics that would rival a most intense training program. Warming up with 100 sit-ups and 30 push-ups is commonplace at many Karate schools. [2]

Wiseman says that the fact that you are able to face your fears during sparring makes you feel that you can do anything. [3]

She also says that women can compensate for their lack of upper-body strength by emphasizing their lower-body strength. "So many guys expect you to be weak," gloats Wiseman, "that once in a while, you have to punch a guy really hard in the face so he knows he is fighting someone better."

—Sidney G. Becker

Controlling Idea:

Map or Outline:

Summary:

_____

_____

_____

_____

_____

_____

_____

_____

_____

_____

Selection 2:

Amelia Bloomer and Women's Dress Reform

The debate began as something of a joke, but for women the problem was real. Women's fashions in the 1850's were impractical, unhealthy, and sometimes dangerous. Skirts flowed in a "great pyramid" from a tiny waist to a wide, floor-length bottom. To achieve the desired effect, women pinched their waists with corsets, sometimes so tightly that they injured internal organs. The skirt, requiring eighteen to twenty yards of material, was so massive that it was difficult to get through doorways and halls. An accidental brush against fireplace, oven, or lighted candle was a constant danger.

A conservative newspaper editor from upstate New York started the debate when he jokingly suggested that female reformers ought to wear pantaloons in imitation of men. Amelia Jenks Bloomer promptly took up the idea. She had long sponsored a variety of reforms, including temperance and women's rights. Her home was Seneca Falls, New York; both she and her husband had attended the Women's Rights Convention of 1848. She also published _The Lily,_ the first newspaper owned and edited by a woman and devoted to the interests of women. In response to the editor's sneer, she took up the cause of dress reform.

Amelia Bloomer was not prepared to cut off her own 3 skirts, however. That bold move was made by a friend of hers, Elizabeth Smith Miller. On her honeymoon in Switzerland, Mrs. Miller visited a hospital where women were recuperating from the damage done by too-tight corsets. For comfort, the patients were wearing Turkish pantaloons gathered at the ankle and partially covered by a knee-length skirt. Elizabeth Miller brought the costume home to Seneca Falls. Amelia Bloomer adopted it and broadcast its advantages in the columns of *The Lily*. Newspapers around the country quickly picked up the story and the bloomer became a symbol of the women's rights movement.

—Norman K. Risjord

Controlling Idea:

_____

_____

_____

_____

Map or Outline:

Summary:

_____

_____

_____

_____

_____

_____

_____

_____

_____

_____

Selection 3:

Drowsiness and Driving

Drowsiness while driving is caused by lack of visual or 1
physical stimulation. This happens frequently on express-
ways and roads where there is very little change in the environment. After continually seeing the same visual images
over and over, the senses stop perceiving any fresh stimuli.
This monotony causes a drop in information processing,
dulled perception, muscle relaxation, and narrowing of the
visual field, or tunnel vision.

What can you do to avoid fatigue and drowsiness? 2

First of all, recognize the symptoms and signs of drowsi- 3
ness. Some of these symptoms are: a lack of concentration,
aching back or hips, staring straight ahead of your vehicle, in-
ability to keep your eyes open, and restlessness.

To avoid drowsiness while driving, add variation to dri- 4
ving operations. Open the window for fresh air, listen to the
radio, stop for a break and exercise. If you are the driver, you
will be more apt to become drowsy if passengers are sleeping.

Ask the person in the passenger's seat to stay awake. Switch drivers every two to four hours.

—National Safety Council

_____

Controlling Idea:

_____

_____

_____

_____

Map or Outline:

Summary:

_____

_____

_____

_____

_____

_____

_____

_____

_____

_____

Selection 4:

The Concept of Occupational Crime

The commission of crime through occupational oppor-   1
tunity is hardly a new phenomenon. More than three thousand years ago, for instance, Horemheb, a pharaoh in Egypt in
the fourteenth century B.C., passed what was probably the
first law carrying a penalty for judicial bribes. Horemheb's
edict called for capital punishment for those who committed
such a "crime against justice." In ancient Greece, there were
the Alcmaenoids, a leading family, who are reported to have
contracted to build a solid marble temple, but instead used
concrete, veneering it with marble. In ancient Persia, bakers
who short-weighted bread or adulterated it with straw were
executed in their own ovens. Henry III passed laws against
"forestalling," which outlawed the practice of buying up large
amounts of foodstuffs, and thereby controlling prices. By
1812, England had adopted complex legal regulations regarding labor practices. And in 1890, the United States Congress
passed the Sherman Antitrust Act which outlawed unfair
competition resulting from practices such as price-fixing.

These are but a few examples along the historical road of   2
crime in the course of occupation. Such crime has aroused

public and official indignation for many centuries. During the past two decades, however, the level of attention and indignation has increased dramatically. Every day's newspaper usually has some item about occupational crime. The stories may involve political bribery, embezzlement, child molestation in day care centers, income tax evasion, insider trading in the stock market, environmental pollution, or police brutality—each episode an example of occupationally related criminal behavior.

—Gary S. Green

Controlling Idea:

_____

_____

_____

_____

Map or Outline:

Summary:

_____

_____

_____

_____

_____

_____

_____

_____

_____

_____

Review: Summarizing

- Use the **previewing** and **main idea strategies.**
- Use the **underlining** and **annotating strategies.**
- Make a **map** or an **outline**
- Begin the **summary** with the **controlling idea.**
- Write the **main ideas** and important **details** in your own words. Keep the sequence of ideas the same as they are in the text.

More Questions about Summarizing

1. Why is it important to be able to write a clear summary of what you have read?

   _____

   _____

   _____

2. How do the other strategies you have learned help you to write a summary?

   _____

   _____

   _____

3. What should you do if you have difficulty paraphrasing the writer's ideas in your summary?

   _____

   _____

   _____

8

Organizing Information with Longer Readings

This chapter consists of four selections on which you can practice your **prereading, reading,** and **postreading game plans.** Two of them are parts of textbook chapters. The other two selections are essays. For them, you need to use the **previewing strategy** for a reading without headings (see Chapter 2).

This is what you need to do for each selection:

1. Preview.
2. Develop three preview questions.
3. Find the main ideas and details. Underline them. Underline signal words.
4. Annotate in the margin.
5. Answer your own preview questions.
6. Make a map or an outline of the selection.
7. Write a summary of the selection.

Practice 1

Preview the selection "Lifestyle Patterns in Adulthood" from a psychology textbook. Show your preview on the text itself.

Write your preview questions here.

_____

_____

_____

_____

_____

_____

_____

_____

After you read the selection, answer your preview questions here.

_____

_____

_____

_____

_____

_____

_____

_____

_____

Lifestyle Patterns in Adulthood

Is the "average household" in the United States still   1
headed by a married couple? Yes, for more than two-thirds of
the population. The majority of people (67 percent) live in a

household headed by a married couple who may or may not have children under age 18 (U.S. Bureau of the Census, 1994).

Singles: Playing the Field

About 24 percent of males and 19 percent of females over age 18 are single (U.S. Bureau of the Census, 1994). Some people believe that if unburdened by a spouse, they will be able to pursue their careers and their interests and have a more interesting and exciting life. Yet the happiest singles seem to be those who have relationships that provide emotional support.

Marriage: Tying the Knot

Despite the growing alternatives to marriage, 67 percent of men and 77 percent of women in the United States either are married or have been married. Though the institution of marriage is still alive and and well, men and women are waiting longer to tie the knot. Since 1970, the average age at first marriage has increased by 3 years, to 25.5 years for males and 23.7 for females (U.S. Bureau of the Census, 1994).

Divorce: Untying the Knot

According to a 1989 Gallup poll, half of those who have ever been married have experienced severe marital problems or divorce, and 26 percent have been divorced at least once (Colasanto & Shriver, 1989). The reasons given for the divorce were basic personality differences or incompatibility (47 percent); infidelity (17 percent); a drug or alcohol problem (16 percent); disputes about money, family, or children (10 percent); and physical abuse (5 percent). People aged 35 to 54 experienced the most severe marital discord, and those over age 55, the least.

The marriages most likely to fail are teenage marriages, those in which the bride was pregnant, and marriages of people whose parents had divorced. And the marriages that do survive are not necessarily happy. Many couples stay together for reasons other than love—because of religious beliefs, for the sake of the children, for financial reasons, or out of fear of facing the future alone.

Parenthood: Passing Along the Genes

According to a 1990 Gallup poll, 90 percent of Americans over age 40 have had children, and despite the difficult task of raising them, only 7 percent say they wish they had never had children (Gallup & Newport, 1990d).

Even though most couples want children, satisfaction [7] with marriage does tend to decline after the birth of the first child (Belsky et al., 1989; Cowan & Cowan, 1992). Women in general find the period of child rearing the least satisfying time of marriage. The problem centers mainly on the division of work—who does what. Even though men are helping with children more than in the past, child care still generally ends up being primarily the responsibility of the woman. Unless she holds very traditional views of sex roles, a woman's dissatisfaction after the birth of the first child often relates to the discrepancy between how much help with child care and housework she had expected from her husband and how much help she actually receives (Hackel & Ruble, 1992). Glass and Fujimoto (1994) found that time spent in housework was related to an increase in depression for both husbands and wives. Several studies have revealed that when husbands in dual-earner families *do* help with child care, they show a decline in mental health (Rosenfield, 1992), a more negative view of their marriage, and an increase in marital conflict (Crouter et al., 1987).

Remaining Childless: No Bundles of Joy

Some couples are choosing not to have children, leaving [8] themselves free to devote their time, energy, and money to pursuing their own interests and careers. A few studies indicate that such couples are happier and find their marriages more satisfying than couples with children (Campbell, 1975). However, this same sense of satisfaction may not continue into middle and old age, when couples may wonder if their decision to remain childless was a good one. A 1990 Gallup poll found that only about 4 percent of Americans are "anti-children"—that is, they don't have any, they don't want any, or they are glad they never had any children (Gallup & Newport, 1990c). In spite of the tremendous emotional and financial investment children require, most parents find their children provide a major source of satisfaction and meaning in their lives and that the investment has been a good one.

—Samuel Wood and Ellen Green Wood

After you go back and answer your preview questions, make an outline or a map of this selection here (an outline with an explanation has been started for you):

Lifestyle Patterns in Adulthood
(title of selection is title of outline)

I. Introduction *(topic which shows information is from the introduction to the article)*

    A. Majority of people still live in households with married heads. *(main idea of introduction)*

        1. 67% of households in U. S. *(major detail)*

        2. May or may not have children *(major detail)*

II. Singles *(topic of this section)*

    A. 24% of males and 19% of females are unmarried *(main idea)*

    B.

Write a summary of this selection:

_____

_____

_____

_____

_____

_____

_____

_____

_____

_____

Practice 2

Preview the selection "Packaging" on pages 159–162.

Write your preview questions:

_____

_____

_____

_____

_____

_____

_____

After you read the selection, answer your preview questions here:

_____

_____

_____

_____

_____

_____

_____

_____

_____

_____

_____

Packaging

Introduction to Packaging

The activities throughout the marketing process that are concerned with the design and construction of the container or wrapping of a product are called packaging. Not too long ago, packaging decisions were based solely on the physical characteristics of the product. Goods were moved from the producer to the final consumer in a manner that would ensure product protection at the lowest possible cost. A prime example of this is the old general store, in which merchandise such as flour, sugar, and crackers was received in bulk containers such as sacks and barrels and distributed to housewives in small unmarked containers by the storekeeper. 1

More recently, the package in which the goods are held has become as much of a sales tool as it is a container. At present, proper package design is one of the most important factors in the competitive battle for sales. The producer with the best package has a decided edge over competitors, and all progressive business managers are constantly researching means to improve their packaging design. 2

Packaging Considerations

The problems of packaging design are not easy to solve. 3
Designing a good package poses many difficulties, and many

people are involved whose preferences may conflict. For example, the transportation and storage department may be primarily interested in the safety of the product and the ease with which it can be handled, whereas the main concern of the sales department is the package's eye appeal as a promotional device.

Packages must be individualized. That is, each type of goods has its own requirements and the design of the package must be unique to the specific goods involved. Several factors must be taken into consideration when packaging decisions are to be made. [4]

An example of a package that is both appealing visually and functional is the Pillsbury packaging for such products as Pizza Crust, Crescent Rolls, Cinnamon Rolls, and so on. Each package is distinctively styled to capture the shopper's attention and is specially packed to ensure freshness during the refrigeration period of transportation and storage on the retailers' shelves. [5]

The Retail Store

To design a package for a retail store, the designer must know the kind of store in which the package will be placed and the kind of customer who will buy the package. In a self-service supermarket, or any other self-service store, the package is an important selling device and the design of the package is vital to increased sales. The package must be visually competitive in order to facilitate the undecided shopper's choice. [6]

The designer must keep in mind the location of the store where the package will be placed. Must it fit on a supermarket shelf? Will it be part of a display? [7]

Transportation

Various transportation companies have standards and requirements that must be taken into account in packaging design. In addition, the size and weight of the shipping carton play an important role in the cost of transportation. Some goods require special treatment as to temperature control, moisture, pilferage, and bugs. [8]

The Consumer

Packages, to be effective, must be designed for home use. A container that is immediately emptied and discarded has different requirements from one that is used to store the product until its consumption. The length of time that the [9] contents will be stored and the method of use are also important. For example, it would be difficult to sell a pound of table salt in a flimsy container without a dispensing device. The packaging designer is also interested in whether or not the package is to be reusable for the same product, reusable for another product, returnable, stored in the kitchen or the basement, and so on.

Safety

While some attention has been given to packaging in terms of the consumer's safety as in the case of aspirin containers, which sometimes require proper alignment of the cap for opening, the Tylenol scare significantly underscored the necessity for safer packaging. Johnson & Johnson, faced with the possible demise of the enormously successful Tylenol, spent huge sums to alter the packaging of the product when tampering caused the deaths of some users. This serious problem clearly dictated to their company as well as others that safety must become at least as important in packaging as eye appeal. 10

Convenience

With the increasing number of women in the workplace and the need for people's quick preparation of prepared foods, the microwave oven has become a necessity in many households. Foods can be prepared in a fraction of the time it takes to cook them in the conventional manner. Bearing this in mind, food producers have repackaged many of their items in microwavable containers which virtually eliminate the need to transfer goods from the package to the cooking utensil. The foods are placed on trays or "pans" that are easily popped into the microwave for cooking. 11

Another convenience package is the "Bowl in the Box." This is not really new, but the reintroduction of a cereal package that was first introduced in the 1940s. It allows the user to discard the package, once used, and only wash the spoon. 12

Important Points

1. Packaging consists of the activities—throughout the marketing process—concerned with the design and construction of the container of a product. In recent years packagers are as much concerned with sales promotion as they are with product protection. 13

2. Since the characteristics of products vary, each package must be designed to fit the needs of the specific merchandise. Complications arise because consideration must be given to a variety of problems, for example, transportation, storage, type of customer, and use in the home. 14

3. The expansion of self-service shopping has placed strong emphasis on the use of the package as a "silent salesperson." Since in many cases the package must sell itself, it must be designed in an unusual eye-catching fashion. 15

—Jay Diamond and Gerald Pintel

After you go back to the beginning of this selection to answer your preview questions, make an **outline** *or a* **map** *of the selection in the space provided. Then write a* **summary** *of it.*

Outline or Map:

Summary:

_____

_____

_____

_____

_____

_____

_____

_____

_____

_____

_____

_____

_____

_____

_____

Questions about the Two Textbook Selections

Compare the two textbook selections to answer the following questions.

1. For which selection was it easier to apply the strategies?

_____

Why?

_____

_____

_____

_____

2. Which strategy did you find most helpful in organizing and re-membering the material?

_____

Explain how the strategy helped you.

_____

_____

_____

_____

3. How did the writer of the marketing selection help you focus on the most important information?

_____

_____

_____

_____

4. What was different about the way in which each selection was organized?

_____

_____

_____

_____

Practice 3

Take a look at the selection that follows, then begin by using ***prereading strategies.***

1. Freewrite or list about "Eating Disorders":

_____

_____

_____

_____

_____

_____

2. Write your preview questions here:

_____

_____

_____

_____

_____

_____

_____

3. After you read the selection, answer your preview questions here:

_____

_____

_____

_____

_____

_____

_____

_____

_____

_____

_____

_____

_____

Eating Disorders—The Tyranny of the Scale

1   Imagine this: The thought of even the slightest layer of fat on your body repels you. You have been dieting and exercising strenuously for months, but you still feel fat, even though your friends comment that you're nothing but skin and bones. And you're unbelievably hungry: You leaf through cookbooks, go grocery shopping, and prepare meals whenever you get a chance, but when you sit down to eat you merely play with your food, because if you ate it you might get fat.

2   Now imagine this: Driven by an uncontrollable urge, you buy a dozen packages of cookies, some soda, perhaps a box of doughnuts. You take them to your room, lock the door, and start eating them. Once you've started, you can't stop—you gorge yourself on cookies and doughnuts until you feel as if you're about to explode. At that point you are overcome with disgust and anger at yourself. You run to the bathroom and thrust your fingers down your throat to get rid of the excess volume of food you have consumed.

3   These two scenarios are not as unusual as you might think. They represent two surprisingly common eating disorders: anorexia nervosa and bulimia nervosa. What causes these disorders, and how can they be treated?

Anorexia Nervosa

4   Although there are some similarities between them, anorexia and bulimia are very different disorders. *Anorexia nervosa* is characterized by an overwhelming, irrational fear

of gaining weight or becoming fat, compulsive dieting to the point of self-starvation, and excessive weight loss. Some anorexics lose as much as 20 to 25 percent of their original body weight. Anorexia typically begins in adolescence, and 90 percent of those afflicted are females (American Psychiatric Association, 1994). About 1 percent of females between ages 12 and 40 suffer from this disorder (Brotman, 1994).

Anorexia often begins with dieting, perhaps in reaction   5
to a gain in weight after the onset of menstruation. Gradually the dieting develops into an obsession. Anorexic individuals continue to feel hunger and are strangely preoccupied with food. They spend inordinate amounts of time thinking about food, reading recipes, shopping for food, preparing it, and watching other people eat, although they may eat only the smallest portions themselves.

Anorexic individuals also have a gross distortion in the   6
perception of their body size. No matter how emaciated they become, they continue to perceive themselves as fat. In fact, they have been found to overestimate their body size by much as 31 percent (Penner et al., 1991). They are so obsessed with their weight that frequently they not only starve themselves but also exercise relentlessly and excessively in an effort to accelerate their weight loss. Among young women, progressive and significant weight loss eventually results in amenorrhea (cessation of menstruation). Anorexics also become weak and highly susceptible to infection. They may experience low blood pressure, impaired heart function, dehydration, electrolyte disturbances, and/or sterility (American Psychiatric Association, 1993).

Unfortunately as many as 20 percent of those suffering   7
from anorexia nervosa eventually die of starvation or complications from organ damage (Brotman, 1994). One casualty of the battle with anorexia and bulimia was gymnast Christy Heinrich who died in 1994 at the age of 22.

Causes and Treatment of Anorexia

It is difficult to pinpoint the cause of this disorder. Most   8
anorexic individuals are well-behaved children and good students (Vitousek & Manke, 1994). Some investigators believe that young women who refuse to eat are attempting to control a portion of their lives, which they may feel unable to control in other respects.

Anorexia is very difficult to treat. Most anorexics are   9
steadfast in their refusal to eat; some actually starve themselves to death while insisting that nothing is wrong with them. The main thrust of treatment efforts, therefore, is to

get the anorexic to gain weight. The patient may be admitted to a hospital, fed a controlled diet, and given rewards and privileges for small gains in weight and increased food intake. Antidepressant drugs may be used if a patient shows symptoms of depression or obsessive-compulsive disorder.

Bulimia Nervosa

Up to 50 percent of anorexics also develop symptoms of *bulimia nervosa*, a chronic disorder characterized by repeated and uncontrolled episodes of binge eating, often in secret (American Psychiatric Association, 1993). An episode of binge eating has two main features: (1) the consumption of much larger amounts of food than most people would eat during the same period of time, and (2) a feeling that one cannot stop eating or control the amount eaten. Binges—which generally involve foods that are rich in carbohydrates, such as cookies, cake, and candy—are frequently followed by purging: self-induced vomiting and/or the use of large quantities of laxatives and diuretics. Bulimics may also engage in excessive dieting and exercise. Athletes are especially susceptible to this disorder. Many bulimics are average in size and purge after an eating binge simply to maintain their weight. [10]

Bulimia nervosa can cause a number of health problems. The stomach acid in vomit eats away at the teeth and may cause them to rot, and the delicate balance of body chemistry is destroyed by excessive use of laxatives and diuretics. The bulimic may have a perpetually sore throat as well as a variety of other symptoms, including dehydration, swelling of the salivary glands, kidney damage, and hair loss. The disorder also has a strong emotional component; the bulimic person is aware that the eating pattern is abnormal and feels unable to control it. Depression, guilt, and shame often accompany the binges and subsequent purging. [11]

Bulimia nervosa tends to appear in the late teenage years and affects about 1 in 25 women during their lifetime (Kendler et al., 1991). An even larger number of young women regularly binge and purge, but not frequently enough to warrant the diagnosis of bulimia nervosa (Drewnowski et al., 1994). And contrary to the notion that bulimia is confined primarily to white, upper middle-class young women, in a survey of high school students, Smith and Krejci (1991) found even higher rates of binge eating among Native Americans and Hispanics. And about 10 to 15 percent of all bulimics are males (Carlat & Camargo, 1991). [12]

Bulimia, like anorexia, is difficult to treat. Cognitive-behavioral therapy has been used successfully to help bulim- [13]

ics modify their eating habits and their abnormal attitudes about body shape and weight (Fairburn et al., 1991; Wilson & Fairburn, 1993). Certain antidepressant drugs have been found to reduce the frequency of binge eating and purging and to result in significant attitudinal change (Agras et al., 1994; Goldbloom & Olmsted, 1993). A combination of medication and cognitive-behavioral therapy seems to be the most effective approach (Agras et al., 1992).

—Samuel E. Wood and Ellen Green Wood

*After you go back and answer your preview questions, use the information you underlined and annotated to make an **outline** or **map** of the selection. Then write a **summary.***

Create your Outline or Map:

Summary:

_____

_____

_____

_____

_____

_____

_____

_____

_____

_____

Group Activity

The selection in Practice 3 suggests that females are more likely than males to become anorexic or bulimic. What do you think are the causes of the higher rate of female anorexia and bulimia? Make a list of your causes, listen to the ideas of other group members, and try to come to a group consensus (agreement) about the main causes. Have a recorder (secretary) list the three main causes that your group agrees on and be prepared to listen to and compare these causes with those listed by other groups.

Practice 4

*Begin by using your **prereading strategies** on the selection title that follows.*

1. Freewrite or list about "The Big Fat Lie":

_____

_____

_____

_____

_____

_____

2. Write your preview questions here:

_____

_____

_____

_____

_____

3. After you read the selection, answer your preview questions here:

_____

_____

_____

_____

_____

_____

_____

The Big Fat Lie

In these days of enlightened political correctness, when   1
most people have learned to tolerate different races, reli-

gions, and sexual orientations, as well as the physically challenged and those who do battle with drug and alcohol addictions, it is still completely acceptable—even fashionable—to be scathingly cruel to those who are overweight.

Fat-bashing is a women's problem. Fat men can be cute, cuddly, even powerful. The expansive physiques of John Goodman, Luciano Pavarotti, Charles Durning, and Charles Kuralt are simply part of who they are: big, splendid guys. Compare them with such equally rich and popular people as Roseanne Arnold, Oprah Winfrey, Delta Burke, and Liz Taylor: The women's excess is considered vile; they are hounded by the supermarket tabloids and are the butt of comedians' jokes. With each pound they gain, their dignity diminishes no matter what their achievements may be.

I know the second-class way fat women are treated because I am one myself. Like just about every other fat woman in America, I have spent the better part of my life on a diet, and like 98% of all those who have lost weight, I eventually regained it. It was on my last diet that I began to think about something my nutrition counselor was telling me, something that I had heard for years but never questioned. Fat women eat to displace anger, to fill an empty place in their lives that thinner women fill with sex, fun, and fashion.

Oh, really?

It is an interesting theory, except for one big flaw in logic: I have not become fat because I am angry. I am angry because being fat means countless assaults on my body and soul no matter where I am or to whom I speak. Here are just a few true-life examples that have happened to me over the last few years:

I am stuck in traffic and spend an hour staring at the bumper sticker on the car ahead of me, which shows a hitchhiker who looks not unlike me with a black slash through her and the slogan No Fat Chicks.

I am in the middle of a business meeting at a magazine I often work for when the male editor stops discussing the project and in front of the rest of the staff tells me that he thinks I am not sexy anymore since I gained weight.

I am sitting next to a large friend of mine watching her cry because some coworkers gave her a gag gift that attaches to the refrigerator and goes, "Oink, oink, oink" when the door is opened.

Some fat-bashing isn't verbal but has the same soul-crushing effect—like the weight chart my insurance company issues and the coach seats on the airlines that I fly. Both are cruel reminders that I am the wrong size for life in these

United States. It doesn't matter to the fat-bashers that I—like many other large women—have a great marriage, a successful career, and wonderful friends. In fact, if anything, that makes matters worse. Fat people are tolerable to thin people only if they live in a state of constant self-hatred. An unrepentant fat woman who feels fine about herself is a walking target, always in the cross hairs of those who see her as an eyesore, a blight upon the landscape.

Sadly because fat women have been trained to be passive and don't have a tough-minded organization like Act-Up or a fearless leader like Malcolm X or any political clout whatsoever, we are at the mercy of anyone who cares to comment negatively on us. Just as it was once assumed that all black people wished they were white and all gay people wished they were straight, it is assumed that all fat people wish they were thin. And thin people seem to think it is their right to show us the error of our ways and lead us out of our misery. 10

The most popular way for fat-bashers to operate is to disguise their hostility as concern about a fat person's health. Personally, I am in fine health. I exercise and ride horses. Despite my robustness, I am routinely approached by virtual strangers who feel that it is their responsibility to advise me about health matters. I wonder how many of them would appreciate it if I offered them my perspective on their bad breath, their curved spines, or their dandruff. They would tell me to mind my own business, and certainly they would be right in doing so. Yet, my only approved response is a meek grin and pathetic litany of how very hard I am trying to accomplish the goal of reducing myself. 11

This is especially aggravating because the average fat person has far more experience with dieting than most thin people do. Personally, I have hired physicians, nutritionists, and a slew of other weight-loss counselors over the years to help me slim down. I have read all the books, seen all the tapes, gone to the spas and the exercise classes. But it is my personal choice to eat more than four ounces of skinless chicken for dinner and not to spend my days kicking my legs in the air to Jane Fonda's encouragement. I am also aware that for every scary medical statistic about obesity, there is a contradictory one that says that big women live every bit as long as thin ones and in addition have far lower suicide rates. 12

So why am I not allowed to look the way I choose? What is it that thin people are so afraid of that they won't leave us alone? Fat is not a passively transmitted health hazard, like cigarette smoke, nor is it contagious. If I eat a 13 brownie, you can be sure you won't find it on your hips the next day.

A few years ago, after a lifetime of being a slave to the scale and sick and tired of forking over my Visa card to anyone with a weight-loss scheme, I decided to get off the diet bandwagon. I was curious and a little bit scared to see what would happen, and I wondered where my body would take me. 14

Where it took me was precisely the place I had been at the start of each new diet. Historically, I never wanted to be that weight, but obviously my body likes it just fine. It was an empowering feeling. There was no longer the "good" me and the "the weight"; there was just me. 15

The truth is that there is something deeply pleasurable about being big. It is perhaps the ultimate feminist gesture. As men have known for years, it can feel good to take up a lot of space and to hear one's footsteps fall meaningfully upon the ground. I must also concede that secretly I relish the thought that, with my size and strength, I could easily grab the next impertinent size 3 I meet around the neck and wring her like a chicken. 16

Recently a man came up to me in our local hardware store and asked if I was an opera singer. At first I flinched, a reflex from a life time of unsolicited remarks: but then I thought of Jessye Norman and the other powerful big women I have admired throughout my life and felt it was a compliment. I thought that at least metaphorically I would move like a diva in stately fashion throughout the rest of my days as a woman warrior from the land of the big and the home of the brave. 17

—Jane Stern

---

*Now that you've read the selection, go back and answer your preview questions. Use the information you annotated to make an **outline** or a **map**. Then write a **summary**.*

Create an Outline or Map:

Summary:

_____

_____

_____

_____

_____

_____

_____

_____

_____

_____

_____

Essay Question

The writer of the selection in Practice 4 thinks that fat women are unfairly picked on and discriminated against. **On a separate paper,** write an essay in which you agree or disagree with her. Be sure to use ideas from this text in your essay.

Group Activity

In a small group, summarize your position on the issues raised in the reading selections in Practice 3 and Practice 4. Listen to the other group members' positions and then see if your group can agree on a single viewpoint.

PART FOUR

CRITICAL READING

CHAPTER

9

Reading Newspapers

Critical reading is a thinking process that helps us interpret information so that we can make intelligent decisions about what we have read. This is different from criticizing something to find fault. When we read critically, we think carefully about what was written so that we can make sense of the text, evaluate the information or ideas that the writer has presented, and come to our own conclusions about what we have read.

In this chapter and the two that follow, you build on the reading strategies that you have already learned to become a more critical reader. You develop critical reading and thinking strategies to:

1. Make sense of information.
2. Evaluate information.
3. Make informed decisions about information.

By working with newspaper and magazine articles and college course materials, you become a good critical reader and thinker.

Newspapers: Critical Thinking and Reading Strategies

Newspapers are one of our major links to the world around us. They give us up-to-the-minute information about issues that affect everyone. We need to evaluate this information to become informed citizens and to understand what other persons are thinking. It is important that you understand the purpose of a newspaper so that the critical thinking strategies you develop make sense to you. Then you can use them with all kinds of reading material in the future. In fact, the critical thinking and reading strategies that you develop for reading newspapers can be applied to all your college reading materials.

Practice 1

*Read the following article about newspapers and critical thinking. The article explains what newspapers do, how they are written, and why you need to be a critical thinker to read them wisely. Use the **reading strategies** that you have already mastered to answer the questions.*

1. Read the title of the following selection. In the space below, freewrite or list what comes to mind about the topic.

   _____

   _____

   _____

   _____

   _____

2. Preview the selection. Write three questions that you think will be answered by the reading.

   a. _____

   _____

   b. _____

   _____

   c. _____

   _____

Newspapers and Critical Thinking

The word *NEWS* is an acronym—a word formed from the first letters of a group of words—for North, East, West, and South. News is information that comes from all directions; from all over the world. The newspaper is one way in which this information is presented. 1

Reading a newspaper is very different from reading a college textbook. Nobody reads a newspaper from cover to cover every day. There is simply too much information in each issue. Also, no two people read a newspaper in the same way. Readers pick and choose what interests them and skip around and preview the different sections of the paper to get the particular information that they need. 2

The first part of any newspaper is usually concerned with what is called "hard news." The articles are reports about events that occur in your neighborhood, your town, the state, the country, and the world. They are written in a pattern called "journalistic style." This is a kind of writing which focuses on the main idea and the most important facts of a news story. These stories are factual; they are not someone's opinion. They simply tell what happened. The titles of these stories are called *headlines*. Headlines are set up to attract the reader's attention. The headline is really the main point of the news story. The headline is also what you preview. It helps you decide whether or not to read the story. 3

If a particular article interests you, you will probably read just the first paragraph or two thoroughly because these paragraphs will give you the main facts by answering the questions, Who? What? When? Where? and, possibly, How? The rest of the article will have more details. Hard news articles are written this way so that they can be shortened if there is not enough room for them in the paper. This is why the most important information is put into the first or first and second paragraphs. 4

A second kind of article is the editorial. An editorial is most similar to your other reading material. There is usually an introduction, a body of information, and a conclusion. An editorial may give you information about a specific topic (e.g., fixing a stereo), present the writer's opinion (e.g., whether or not to have gun control), or discuss a political issue (e.g., a candidate who is running for office). 5

When reading an editorial, it is important that you evaluate the information with respect to the facts presented. You evaluate by asking questions: (1) Are the facts true? (2) How 6 does the writer present his or her argument? (3) What is the writer's opinion? (4) What is your opinion about the topic? (5) Can you challenge the argument? When reading this type of material, you will need to make inferences, come to your own conclusions, and develop your own opinion about what the writer is saying.

The third general kind of information that appears in the newspaper is advertising. Since newspapers have such a wide readership, advertising takes up a sizable portion of any newspaper. Companies pay newspapers to print their ads. Because newspapers do not judge the content of their advertisements, it is up to the reader to use critical thinking strategies in order to decide whether or not to buy a product or to determine whether or not an advertiser's claim is valid. 7

The newspaper gives you the opportunity to understand the world around you, develop your own opinions about issues that could affect your life, and make wise personal decisions. It is most important for you, the reader, to read and think critically about the information that is presented to you in newspapers and other media so that you can become an informed citizen and an intelligent consumer. 8

—Myrna B. Skidell

1. Answer your preview questions here.

_____

_____

_____

_____

_____

If you were unable to answer your preview questions, explain why here.

_____

_____

_____

2. What is the controlling idea of the selection?

_____

_____

_____

3. What is the purpose of newspapers?

_____

_____

_____

4. What is a headline?

_____

_____

_____

5. How is journalistic style different from editorial writing?

_____

_____

_____

6. Why is it important to read an editorial critically?

_____

_____

_____

_____

Making Sense of Information

Making sense of information "sets the stage" or prepares you for critical thinking. To make sense of information means to understand the main points and major details about what you are reading. You already have a **main idea strategy** with which to do this. Simply ask yourself two questions:

1. What is this about? (Topic)
2. What is the most important point the writer is making about the topic? (Main Idea)

In this section, you will practice your **main idea strategies** to make sense of the information in hard news stories and editorials.

News Stories

Hard news stories are written in what is called **journalistic style.** These stories contain only facts, not opinions, and the facts may not always be accurate. The **headline** (or title) of a hard news story is really the main idea written in language designed to attract the reader's attention. The article itself usually gives the most important information (the main points and major details) in the first or first and second paragraphs. The information answers the questions, Who? What? When? Where? and, sometimes, How? Other, less important details are presented in the paragraphs that follow. Journalistic style allows the reader to get the most important information by reading a small amount of text. This is helpful because there is so much information in a newspaper that it would be almost impossible to read everything in it each day.

The titles of hard news (or news stories) are called headlines because they appear at the top, or head, of the news story. Headlines tell the main idea of a news story. They may include abbreviations, **bold face type,** CAPITAL LETTERS, or anything else the editors think will capture the reader's attention.

Practice 2   Writing Headlines from Main Ideas in Hard News Stories

*In this section, you need to find the **main ideas** of **news stories** and write **headlines** to attract readers' attention.*

Example:

Headline: _Double Lottery Winner! One in Millions!_

News Story: Everyone would like to win the lottery. Frank Jones, 34 and unemployed, bought lottery tickets in New York and New Jersey. He was shocked to find that he won two jackpots! It's unusual to win one jackpot. The odds of winning two jackpots are one in many millions.

Explanation: Note how the headline puts the main idea—that the chances of winning one lottery jackpot are slim, but winning two is even less likely—into symbols and words to attract attention. Be creative in writing headlines for the following news stories.

1. *Headline:* _____

News Story: The family is furious about hidden camera photos of their daughter in skimpy work-out clothes at a private gym.
    The photos appeared in the London *Sunday Mirror* as an "exclusive." The family is "red faced" about how easily the photographer was able to get through their security.

2. *Headline:* _____

News Story: According to campus health experts, more students than ever before are getting tested for AIDS—some of them several times. College health offices cannot keep up with the demand.
    They are assuming that this upsurge is because many celebrities and athletes have come forward to say that they have contracted AIDS.

3. *Headline:* _____

News Story: A drunken unlicensed driver who ran over and killed an elderly woman and her companion had had his license revoked twice and suspended 120 times for 40 incidents.
    A police spokesman said that Harry Strong, 32, of Smith Street, was charged with driving while intoxicated.

4. *Headline:* _____

News Story: A new survey shows that even though most Americans know that exercise is good for them, most are too lazy or too busy to do so. The President's Council on Physical Fitness and Sports surveyed 1,018 couch potatoes last month. Sixty-four percent said that they would like to exercise more. They simply can't find the time. However, TV watching occupied at least three of the ten hours of weekly leisure they had for 84% of the group. Their responses suggest that they have time for exercise but are too lazy or prefer TV.

Group Activity

Work in groups of four. Bring in **hard news** stories from your newspaper. Separate the **headlines** from the articles. Use the main ideas of the stories to write headlines. Compare your headlines and stories with what actually appeared in the newspaper.

Editorials

Editorials are written to influence readers' opinions about current issues. Some represent a newspaper's **point of view** (opinion) about an issue. These editorials have no byline—a byline is the writer's name in newspaper language. Other editorials may be written by individual reporters who are called columnists or journalists and will have a byline. Articles written by columnists in the editorial section reflect that person's opinion, point of view, or bias about a particular topic. The journalist's opinion may or may not agree with the newspaper's point of view.

Because an editorial reflects someone else's viewpoint, you need to decide whether you agree with it. Then you must decide whether the position taken in the editorial will influence your own thinking. The ability to think critically helps you understand and make sense of the information presented and develop an informed opinion about the issue.

Editorials deal with topics (e.g., gun control) and issues (or questions) about topics (e.g., Should we have gun control laws?). An **issue** is a question about a topic that people dispute or disagree about. Writers (as well as other persons) have different opinions, or points of view, about different issues.

Very often, the topic, the issue, and the writer's point of view are stated in the title of an editorial. The issue is not usually stated as a question, but you can guess what the issue is from the other information given. When this happens, you can predict what the editorial is about and what the writer thinks about it.

To make sense of editorial information, you need to ask yourself three questions:

1. What is the topic?
2. What is the issue? (The issue is some question about the topic that can be disputed, argued, or questioned.)
3. What is the writer's point of view?

Remember, if the topic, issue, or the writer's point of view is not clear from the title, you need to preview the editorial.

Practice 3

*Use the following titles of editorials to identify the **topic, issue,** and writer's **point of view,** or opinion. Remember: The issue is always a question that can be argued or disputed. You will have to make up your own question about the issue, based on the title of the editorial.*

When you do the following exercises, do not forget to use the three question strategy.

1. What is the topic?
2. What is the issue?
3. What is the writer's opinion, or point of view?

Following is the way one student made sense of the information presented in a newspaper editorial.

Example:

Title: ASSISTED SUICIDE SHOULD BE OUTLAWED!

Topic: *Assisted suicide.*

Issue: *Should assisted suicide be legal?*

Writer's Opinion: *Assisted suicide should be illegal.*

Explanation: The topic and the writer's point of view are clearly stated in the title. Notice how the student developed the issue question—she concluded that there was a dispute about whether assisted suicide should be legalized.

1. Title: **TREAT TEENAGE CRIMINALS AS ADULTS!**

   Topic: _____

   Issue: _____

   _____

   Writer's Opinion: _____

   _____

   _____

   _____

2. Title: *Unfair Election: We Need a Recount!*

   Topic: _____

   Issue: _____

   _____

   Writer's Opinion: _____

   _____

   _____

   _____

3. Title: USE FEWER PESTICIDES

   Topic: _____

   Issue: _____

   _____

   Writer's Opinion: _____

   _____

   _____

   _____

4. Title: **Don't Tolerate Sexual Harrassment—It Is Against** *YOU* **. . . As Well As the Law!**

   Topic: _____

   Issue: _____

   _____

   Writer's Opinion: _____

   _____

   _____

   _____

5. Title: **Gun Control Is a Bad Idea**

   Topic: _____

   Issue: _____

   _____

   Writer's Opinion: _____

   _____

   _____

   _____

Evaluating Information

When a newspaper or magazine editorial is written to influence your thinking, the writer tries to persuade you to agree with his or her point of view. The writer gives reasons to support the argument presented in the editorial. You need to decide whether you share the writer's opinion by examining the evidence given to support the argument. To critically examine the evidence, you have to decide whether it is truthful, logical, and really supports the facts that are given. You need to follow the writer's argument and reasoning.

Following a Writer's Argument and Reasoning

Following are some of the kinds of reasoning used to persuade you to agree with an editorial point of view.

Emotional Reasoning

Some issues (e.g., abortion) cause more disagreement than others (e.g., wearing seat belts). The more pros and cons about an issue, the stronger people tend to feel about it. Examples of issues that cause arguments might be gun control, AIDS, and capital punishment. When emotional reasoning is used, you should realize that the writer has very strong and possibly biased (one-sided) feelings about the topic. Here are some examples of emotional reasoning:

Intimidation. The writer might want to frighten you or make you feel threatened about something.

> **Example:** "Unless this gun control law is passed, no American will be safe in his or her own home!"

Clearly, the writer feels very strongly about the need for gun control laws and wants to frighten you into agreeing with his or her point of view.

Power, expert opinion, authority. People tend to believe experts. Writers often quote authorities to impress readers. They want you to believe that the experts know more than you do, so you will be influenced by them.

This type of reasoning should alert you to question whether the so-called expert is really qualified to comment about the issue.

Examples:

1. Professor Mary Jones has stated that the earth is definitely getting warmer.
2. According to Joe Smith, a well-known tax attorney, the accused murderer should appeal the verdict.

In the first example, you need to be alert to titles. The fact that Mary Jones is a professor does not necessarily mean that she is a scientist or an expert about global warming.

In the second example, Joe Smith may be a tax attorney, but is he an expert in criminal law? Is his opinion in line with most criminal lawyers who are the real experts in this case? As a critical reader, you should avoid accepting a point of view just because an expert is quoted.

Association.   Sometimes a writer wants you to feel comfortable with his or her point of view.

> **Example:** Everyone should vote for Frank Gold. He is kind, good, and very much like the wonderful grandfather that we all had.

Notice how the writer tries to persuade you to vote for the candidate based on his grandfatherly appearance. Is there any information given to convince you of the candidate's ability?

Tone.   A writer's "tone of voice" (use of descriptive language) should make you aware of his or her attitude or bias toward the issue.

> **Example:** The obnoxious television reporter stood very close to the poor earthquake victim. He then asked her how she felt after just having lost all of her belongings. How absurd!

You should conclude that the writer does not approve of the reporter's action by the use of words such as *obnoxious* and *absurd*.

Personal Attack

This type of reasoning is used to influence you to ignore the argument. When a writer ridicules someone or calls another person names, it is usually a personal attack on someone with a different point of view and is not logical support for the issue itself. These personal attacks might influence you, but they almost never provide valid support for an argument.

> **Example:** The senator voted against the AIDS bill. He should have voted for it. He has a long history of alcoholism. How can anybody trust his judgment?

In this example, the writer attacks the senator for his drinking problem but does not give any support for the argument that the senator should have voted for the AIDS bill.

Use of Statistics

Statistics are numbers (called data) that are put together or classified to present information about some issue. Statistics are often used to support an argument. Many individuals believe that statistical proof is always true. You must understand that it is extremely difficult to use statistics clearly. When you are given statistics to support an argument, be aware of the following:

Statistics that cannot be verified.

Example: One of every million newborn babies will grow up to be a genius.

Can this statement be verified? Of course not! To prove it, you would need to follow the growth of every newborn baby to determine if one baby per million grows up to become a genius.

Statistics that are used alone.

Example: American people are getting thinner by two pounds per person each year. Last year, they lost a total of two million pounds.

Do you believe this statement? It sounds like a great weight loss, but it does not tell very much. How many individuals were counted as losing weight? What was the age group? You need to be alert to overgeneralizations—this means that the person who made this statement wants you to believe that every American is getting thinner. How can this be proven?

Statistics that have no basis for comparison.

Example: The number of people who bought New York State lottery tickets grew by 9 percent last year, while the growth rate of the Florida lottery was 11 percent.

This statement implies that the Florida lottery is doing better than the New York lottery. However, we do not know what the growth rate of each lottery was until last year. If the New York base was greater, then it could be growing more than Florida. To make sense of some statistics, you need to find out the basis for comparison.

Practice 4

*Read each of the following paragraphs to identify the type of **reasoning** the writer uses to support his or her argument, opinion, or point of view. Write and explain your answers in the spaces provided after each paragraph.*

Example: Fifty percent of subjects taught in school have nothing to do with education. Subjects such as driver education and cooking do not prepare students for the job market. These subjects should be taught at home. Too many students cannot read, write, or do arithmetic.

Explanation: After reading the above example, one of our students wrote that the statistic—50 percent—cannot be verified. He also stated that the writer is attacking education but does not give facts to support his or her point of view.

1. The health care situation in the United States is getting worse over time. Physicians do not want to treat patients unless they will receive payment immediately. What about poor patients who cannot put out the money for a physician's visit and depend on their health plan. Too many physicians have become self-serving and do not care about their patients any longer. This is a disgrace!

   _____

   _____

   _____

   _____

2. Feminists are concerned that football games, particularly the Super Bowl, give rise to more wife-beating than usual. They say that statistics show a tremendous rise in these beatings as soon as the football season starts and that they go down after the Super Bowl.

   _____

   _____

   _____

   _____

3. The U.S. Senate voted to end America's embargo against North Vietnam. They made a wise decision. The Vietnamese people are gentle and hardworking. Few Americans think that they should be punished. They are moving toward many of the goals in which America believes. Their government has been very

cooperative in providing information about missing soldiers. Why punish this poor country any longer?

_____

_____

_____

_____

4. Lead poisoning is a major health threat to children. Lead in the water supply affects 30 million people. It is estimated that 25% of white children and 55% of black children have unhealthy levels of lead in their bodies. Continual exposure to lead can cause stunted growth and brain damage. Lead contamination can play a vital role in school failure. State and local governments should get moving to clean up their water supplies.

_____

_____

_____

_____

5. The idea of a four-day work week is too good to be true. What lazy person would complain about three-day weekends every week? A short work week would only cause higher production costs. The guru of the shorter week, Frank Morgan, a consultant, probably earns six figures. He doesn't care how unproductive factories are. His belief that a 15 percent reduction in hours would be more efficient sounds crazy.

_____

_____

_____

_____

Working with Complete Editorials

When you evaluate the information in longer selections, you should use your **marking** and **annotating strategies,** as well as the critical thinking questions, to understand and analyze all of the information. In the next practice, you can use all these skills.

Practice 5

*Read the following newspaper **editorials**. Identify the **topic, issue,** and the writer's **point of view.** Then, determine the **reasoning** used to support the writer's argument. Explain why you agree or disagree with the reasons given.*

Selection 1:

Tougher Standards for College Athletes

1 A new move is under way to ensure that college athletes have the ability to absorb at least a bit of education during their four years on campus. But this effort has some folks crying foul.

2 At present, to play in their freshman year athletes must maintain a C average in high school and score 700 out of a possible 1600 points on the SAT tests. Potential players with lower scores cannot compete, and they need to show acceptable grades before becoming eligible for athletic scholarships.

3 The new standards, proposed by the NCAA and its Presidents Commission, are somewhat more serious: A player with a 2.0 (C) average in high school must score at least 900 on the SATs; one with a 2.5 average needs only 700 to qualify.

4 The requirements remain relatively minimal. But, unlike the standards now in place, they aren't a total joke.

5 Sad to say, many of the nation's top basketball coaches—led by the outspoken John Thompson of Georgetown—term the new standards too restrictive. And some have managed to inject race into the debate, in the process gaining the support of Rep. Kweisi Mfume, chairman of the Congressional Black Caucus.

6 Thompson long had led the effort to abolish even the most minimal academic standards for college athletes, many of whom are black. By placing such a heavy emphasis

on athletics, the Georgetown coach—and his ally, Rep. Mfume—reinforce the outdated and insidious notion that playing ball is a major avenue of escape from the travails of inner-city life.

In reality, only one in 10,000 high school basketball 7 players ever makes it to the NBA. Moreover, even college athletic scholarships are rare and difficult to obtain. Black youngsters who dream of playing before thousands in huge arenas on subsidies provided by eager universities are all too often dwelling in a dream world.

As for standards, tougher restrictions on athletic eligi- 8 bility are not remotely discriminatory. Quite the opposite: They ensure that minority youths are not simply exploited for their athletic prowess and then sent off to fend for themselves.

Minority youth would do well to heed the Rev. Jesse 9 Jackson, who's traveling the nation urging black students to pledge "to push for excellence by striving to learn as much as I can . . . (to) work to achieve success in school to prepare myself for success in life." Success at sports on a level that offers professional opportunities is a rare, God-given gift. Let's not pretend otherwise: There isn't a Michael Jordan on every playground.

—*New York Post*

Topic: _____

Issue:_____

_____

Point of View:_____

_____

_____

_____

Reasoning Used: _____

_____

Analysis of Reasoning: _____

_____

_____

_____

_____

_____

_____

Selection 2:

Air Safety Need Not Be Pie in the Sky

The flying public is not well served by a new book on   1
air safety written by the former inspector general of the U.S.
Department of Transportation. Mary Schiavo's *Flying Blind,
Flying Safe* will only bolster travellers' fears without making
the skies any safer.

Why is she tearing down the industry with her claims   2
regarding safety that are out of proportion to the risks
involved?

At one point, Schiavo bemoans the fact that Federal Avi-   3
ation Administration administrators have all been men [al-
though a woman has now been appointed] and complains
that she was discriminated against because she is a woman.
Granted, that is deplorable. But besides trying to capitalize
on her almost 10 years as a public servant, did she write this
book to get back at them? Schiavo certainly deserves no
credit for scaring people needlessly just to settle a score.

The likelihood of being killed in an air-transportation   4
accident is but a fraction of that of dying on a highway. Air-
transportation accidents killed 26 people in America in 1992,
none in 1993, 228 in 1994, 152 in 1995 and 319 in 1996. During most years, more people are killed driving to or from air-
ports. Yet, a majority of us insist on flouting speed limits or
driving fast with one hand on the steering wheel while using
the other to dial a cellular telephone, apply makeup or sort
through files.

Schiavo is correct in pointing out that there are many as-   5
pects of comercial aviation in need of safer practices. But not
all "up and coming" airlines are "accidents in the making,"

as she claims. When I began working for Douglas Aircraft in December, 1964, Southwest Airlines did not exist. When I left four years later, Southwest was a 21-month-old "up and coming" carrier flying intrastate, low-fare services in Texas. Today it is one of the largest and safest airlines in the United States.

Some of today's newcomers will be tomorrow's industry 6 leaders unless Schiavo and her like succeed in scaring away customers before these new airlines have a chance to prove that they really are safe. Likewise, aircraft that early on earned a poor safety record, such as the Boeing 727, developed into highly reliable machines. (Even Schiavo admits, "I must confess, I like the 727.")

Schiavo is also right when expressing concern about 7 "aging airplanes." Taking care of that problem is easy, however. The almighty dollar can rejuvenate the fleet of just about any airline. But who is to pay for these aeronautical "face-lifts" and "liposuctions"? Stockholders cannot absorb such costs and the airlines will have to pass them on to customers by raising fares.

Similarly, federal, state and local governments cannot 8 ask taxpayers to pay the costs for improving airport security and so those costs are passed on to the airlines and their passengers. Yet, most of us clamor for cheap, safe air transportation but are quite unwilling to pay for it.

In air transportation, there is no such thing as a "win- 9 win" situation if one seeks to balance "assured technical safety" and "affordable transportation" or "assured security against terrorism" and "passenger convenience." We can make air transportation safer, but do we want to open every piece of baggage and strip-search each passenger on every flight to ensure that no one carries a bomb aboard an aircraft? Should we require that passengers be at the airport three hours before departure in order to have time for such searches?

Should pilots be tested for alcohol and drugs before 10 every flight? Should airliners be retired after X number of flight hours or Y number of landings in order to avoid the possibility of equipment failure? If so, are we passengers willing to pay substantially higher fares so that the airlines can continuously purchase new aircraft?

Impressive as her knowledge may be to the layperson, 11 Schiavo displays many gaps and biases in her aviation education. Here are two examples: She states that "in 1924, the first commercial airplane service in the U.S. began with a 22-mile route between Tampa and St. Petersburg, Florida." In fact, the first fare-paying passengers in the United States had been transported five years earlier between New York and Atlantic City.

Later in the book, she writes fondly about experience with her first aircraft, a Beech Musketeer. That aircraft happens to have a below-average safety record, according to the National Transportation Safety Board (an organization she cites as being more responsible than her former employer), but she never mentions that. Many other errors or omissions are found in the rest of the book but few of her readers will have the knowledge or experience to challenge her. 12

We can only hope that people like Schiavo will come down from their soap boxes and face reality. The air-transportation industry is not as safe as it could be, but it is far safer than many other daily activities. 13

Scaring the traveling public away from the low-cost airlines, as Schiavo seems to be doing with her book, is playing into the hands of major airlines. Maybe the big companies are interested in safety, but without competition their fares would certainly soar. Readers should leave *Flying Blind, Flying Safe* on the ground. 14

—René J. Francillon

Topic: _____

Issue:_____

_____

Point of View:_____

_____

_____

_____

Reasoning Used: _____

_____

Analysis of Reasoning: _____

_____

_____

_____

_____

_____

Group Activity 1

1. Compare your analysis of the writer's argument in Selection 1 with that of your classmates'.
2. Discuss each other's points of view. See if anyone in the group changes his or her opinion because of the discussion. Did everyone understand the way reasoning was used to influence thinking?

Group Activity 2

Discuss your feelings about air safety in small groups by focusing on the way the writer in Selection 2 specifically defines it in terms of the United States. Then write your own opinions about the issues. Compare your points of view and analyze each other's reasoning. Write your point of view here.

Point of View: _____

_____

_____

_____

_____

_____

_____

10

Make Informed Decisions about Information

Earlier in this section, you learned how to make sense of information by identifying topics, issues, and a writer's point of view. You also learned how to evaluate information by following a writer's argument and testing his or her reasoning and evidence to support that point of view.

In this chapter, you learn how to make **informed decisions** about information and come to intelligent **conclusions** about what you read by mastering strategies to:

1. Separate fact from opinion.
2. Make inferences.
3. Make notes and take notes.
4. Write informed opinions about what you read.

Separate Fact from Opinion

Facts

In the "Hard News" section of Chapter 9, you learned about facts. Facts describe the actual way things are. Facts can be observed, proven, or verified. Here are some factual statements:

- John F. Kennedy was assassinated in 1963.
- The snow was six inches deep.

- Sidney got an "A" on her report.
- The title of this book is *The Main Idea.*
- The Bill of Rights is part of the U.S. Constitution.

All the above statements can be easily checked out and will hold up under examination. They are **facts.**

Opinions

Opinions are statements that cannot be proved. They are based on a person's feelings or beliefs. It is important for you to understand that these feelings or beliefs may be based on facts, but by themselves, they are opinions. Here are some opinion statements based on the facts that you have just read.

- John F. Kennedy was assassinated because he was a bad president.

Although stated as a fact, this statement may or may not be true. It cannot be proved. It is only one person's opinion. Other persons may agree or disagree with it.

- The six-inch snow was great fun.

Not everyone likes snow. Consider the individuals who have to clean it up. The statement that snow is fun is a matter of opinion.

- I think that Sidney is the smartest person in the class.

It is a fact that Sidney got an "A" on her report. She might also be the smartest in the class. But the clue here is the word *think.* This is an opinion word, which should alert you to the idea that the statement reflects the writer's point of view. Other words that should alert you to an opinion are *feel, suggest, believe, hope, in my opinion, it seems that, most likely, probably, perhaps,* and *often.*

- This textbook, *The Main Idea,* will make you a better reader.

You might become a better reader if you use this book, but the statement cannot hold true for everyone. Some students may not do the exercises or understand the material. Be aware that when a writer overgeneralizes (includes everyone), he or she is making a judgment.

- The Bill of Rights needs to be updated.

This statement is controversial. Some individuals might think that it is fine just the way it is. This statement simply reflects one person's opinion.

You can test for yourself whether a statement is fact or opinion by asking the following questions:

1. Can the statement be proved or verified?
2. Can the statement be disputed?

Facts and Opinions

Much of what you read will be a combination of fact and opinion. Individuals have opinions about the facts that they know. Sometimes a writer may sincerely believe that his or her opinion is a fact. Other times, he or she may hope that because only part of a statement is fact you will believe the whole statement and agree with his or her point of view.

Practice 1

Read the following statements taken from newspaper editorials. Determine whether they are facts, opinions, or combinations of fact and opinion. State the reasons for your choices.

Example:

There is nothing unfair about athletes using steroids. They are allowed to wear special shoes, use exercise machines and eat foods that they believe will give them a competitive edge. The use of steroids fits into the special things that athletes do in order to win.

Fact? Opinion? Why?: *This paragraph is a combination of fact and opinion. The facts are that athletes are permitted to do certain things to help them compete. The opinion part is that they should be allowed to take steroids. The use of steroids is controversial, and many people would disagree with this writer's point of view.*

1. It would be unconstitutional for the government to limit the amount of personal money that individuals could spend on health care products.

   Fact? Opinion? Why?:_____

   _____

   _____

   _____

2. I strongly believe that individuals who are born in any city neighborhood are anxious to move away when they become adults and have children of their own. Who would want his or her children to grow up in a crowded environment when they could live in a house in a beautiful suburb?

   Fact? Opinion? Why?:_____

   _____

   _____

   _____

3. When a person diets, there is no such thing as a forbidden food. A dieter may eat whatever he or she wants, provided the portions are small. It is a myth that when you diet you must avoid certain foods.

   Fact? Opinion? Why?:_____

   _____

   _____

   _____

4. According to the local newspaper, the amount of money raised by the Girl Scouts through their cookie sales has dropped quite a bit because people are watching their sugar intake.

   Fact? Opinion? Why?:_____

   _____

_____

_____

5. It is estimated that a million individuals are now infected with tuberculosis. More than 121,000 cases have been diagnosed since 1990. The medical community believes that thousands of persons are afraid to be tested. Costs for care may reach more than $5 million.

Fact? Opinion? Why?:_____

_____

_____

_____

Group Activity

Work with a partner to develop statements that are combinations of fact and opinion. Present the statements to the rest of the group for discussion and analysis.

Practice 2

Read the following **editorial.** Evaluate it by identifying the topic, issue, writer's point of view, and line of reasoning and, finally, by determining which parts of it are **fact, opinion,** and/or **combinations** of fact and opinion. There is space after the editorial for your analysis.

Blacks Need Uncle Sam

For too long, African-Americans have been told that we   1
could succeed if only we believed and tried a little self-help. We should pull ourselves up by our bootstraps, wearing boots or not. We should turn the other cheek until our cheekbones are slapped raw. We should stare racism in the face without blinking.

These noble myths wear thin in the face of reality. Black   2
people are twice as likely as whites to be unemployed, three times as likely to be poor. Our kids are more likely to die as infants, our men more likely not to live to retirement age.

Between birth and death, there are the awful gaps that African-Americans are slapped with, whatever the indicator—income, wealth, health, education. These are gaps some say we can overcome if we only believe.

When James Barrie wrote *Peter Pan,* he said people could fly if they believed. Irate parents, daunted by children leaping out of windows, asked Barrie to amend his myth. In later versions, he said people could fly if they believed *and* had some magic dust. The connection between belief and implementation speaks to African-Americans today.

How can we believe in an American dream unless we see it implemented? Who will provide the magic dust for black America, if not our government? We need leadership that will not stoop to the use of racist images and rhetoric. We need a programmatic commitment, an urban Marshall Plan that provides jobs, services, opportunities. We need strong civil rights laws, and we need them enforced. Government offered this in Great Society programs a generation ago. Are the self-help gurus grinches who snatched away the magic dust?

—Julianne Malveaux

Topic: _____

Issue: _____

_____

_____

Point of View: _____

_____

_____

_____

Reasoning: _____

_____

_____

_____

_____

Fact? Opinion? Why? _____

_____

_____

_____

_____

_____

Make Inferences

Writers do not spell everything out for you. They supply a certain amount of information and expect you to make inferences about it. **Inferences** are educated guesses, conclusions, or judgments that you make based on what you have read. When you make inferences, you are interpreting and understanding information. Making inferences is sometimes called "reading between the lines."

You make inferences all the time. Suppose that your psychology teacher returns an "A" paper to you. He or she smiles and says, "This is a great job!" The combination of the smile and the good grade leads you to infer that the teacher is pleased with the work you have done.

However, if your paper was an "F" and your teacher said, "This is a great job!" you would infer that the teacher was being sarcastic and certainly not pleased with your work.

Throughout this textbook, you have been using **inference strategies.** In Chapter 1, "Getting Started," you made inferences when you did **freewriting.** You used your personal experience and background information to predict or infer what a reading selection might be about, based on the information given in the title.

When you looked for **unstated main ideas** in Chapter 4, you used the examples and details that the writer gave you to determine the main idea.

All the critical thinking and reading strategies that you have developed in this chapter require you to use inferential thinking. In fact, all written information assumes that the reader will make inferences. The writer suggests or implies ideas, and it is up to the reader to interpret these ideas to fully understand the material. To make correct inferences, you must first read the information. Then, look for hidden meanings and analyze the writer's language, purpose, attitudes, bias, and feelings. It is most important for you to understand that inferences must be supported by information. You must be careful not to make foolish guesses or misinterpret what the writer has to say or really means.

Practice 3

*Read the following paragraphs from **newspaper editorials**. The sentences are numbered for you. List the kinds of **inferences** that you can make from the information given in each sentence in the space given below the paragraph. Choose a reason for making each inference from the following choices:*

1. Background information
2. Writer's opinion
3. Writer's language
4. Hidden meaning (between the lines)

Compare your inferences with those of other students. Remember: Do not make foolish guesses or misinterpret what the writer has to say.

Example:
We doubt that a rating code will keep violent and sexually explicit video games out of young peoples' hands. A code might be good public relations for worried parents, but any law that would regulate video games would come close to regulating freedom of speech.

Here are the inferences that one student made from the above paragraph.

Inferences: Sentence 1: background information, writer's opinion
Sentence 2: writer's opinion, hidden meaning

Student Explanation:
1. *We know that rating codes give some idea of how appropriate something is for a particular age group, such as a PG13 rating of a movie. (background information)*
2. *The word doubt tells us that the writer does not think that a rating system is a good idea and will not stop young people from using the games. (writer's opinion)*

3. *The statement, "A code might be good public relations among worried parents," suggests that the only persons who might think a rating code is a good idea are those in a special interest group. (writer's opinion)*

4. *The statement that a rating system could possibly regulate freedom of speech raises a much more controversial issue than a simple rating system. Because freedom of speech is guaranteed by the Constitution, a rating code, according to the writer, could set off a major dispute. (hidden meaning)*

1. [1]The U.S. prospered for more than 120 years without a federal income tax. [2]The tax is the 16th amendment to the Constitution and was enacted in 1913. [3]It is unfair because some parts of the country have a much higher cost of living than others.

   Inferences: _____

   _____

2. [1]It is already against the law to beg in public places. [2]Now, panhandlers who persist can face up to fifteen days in jail. [3]But what happens on day 16? [4]Last year, more than 300,000 summonses were issued for panhandling. [5]Hint: The problem did not evaporate.

   Inferences: _____

   _____

3. [1]Under current Food and Drug Administration regulations, cigarettes would not be accepted for marketing if they were introduced today. [2]But cigarettes have never been classified as either food or drug, which would require them to be safe and effective; they're classified as a "device of pleasure." [3]Tobacco has always had friends in high places.

   Inferences: _____

   _____

4. [1]It is hard for me to understand women who are jealous of the First Lady of the United States. [2]These women probably disagree with her husband's politics. [3]Or they might wish that they had all of her perceived material possessions. [4]What they don't understand is that she lives in a fish bowl and needs to mind her manners even in the 1990s. [5]It is a difficult position to be in at best, but wouldn't all of us want to be in her shoes for at least one day?

Inferences: _____

_____

5. [1]Bills for the care of AIDS patients are paid haphazardly, forcing hospitals to absorb huge losses. [2]Private insurers shrink from the problem. [3]The poor are entitled to some help from Medicaid, the federal-local insurance program. [4]But state reimbursement rules differ; rates are not always sufficient to cover actual costs of treatment, and not all poor patients get covered. [5]One recent study showed that a quarter of all AIDS patients have no insurance at all.

Inferences: _____

_____

_____

_____

_____

Practice 4

Read the following selections. Use your inference skills to answer the questions after each one.

Selection 1:

Delivering Your Speech

The day arrives and you are ready. Using information   1
about your audience as an anchor, you have developed a speech with an interesting topic and a fine-tuned purpose.

Your central idea is clearly identified. You have gathered interesting and relevant supporting material (examples, illustrations, statistics) and organized it well. Your speech has an appropriate introduction, a logically arranged body, and a clear conclusion that nicely summarizes your key theme. You have rehearsed your speech several times; it is not memorized, but you are comfortable with the way you express the major ideas. Your last task is calmly and confidently to communicate with your audience. You are ready to deliver your speech.

As you approach the time for presenting your speech to 2
your audience, consider the following suggestions to help you prepare for your successful performance.

• At the risk of sounding like your mother, we suggest that 3
you get plenty of rest before your speech. Last-minute, late-night final preparations can take the edge off your performance. Many professional public speakers also advocate that you watch what you eat before you speak; a heavy meal or too much caffeine can have a negative effect on your performance.

• Review the suggestions in Chapter 2 for becoming a confi- 4
dent speaker. It is normal to have prespeech jitters. But if you have developed a well-organized, audience-centered message on a topic of genuine interest to you, you are doing all the right things to make your speech a success. Remember some of the other tips for developing confidence. Re-create the speech environment when you rehearse. Use deep breathing techniques to help you relax. Also make sure you are especially familiar with your introduction and conclusion. Act calm to feel calm.

• Arrive early for your speaking engagement. If your room is 5
in an unfamiliar location, give yourself plenty of time to find it. As we suggested in Chapter 5, you may want to rearrange the furniture or make other changes in the speaking environment. If you are using audiovisual equipment, check to see that it is working properly and set up your graphic support material carefully. You might even project a slide or two to make sure they are in the tray right side up. Relax before you deliver your message; budget your time so you do not spend your moments before you speak harriedly looking for a parking place or frantically trying to attend to last-minute details.

—Steven A. Beebe and Susan Beebe

1. What does the writer assume about how you have prepared your speech?

_____

_____

_____

_____

2. What comes to mind when the writer says, "At the risk of sounding like your mother?" Why do you think he or she chose those words for this particular paragraph?

_____

_____

_____

_____

_____

3. Why do you think that acting calm will make you feel calm?

_____

_____

_____

_____

4. What are the advantages of arriving early for a speaking engagement?

_____

_____

_____

_____

Selection 2

A Party for Mickey Mouse

I remember Riverview. This vast amusement park was located on Chicago's North Side. It was magnificent, dangerous, and thrilling. There were freak shows; there was the renowned Bob's roller coaster, the fastest in the world; there was the Rotor, a room-sized cylinder in which one stood back against the wall and was spun around, while the floor dropped away; there was the PARACHUTE JUMP, the symbol of Riverview, and visible for a mile. 1

There was illicit gambling; one could die on the rides; the place reeked of sex. A trip to Riverview was more than a thrill; it was a dangerous dream adventure for the children and for their parents. 2

My father took me up in the Parachute Jump. We were slowly hoisted ten stories in the air, seated on a rickety board, and held in place by a frayed rope. We reached the top of the scaffold, the parachute dropped, the seat dropped out from under us, and my father said under his breath: "Jesus Christ, we're both going to die here." 3

I remember wondering why I was not terrified by his fear. I think I was proud to be sharing such a grown-up experience with him. 4

Black men in jump suits sat suspended over tubs of water. White men paid to throw baseballs at a target. When the target was hit, the black men were dropped into the tubs below. The black men Uncle-Tommed in thick Southern accents. 5

The fix was in. Everyone was getting fleeced *and* short-changed to boot at the ten-in-one. Hell, that's why we *came* here. This was a *carnival*, this wasn't a merry-go-round and cotton candy; this was a *carnival*, and we were making fun of the horror of existence, saying, "Tonight, I'm going to *party*." And this was our Family Entertainment. 6

Did it bring the family together? You bet it did. And thirty-five years later I prize the memories. As does every other kid who went there with his family. As does everyone who ever went there, *period*. You got the bang for your buck that you were promised. Riverview; the very *name* is magic, to a kid from those days in Chicago; as magic as the first girl you ever loved, and that's the truth. 7

My family took me to Disneyland the first year it was opened. I was eight, the year was 1955, and it seems to me that much of the park was still under construction. 8

I came back with my five-year-old, thirty years later. 9
And I remembered it all. I remembered the route from one
ride to the next. I remembered where the hot-dog stands
were. Nothing had changed. I was charmed to remember the
Pirate menus in the restaurant, and how one punched out the
ears of the menus, and could wear them as masks. I remembered the souvenirs. I went on the Dumbo Ride, and my wife
took a picture of me and my kid, and it looks just like the picture of me and my mom on the same elephant.

Leaving the park, we ran into a parade on the Main 10
Street of Disneyland. The parade was commemorative of the
Sixtieth Anniversary of Mickey Mouse. The parade was a lav-
ish panegyric designed to evoke feelings of fealty.

A part of the parade was a musical variation of the 11
Mickey Mouse Song: "M–I–C—see you real soon—K–E–Y
. . . why? Because we *like* you . . ." et cetera; which song I
both heard and sang along with weekdays for the several
years I watched *The Mickey Mouse Club* on television. I remembered Jimmy Dodd, the *compere* of the Club, singing to
us viewers, rather sententiously, and I remembered being
moved by his affection.

Well, here we were, kids and adults alike, smiling at 12
that same Anthem, wishing Mickey well, thirty years later.

But I asked myself, what *actually* were we endorsing? 13
What *was* it that we were wishing well? How, and to what
end, was this warm feeling evoked?

Were we feeling "good" about wishing Happy Birthday 14
to a mouse? It's not a mouse, it's a character in a cartoon.
Were we wishing well to a commercial enterprise? For surely
Disneyland is the most commercial of enterprises. It is the
State of the Art in crowd control; it is terrifying to reflect
that one stands in line for approximately fifty-five minutes
out of every hour on a moderately crowded day at the park,
that a five-hour sojourn at the park contains twenty-five
minutes of "fun." The turns and bends and sights in the waiting line are designed to create the illusion that the line is
shorter than it actually is. One sets one's sights and hopes on
a Crest Up Ahead, which, surely, must be the entrance to the
ride, only to find, on reaching that crest, that yet another
stretch of waiting is in store, that one must wait, further,
until one passes under the arches up ahead, certainly not too
long a time. But on *reaching* those arches, one finds, et
cetera.

Why does no one complain? Why does everyone return? 15
Are the rides that thrilling? No, they are enjoyable, and some
are rather good, but they aren't any more thrilling than the

run-of-the-mill traveling carnival rides. Is the atmosphere that enjoyable? No. I think, to the contrary, that the atmosphere is rather oppressive. It is racially and socially homogeneous, which may, to a large extent, be a function of its geographical reality. But there is, more importantly, a slight atmosphere of *oppression* in the park. There is the nagging feeling that one is being watched.

And of course, one *is* being watched. One is being watched by those interested in crowd control, both to extract the utmost in dollars from the visitors, and, also, to ensure their safety. The atmosphere and oppression come, I think, from this: that the park's concern for extraction far outstrips the concern for safety, but the regimentation is presented, as foremost and finally, a desire to *care for* the visitor—to protect, to guide, to soothe.

One creates for oneself the idea that things at Disneyland are being done *for one's own good*. And, far beyond obeying the rather plentiful signs forbidding one or another thing, one finds oneself wondering, "I wonder if this is allowed here . . ." "This" being, for example, smoking, eating-in-line, et cetera.

At Disneyland one creates (with a great deal of help) the idea that Every Thing Not Required Is Forbidden. And so we see, as in any other totalitarian state, the internalization of authority, and its transformation into a Sense of Right.

We see the creation of a social Superego, which is sometimes a handy tool, but perhaps out of place at an amusement park. I.e., (1) the Id says: "Well, hell, I'm going to Cut in Line and get to Space Mountain sooner"; (2) the Ego says: "Don't *do* it, They will get you and, in some way, punish you"; and so, to overcome the anxiety and humiliation of being subject to a superior force, (3) the Superego is created and says: "No, it is not that you are *afraid* of authority, not at all, you are just concerned with Right and Wrong, and *you* want to go to the back of the line because it is the correct thing to do."

And it is *this* feeling that one is celebrating, I think, in singing paeans to Mickey Mouse, the feeling that I am a Good Person. I am one of the good, and *happy*, people, and I would never do anything wrong. It is the feeling that is being sold in the park. As an amusement park, it just ain't worth the money—far from being Riverview, it's not as much fun as a video arcade. The Mickey Mouse phenomenon is compelling not in spite of, but because of, its authoritarian aspect.

—David Mamet

1. What is the writer's point of view (bias) about Disneyland? What is the writer's point of view (bias) about Riverview?

_____

_____

_____

_____

2. Does his comparison between Disneyland and Riverview, the amusement park of his childhood make sense to you? Why? Why not?

_____

_____

_____

_____

3. In what ways do you think that his point of view might have been shaped by the fact that he went to Riverview as a child and to Disneyland as an adult?

_____

_____

_____

_____

4. How did you feel the first time that you went to an amusement park, a carnival, or even a circus? If you ever went to Disneyland or Disneyworld, did you feel the way the writer did? Why? Why not? What made you feel that way?

_____

_____

_____

_____

5. Why do you think the writer titled his essay, "A Party for Mickey Mouse?"

_____

_____

_____

_____

Make and Take Notes: Double-Entry Journals

You are already familiar with the process of note taking and note making from your work with text annotation. Now you are going to learn a strategy called the **double-entry journal** so that you can take notes and make notes about information to develop intelligent opinions about what you read. This strategy will help you to understand and interpret college course material as well.

A double-entry journal shows the notes that have been taken from text material side by side with your own ideas about what you have read. By showing your own ideas next to those of a writer, you can analyze information more easily, think about it more carefully, and write about it intelligently. You will develop your double-entry journals based on your work with editorial information. A double-entry journal looks like this:

Title of Editorial

Editorial Ideas	*My Ideas*
In this column, you note any facts, issues, writer opinions, examples, and details that you think will help you make a decision about the issue.	In this column put any difficult vocabulary, background information, questions, inferences, and/or anything that you think about the issue.

Practice 5

Read the following editorials. Use the double-entry journal form at the end of each article to take and make notes.

Example: The following editorial deals with saying the Pledge of Allegiance in school classrooms. From the title, it is easy to predict that the topic is the Pledge of Allegiance. The writer's point of view is that the Pledge of Allegiance should be recited in school classrooms each day. What do you think? First, read the editorial. Then, consider how one student set up a double-entry journal to develop his or her own opinion.

Say the Pledge!

I SAT—completely dumbfounded—in the corner chair 1
at a large table at a religion-and-democracy conference.

One by one, teachers from across the country—Ohio, 2
Oklahoma, Mississippi, California and even New York—
were defining the act of reciting the Pledge of Allegiance in
the morning as a violation of individual students' freedom.
Most did not require their students to stand or to participate
in any way. Several clearly identified the ritual as an anachro-
nistic tribute to the Cold War era.

I pictured the students in my inner-city high school 3
standing as we begin the pledge each day. In a homeroom
class of 32, there were six immigrants and 20 first-generation
Americans, speaking five languages and sharing four major
religions. When I looked at my students, I saw the diversity
that earned America the title "melting pot."

Against this background, the pledge may be much more 4
than a relic. It might be the one thing that reminds us every
day that we as Americans have something in common. We
are here, given the opportunity for education and the experience of freedom, because of the people who went before us in
sculpting the America of today.

We need to remember what binds us together as a peo- 5
ple rather than what divides us as a nation. This land we
share is the common denominator. It is that sense that the
people sandbagging flood-threatened districts of North
Dakota share something with Hawaiians who dwell in the
shadow of volcanoes.

The flag is a symbol of the breadth of what America 6
truly is. And the pledge offers a moment to recall that, in
spite of our differences, we are all Americans.

As an educator, I want the next generation to appreciate 7
all that America offers her citizens: the option to choose government officials, appeal court decisions, freely express opinions, experience protection of individual rights. I want them
to envision the bonds between persons rather than exploit
the differences. And my hope is that they will work with an

intensity inspired by mutual- and self-respect to create an improved America in the next millennium.

I want my students to stand during the Pledge of Allegiance and recite the words with deliberate calm. Perhaps repetition will bring recognition that the whole is greater than the sum of its parts. Maybe the words, "I pledge allegiance to the flag of the United States of America and to the republic for which it stands . . . " can begin to inspire unity among many diverse parts. 8

I believe we, as educators, have the responsibility to challenge our students to a deeper understanding of what it means to be an American. We are, after all, educating young people to become the citizens, voters and leaders of America. Consciousness of that mantle of responsibility will mature as they do. Reciting the pledge now may actually be sowing seeds for the future. The quiet young teacher from Florida sitting next to me agreed. Her students say the pledge each day. 9

—AnnMarie McLeod

Example: Double-Entry Journal Example

Say the Pledge!

Writer's Ideas	*My Ideas*
1. She was surprised that other teachers did not require their students to say the pledge.	1. I never said the pledge in school.
2. The writer's class has many different kinds of people.	2. Never realized what the pledge really stands for.
3. The pledge gives everyone a patriotic feeling.	3. Not a bad idea.
4. All Americans share the same history.	4. The pledge doesn't violate any freedom—probably makes people happy to be part of something.
5. She wants all future generations to appreciate America.	5. Not a bad idea.
6. Educators have the responsibility to make students understand that they are the future of America.	6. O.K. to say it.

Explanation: Notice how the double-entry journal clearly shows both the writer's and the student's ideas. Not all double-entry journals about this editorial will be the same. The student chose what he or she thought was the important information from the article. The student's ideas are very personal. The student's notes are in his or her own shorthand, and he or she used abbreviations as well. If you were to do a double-entry journal about this editorial, your entries might be different because they would reflect what was most important to you. It is important to remember that the "Writer's Ideas" column must contain only information from the text.

Now, you read the following editorials and develop your own double-entry journals.

Selection 1:

Should Marijuana Be Legalized for Medical Uses? [No]

Marijuana lobbyists want to legalize marijuana as a medicine. This legalization effort is a cruel hoax being played on very sick people. These patients are being used by the marijuana lobbyists in hopes of bringing attention to what they really want to do, which is to legalize marijuana in general. The way they portray it, the government is the bad guy and they're the good guys. But in fact, their compassion isn't compassion at all.

The marijuana lobbyists have promoted the idea that marijuana is good medicine. To support their claims they've cited pseudo-scientific sources and a number of nameless testimonials. But here are the facts: Twenty years of research have produced no reliable scientific proof that marijuana has medical value. If you call the American Cancer Society, the American Glaucoma Society, the National Multiple Sclerosis Society, the American Academy of Ophthalmology, or the American Medical Association, they'll all say there is no evidence that marijuana is a medicine.

Americans take their medicines in pills, solutions, shots, or drops. But never, ever by smoking. No other drug prescribed today is smoked. And there's no doubt that smoking causes lung cancer. Think about that before you swallow the quack medical claims from the marijuana lobbyists.

Plus, there's new evidence that the active ingredient in marijuana actually reduces your body's ability to fight disease. This is a serious concern for AIDS patients or for peo-

ple on chemotherapy, whose bodies are already very susceptible to disease. Without reliable evidence showing that marijuana helps, it's irresponsible to advocate its use by the
seriously ill.

—William Razzamenti

Double-Entry Journal:

Marijuana Should Not Be Legalized for Medical Uses

Writer's Ideas	*My Ideas*

Selection 2:

Should Organ Donation Be Automatic unless a Person Has Expressly Forbidden It? [Yes]

Every year, many people who could live productive lives 1
with a transplant die before a replacement heart or liver can
be found. A "presumed consent" law would help save those
lives at virtually no cost to the person from whom the organs
are taken. Currently, when a person dies, hospital staff members are required in most states to ask next of kin if they
would donate the organs. But that's a terribly difficult time
to be asking such a question, and many doctors and nurses
simply don't.

Giving up our organs after we're dead isn't charity in my 2
view. It's a moral duty. Suppose you're jogging through the
park and a toddler wading in a pond slips and is suddenly face
down in the water. If you stop and pull her out, you've
averted a tragedy, and all it has cost you is a few seconds of
your time. Most people agree that's the sort of "easy rescue"
we all have a moral duty to perform. I would argue that donating our organs is the same sort of easy rescue, and it
should be presumed that we would consent to it. Now if you
or your family object for any reason, for religious reasons or
just because you have a visceral aversion to it, then the rescue is no longer easy for you, and you can opt out—maybe by
checking a box on your driver's license.

Despite our much vaunted individualism, we aren't 3
total atomistic strangers to each other. We need to see donating organs in light of other duties like paying taxes and
jury duty. It might be better if we as a society could reflect
on this issue in a cooler moment and not rely on deathbed
decision making.

—James Lindeman Nelson

Double-Entry Journal:

*Organ Donation Should Be Automatic
unless a Person Has Expressly Forbidden It*

Writer's Ideas	*My Ideas*

Write Your Own Opinion

By this time, you have probably developed **informed opinions** about the issues in the editorials that you have just read. Now, it is time to write them down. Here is a **question strategy** to organize your thinking to write your opinions effectively. When using this strategy, you do not need to answer all the questions—only answer the ones that apply. Writing the questions and your answers may be helpful. If you do not write them down, think about them as a guide for your writing.

1. What is the major issue?
2. What are the most important facts presented?
3. Does any information seem to be left out?
4. How does the writer support his or her point of view?
5. Can the point of view be supported by the facts?
6. Can you accept or reject the argument based on the information given?
7. What, if any, questions do you still have?

Practice 6

*Write your own **opinion** for each of the **double-entry journals** that you have already developed about marijuana and organ donations. First, take a look at the example and answer the questions.*

Example: On the basis of the double-entry journal about saying the Pledge of Allegiance, the student wrote the following opinion about the issue.

I never thought of the Pledge of Allegiance as a violation of my individual freedom. In fact, I have never been asked to say the Pledge in school at all. Even so, I agree with the writer's point of view. Maybe if we said the Pledge of Allegiance in school, we would feel more patriotic and proud of our country. The writer's examples really supported that point of view.

Explanation: The student used the question strategy to frame his or her opinion. The information was evaluated based on the double-entry journal. The student admitted that although he or she never said the Pledge of Allegiance in school, it might be a good idea to do so. On the basis of the information presented, the student agreed with the writer's point of view. The student used critical thinking strategies to come to his or her conclusion.

Do you agree with the writer and the student? Why? Why not?

_____

_____

_____

_____

1. Marijuana Should Not Be Legalized for Medical Uses

_____

_____

_____

_____

_____

_____

_____

2. Organ Donation Should Be Automatic unless a Person Has Expressly Forbidden It

_____

_____

_____

_____

_____

_____

_____

Practice 7

*Read the following two editorials, which present opposing views to the previous two editorials. Set up a **double-entry journal** and write your own **opinion** based on the information given. Remember to use all your critical reading and thinking strategies. Use the question strategy to guide your thinking.*

Selection 1:

Should Marijuana Be Legalized for Medical Uses? [Yes]

Many doctors already recommend that their patients break the law and get marijuana. A recent Harvard survey of oncologists showed that almost half would prescribe marijuana if it were legal. That's because there's very strong evidence that marijuana works as a medicine. It's effective in controlling muscle spasms for people with neurological problems, in controlling nausea and increasing appetite for cancer and AIDS patients, and in controlling the eye pressure that causes damage in glaucoma.

The Physician's Association for AIDS Care sued the DEA in an effort to free marijuana for medical use. The National Lymphoma Foundation, a major cancer group, did the same thing. During the 1980's we had two and a half years of hearings before the DEA's own administrative law judge on whether the medical use of marijuana should be allowed. We put our best case forward. The DEA put its best case forward. And the judge, who was paid by the DEA, ruled in our favor. He said the DEA acted in an arbitrary and capricious manner in classifying marijuana as a drug with no medical use. Still, they haven't changed their policy.

Here's how the DEA sees this issue: If they allow marijuana as medicine, there will be thousands more patients using it. People will see that they're functioning fine. And that will raise questions about why marijuana is illegal at all. That's their fear. But I don't think it's a reasonable fear. Right now cocaine and morphine are prescribed legally as medicines. And those legal uses aren't adding in any significant way to the country's drug problems. Marijuana wouldn't either.

—Kevin Zeese

Double-Entry Journal:

Marijuana Should Be Legalized for Medical Uses

Writer's Ideas	*My Ideas*

Opinion: _____

_____

_____

_____

_____

_____

_____

_____

Selection 2:

Should Organ Donation Be Automatic unless a Person Has Expressly Forbidden It? [No]

"Presumed consent" is exactly that: presumptuous. I agree that organ donation is a moral good—even a moral duty. But the state is not justified in compelling us to fulfill every moral duty we have. Unless I've expressly told you it's okay to take my organs, who are you to presume that I have given my okay? There's already a fear in this country that if doctors know you're a donor, they might not work as hard to keep you alive. That mistrust is unfounded, but is widespread nonetheless. Any move toward a system that even looks coercive—a kind of state mandated snatching of organs—will meet intense resistance from families; we could wind up having fewer organs available rather than more.

I don't think consent on the part of the dead person is the most important factor anyway. In most states, doctors can already retrieve the organs of any dead person who carries a donor card, without bothering to check with next of kin. But in practice, the family is always consulted. We take the family's need to grieve very seriously, and strongly believe that what happens to the relative's body is their business. The needs of a stranger come second—even if the stranger's need for an organ is a matter of life and death.

Part of the value of donating an organ comes from its being a gift. It's a powerful opportunity to find some good in tragedy, and that's why most families do say yes when asked. If you take away that opportunity for generosity and instead legally compel people to donate, something is lost—by the family and by society.

—Thomas Murray

Double-Entry Journal:

*Organ Donation Should Not Be Automatic
under Any Condition*

Writer's Ideas	*My Ideas*

Opinion: _____

_____

_____

_____

_____

_____

_____

_____

Group Activity

You have written opinions after reading both sides of the issues of medical uses of marijuana and automatic organ donation. Were you consistent in your opinions? Different individuals will have opposite views about these issues. Try the following activities:

1. Compare your opinions with those of your classmates and discuss them.
2. Discuss the pros and cons of each argument.
3. Can you convince any of your classmates to change his or her opinion? How might you do this?

Review: Critical Reading Strategy

1. Make Sense of Information
   Ask yourself: • What is the topic?
   • What is the main idea?
   • What is the issue?
   • What is the writer's viewpoint?

2. Evaluate Information
   • Be alert to the writer's argument and reasoning.
   • Decide whether the evidence is logical, truthful, and really supports the information.

3. Make Informed Decisions about Information
   • Separate fact from opinion.
   • Make appropriate inferences.
   • Make notes and take notes.
   • Write informed opinions about what you have read.

11

Reading College Text Material

In Chapter 9, you learned how to critically read and think about materials in newspapers and magazines. The strategies that you learned to use with those kinds of materials are the same ones that you need to critically read and think about your academic course materials.

College instructors are specific and demanding with respect to what you will read in their courses and how they expect you to respond to what you have read. In most of your courses, you will be required to understand, analyze, and write about a variety of new reading materials. You will probably be asked to compare and contrast ideas of different writers as well.

The **P.A.S. strategy** that follows was developed to help you meet the demands of your academic course work. It is a summary of all the critical reading and thinking skills that you have developed—written in an easy-to-remember format. The letters represent three words: **purpose, assumption,** and **support.**

P.A.S. Strategy

To use the P.A.S. strategy, you need to ask yourself the following:

1. What is the **purpose** of the reading? It is important for you to understand that two purposes come together whenever you read something. First, the writer has a reason for writing the text, and second, you have a reason for reading the text. The usual purpose of college reading will be to inform or persuade. A critical reader asks himself or herself, What does the writer want me to learn? How will this information fit into my coursework? What might I need to do with the information?

For example, the purpose for writing a chapter in a science textbook most certainly will be to inform or give you specific information. Your purpose in reading this chapter would be to learn the information that was given. You would probably need to memorize all or some of this information as a course requirement. However, an essay that you read in your English course might have been written to persuade you to agree with the writer's point of view. In this case, you might first need to understand his or her viewpoint. Then you might have to develop your own ideas about the material.

2. What **assumptions** does the writer make about the reader's knowledge? What does the writer say are the facts? What is the writer's opinion or point of view? What inferences can you make from what has been written?

3. How does the writer **support** what he or she has written? What kinds of examples does the writer use? Is the information supported by facts? How does the writer present his or her argument?

Practice 1

*Use your **P.A.S. strategy** on the two selections from previous chapters as instructed below and the new selection that follows.*

1. "Say the Pledge!" (page 216, Chapter 10). You already have done a double-entry journal about the article.

   Purpose of Writer: _____

   _____

   _____

   _____

   Purpose of Reader: _____

   _____

_____

_____

Assumptions: _____

_____

_____

_____

Support: _____

_____

_____

_____

_____

2. "Death and Justice" (pages 26–31, Chapter 2). You have already previewed this selection.

Double-Entry Journal:

Death and Justice

Writer's Ideas	*My Ideas*

Purpose of Writer: _____

_____

_____

_____

Purpose of Reader: _____

_____

_____

_____

Assumptions: _____

_____

_____

_____

Support: _____

_____

_____

_____

_____

_____

3. Now use the strategy with a new reading.

*Following is a new selection. After reading it, use your **P.A.S.** strategy.*

The Cordless Tie That Binds People to Work

I am standing in the lobby of a large office building when   1
the man beside me starts talking into his briefcase. The fel-
low looks buttoned up and rational, so I assume if he is hearing voices, they are real ones. There is a phone in his briefcase.

I am sitting at a red light in traffic, when the car beside   2
me starts ringing. The driver picks up the receiver and begins
a now common routine. She steers her car with one hand and
her business with the other.

I am somewhere over Connecticut on a one-hour shut-   3
tle from Boston to New York when my companion sticks his
credit card into the chair before us and calls his office to find
out if there are any messages. At 22,000 feet, he leaves a
phone message in Boston about where to forward his phone
messages in New York.

Once upon a time, a sitcom hero named Maxwell Smart   4
used to talk into his shoe, and we laughed. But somewhere
along the line, the high-touch gadgetry of the spy films got
transformed into the tools of everyday trade. Today there are
people within reach of a phone every moment of their lives
except takeoff, landing, and a long tunnel ride. The workworld is now an interlocking network of communications
and messages, a proliferation of phones, a great babbling
overkill of Touch-Tone technology. We live from call-waiting
to call-forwarding, from answering machines to voice mail.
We are surrounded by cellular phones and portable phones.
We even have a little pocket phone to form a "personal communications network."

In theory, this population explosion of phones and their   5
fax-similes has sprung into being to offer mobility and freedom from the office. Indeed, people who take phones to the
gym, the restaurant, even the bathroom, swear by the freedom they gain with this telephone tether. But watching my
colleagues-on-call, I have become convinced that this network is a tie that binds more and more people to work. The
executives who go to the beach with a towel and a telephone
aren't liberated from the office: They are only on work-
release. The cellular commuters haven't changed the work
environment; they have turned every environment into
workspace. The new touchable class reminds me of parolees
let out of jail after being collared by a tracking device.

I admit to being somewhat phonephobic. One of the   6
great pleasures of life is being out of touch. If I were to devise
a home voice mail, it would say: Touch 1 if this is a life-
threatening emergency. Touch 2 if you are a family member
with a flat tire on a dark corner. Touch 3 if you are a junk
phone call and would like to be immolated.

But even by normal standards, we've gone too far. In the   7
workworld, we are constantly seduced by the notion of how
efficient it is to be in constant contact with each other. The
phone in all its forms has become a kind of endless meeting
that entices us to spend more time communicating than

producing. And the operative phrase is "more time." The Bureau of Labor says that Americans are working longer hours than we used to. Twenty million or so have bumped the workweek over the forty-nine-hour mark. There are no figures that tell us how many of those hours are spent leaving messages for people who left messages to call. Nor do we know how much time is spent responding to questions that we're asked only because of the availability of the instant-information-gratification system. In the constant-contact future, it's easy to see an insidious expansion of work and a more insidious extension of the workplace. In the industrial age, the factory foreman controlled his workers from nine to five. In the information age, workers are always available. Today it is possible to begin work with the first commuting mile on a cellular phone, continue it through a lunch accompanied by a "personal communications network," and end with a bedtime chat into your briefcase. In twenty-four-hour contact, we haven't missed a thing. Except, of course, the time for rumination, the solitude and space for the work we call thinking.

For years the pitch of the telephone company was 8 "Reach out and touch someone." Now we're all tied up, workers of the world united by the Touch-Tone, and we need a new slogan. How about this one: "Let my people off the hook."

—Ellen Goodman

_____

Purpose of Writer: _____

_____

_____

_____

Purpose of Reader: _____

_____

_____

_____

Assumptions: _____

_____

Support: _____

_____

_____

_____

_____

TIPS Strategy with P.A.S.

Most course assignments will be to read a textbook chapter. It is not a good idea to "jump into" a chapter without previewing it first. When you first developed your reading game plans, you previewed a whole textbook as well as individual readings. Now, we are going to show you a strategy called **TIPS.** By using TIPS, you can understand how any textbook chapter is organized, as well as what kinds of information you can expect to learn from it.

TIPS works as a team with your P.A.S. strategy when you read textbook chapters because it helps you focus on the material that you need to learn and remember.

First, read the explanation of TIPS that follows. Then, use the TIPS game plan to preview the chapter from a marketing textbook that follows the explanation. After that, use your P.A.S. strategy to help you critically read and understand the chapter information.

TIPS Strategy

T. Read the chapter **title.** Write it in your own words.

I. Read the **introduction.** Find the general topics to be covered and the chapter goals and objectives if they are included. Write down the most important ideas.

P. Read the headings and subheadings. Mark the main **parts.** Write the most important headings on your worksheet.

S. Find and read the **summary** at the end of the chapter. Also read the study questions or questions for discussion. Rewrite the summary in your own words.

Practice 2

*Use **TIPS** to preview the following chapter from a marketing textbook. The title of the book is* Consumer Behavior *by Leon G. Schiffman and Leslie Lazar Kanuk.*

1. Before you preview the chapter, freewrite or list what you know or think about consumer behavior in the spaces below.

_____

_____

_____

_____

2. Title (What do you think the chapter will be about?)

_____

_____

3. Introduction (Do not copy from text; rewrite it in your own words.)

_____

_____

_____

_____

4. Parts (Write down the most important headings and/or sub-headings.)

_____

_____

_____

_____

5. Summary (Write it in your own words.)

_____

_____

_____

_____

_____

_____

_____

Consumer Needs and Motivation

Introduction

We have all grown up "knowing" that people are differ- 1
ent. They seek different pleasures, spend their money in different ways. A woman may save her household money to
carpet her bedrooms; her neighbor may save hers to buy a
second car. A couple may spend their vacation traveling to
Europe; their friends are content with two weeks in a cottage
by the sea. A doting father may buy his son a set of encyclo-
pedias; another may buy his son a set of electric trains. Different modes of consumer behavior—different ways of
spending money—do not surprise us. We have been brought
up to believe that the differences in people are what makes
life interesting.

However, this apparent diversity in human behavior 2
often causes us to overlook the fact that people are really
very much alike. There are underlying similarities—con-
stants that tend to operate across many types of people—
which serve to explain and to clarify their consumption
behavior. Psychologists and consumer behaviorists agree that
basically most people experience the same kinds of needs and
motives; they simply express these motives in different

ways. For this reason, an understanding of human motives is very important to marketers: it enables them to understand, and even anticipate, human behavior in the marketplace.

This chapter will discuss the basic needs that operate in most people to motivate behavior. It explores the influence such needs have on consumption behavior. Later chapters in this section explain why and how these basic human motives are expressed in so many diverse ways. 3

What Is Motivation?

There are several basic concepts which are integral to an understanding of human motivation. Before we discuss these, it is necessary to agree on some basic definitions. 4

motivation

Motivation can be described as the driving force within an individual that impels him or her to action. This driving force is produced by a state of tension, which exists as the result of an unfilled need. Individuals strive—both consciously and subconsciously—to reduce this tension through behavior that they anticipate will fulfill their needs and thus relieve them of the stress they feel. The specific goals they select and the patterns of action they undertake to achieve their goals are the results of individual thinking and learning. The motivational process is a state of need-induced tension, which exerts a "push" on the individual (i.e., drives him or her) to engage in behavior that is expected to gratify the needs and thus reduce tension. Whether gratification is actually achieved depends on the course of action pursued. (If a high school girl pins her hopes of being asked to the senior prom on her switch to a highly advertised "sexy" toothpaste, she may be disappointed.) 5

The specific course of action undertaken by a consumer and the specific goal chosen are selected on the basis of his or her thinking processes (i.e., cognition) and previous learning. Thus, marketers who understand motivational theory attempt to influence the consumer's thinking or cognitive processes. 6

needs

Every individual has needs; some are innate, others are acquired. Innate needs are physiological (i.e., biogenic); they include the needs for food, for water, for air, for clothing, for shelter, and for sex. Because all of these factors are needed to sustain biological life, the biogenic needs are considered primary needs or motives. 7

Acquired needs are needs that we learn in response to our culture or environment. These may include needs for esteem, for prestige, for affection, for power, and for learning. Because acquired needs are generally psychological (i.e., psychogenic), they are considered secondary needs or motives. They result from the individual's subjective psychological state and from his or her relations with others. For example, all individuals need shelter from the elements; thus, finding a place to live fulfills an important primary need for a newly transferred executive. However, the kind of house he or she buys may be the result of secondary needs. A place to live may be seen as one where large groups of people may be entertained to fulfill social needs; furthermore, he or she may want to buy a house in an exclusive community in order to impress friends and family (and fulfill ego needs). The house that is ultimately purchased thus may serve to fulfill both primary and secondary needs. 8

goals

Goals are the sought-after results of motivated behavior. All behavior is goal-oriented. Our discussion of motivation in this chapter is in part concerned with consumers' generic goals; that is, the general classes or categories of goals they select to fulfill their needs. Marketers are even more concerned with consumer's product-specific goals; that is, the specifically branded or labeled products they select to fulfill their needs. For example, the Thomas J. Lipton Company wants consumers to view iced tea as a good way to quench summer thirst (i.e., as a generic goal). However, it is even more interested in having consumers view Lipton's iced tea as the best way to quench summer thirst (i.e., as a product-specific goal). As trade association advertising indicates, marketers recognize the importance of promoting both types of goals. The American Dairy Association advertises that "milk is a natural," while Borden's, a member of the association, stresses its own brand of milk in its advertising. 9

Summary

Motivation is the driving force within an individual that impels him or her to action. This driving force is produced by a state of uncomfortable tension, which exists as the result of an unfilled need. All individuals have needs, wants, and desires. The individual's subconscious drive to reduce need-induced tension results in behavior that is anticipated will satisfy needs and thus restore him or her to a more comfortable state. 10

All behavior is goal oriented. Goals are the sought-after 11
results of motivated behavior. The form or direction that behavior takes—the goal that is selected—is a result of thinking processes (cognition) and previous learning. Marketers talk of two types of goals: generic goals and product-specific goals. A generic goal is a general goal or category of goal that may fulfill a certain need; a product-specific goal is a specifically branded or labeled product that the individual sees as a way to fulfill that need.

Innate needs—those an individual is born with—are pri- 12
marily physiological (biogenic); they include all the factors required to sustain physical life (e.g., food, water, clothing, shelter, sex). Acquired needs—those an individual develops after birth—are primarily psychological (psychogenic); they include esteem, fear, love, and acceptance. For any given need, there are many different and appropriate goals. The specific goal selected depends on the individual's experiences, physical capacity, prevailing cultural norms and values, and accessibility in the physical and social environment.

Needs and goals are interdependent, and change in re- 13
sponse to the individual's physical condition, environment, his or her interaction with other people, and experiences. As needs become satisfied, new, higher-order needs emerge which must be fulfilled.

Failure to achieve a goal often results in feelings of frus- 14
tration. Individuals react to frustration in two ways; they may cope by finding a way around the obstacle that prohibits goal attainment or by finding a substitute goal, or they may adopt a defense mechanism that enables them to protect their self-esteem.

Discussion Questions

1. What is motivational research? What are its strengths and 15
   its weaknesses? How can it best be utilized in the development of marketing strategy?
2. Why should marketers understand motivational theory? 16
   How can a marketer attempt to reduce consumer frustration through his promotional strategy? Find an advertisement that illustrates this attempt.
3. Consumers have both innate needs and acquired needs. 17
   Give examples of each kind of need and show how the same purchase can serve to fulfill either or both kinds of needs.

—Leon G. Schiffman and Leslie L. Kanuk

Now that you have used your TIPS strategy on the chapter about consumer needs and motivation, read the chapter and use your P.A.S. strategy to help you understand the information that was presented.

Purpose of Writer: _____

_____

Purpose of Reader: _____

_____

Assumptions: _____

_____

Support: _____

_____

Practice 3

Now use both TIPS and P.A.S. to understand a chapter about stress from a psychology textbook.

Freewrite or list what you know or think about stress in the spaces below.

_____

_____

_____

_____

Title (What do you think the chapter will be about?)

_____

_____

Introduction (Do not copy from text; rewrite it in your own words.)

_____

_____

_____

_____

Parts (Headings and/or subheadings—write most important ones down.)

_____

_____

_____

_____

Summary (Write it in your own words.)

_____

_____

_____

_____

_____

_____

_____

Sources of Stress: The Common and the Extreme

Some stressors produce temporary stress, while others produce chronic stress—a state of stress that continues unrelieved over time. Chronic health problems, physical handi- [1]

caps, poverty, and unemployment are sources of chronic stress. The burden of chronic stress is disproportionately heavy for the poor, for minorities, and for the elderly.

Choices: Everyday Sources of Stress

Sometimes conflicting motives can be sources of stress. When we must make a choice between two desirable alternatives, known as an **approach-approach conflict,** stress may be the result. Some approach-approach conflicts are minor, such as deciding which movie to see. Others can have major consequences, such as whether to continue building a promising career or to interrupt the career to raise a child. In approach-approach conflicts, both choices are desirable. 2

In **avoidance-avoidance conflicts** we must choose between two undesirable alternatives. You may want to avoid studying for an exam, but at the same time want to avoid failing the test. **Approach-avoidance conflicts** include both desirable and undesirable features in the same choice. We are simultaneously drawn to and repelled by a choice—wanting to take a wonderful vacation but having to empty a savings account to do so. 3

Unpredictability and Lack of Control: Factors That Increase Stress

Unpredictable stressors are more difficult to cope with than predictable stressors. Laboratory tests have shown that rats receiving electric shocks without warning develop more ulcers than rats given shocks just as often but only after a warning (Weiss, 1972). Likewise, humans who are warned of a stressor before it occurs and have a chance to prepare themselves for it experience less stress than those who cannot predict when a stressor will occur. 4

Our physical and psychological well-being is profoundly influenced by the degree to which we feel a sense of control over our lives (Rodin & Salovey, 1989). Langer and Rodin (1976) studied the effects of control on nursing-home residents. One group of residents were given some measure of control over their lives, such as choices in arranging their rooms and in the times they could see movies. They showed improved health and well-being and had a lower death rate than another group who were not given control. Within 18 months, 30 percent of the residents given no choices had died compared to only 15 percent of those who had been given some control over their lives. Control is important for cancer patients, too. Some researchers suggest that for cancer patients a sense of control over their daily physical symptoms and emotional 5 reactions may be even more important than control over the course of the disease itself (Thompson et al., 1993).

Several studies suggest that we are less subject to stress when we have the power to do something about it, whether we exercise that power or not. Glass and Singer (1972) subjected two groups of subjects to the same loud noice, but one group was told that they could, if necessary, terminate the noise by pressing a switch. The group that had the control suffered less stress even though they never did exercise the control they were given. Friedland and others (1992) suggest that when people experience a loss of control because of a stressor, they are motivated to try to reestablish control in the stressful situation. Failing this, they often attempt to increase their sense of control in other areas of their lives.

Catastrophic Events and Chronic Intense Stress

Environmental, social, bodily, and emotional stressors are a fact of life for most people, but some people also experience catastrophic events such as plane crashes, fires, or earthquakes. Panic reactions are rare, except in situations such as fires in which people feel that they will survive only if they escape immediately. Many victims of catastrophic events react initially with such shock that they appear dazed, stunned, and emotionally numb. They seem disoriented and may wander about aimlessly, often unaware of their own injuries, attempting to help neither themselves nor others. Following this stage, the victims show a concern for others, and although unable to act efficiently on their own, they are willing to follow the directions of rescue workers. You may have observed these reactions in TV coverage of the Oklahoma City bombing.

As victims begin to recover, the shock is replaced by generalized anxiety. Recovering victims typically have recurring nightmares and feel a compulsive need to retell the event over and over. Reexperiencing the event through dreaming and retelling helps desensitize them to the horror of the experience. Crisis-intervention therapy can provide victims with both coping strategies and realistic expectations about the problems they may face in connection with the trauma.

Posttraumatic Stress Disorder: The Trauma Is Over, but the Stress Remains

Posttraumatic stress disorder (PTSD) is a prolonged and severe stress reaction to a catastrophic event (such as a plane crash or an earthquake) or to chronic intense stress (such as occurs in combat or imprisonment as a hostage or POW).

Breslau and others (1991) found that 9 percent of a random sample of 1,007 adults aged 20 to 30 in metropolitan Detroit had suffered from posttraumatic stress disorder from a variety of events; 80 percent of the women with PTSD had been raped. The disorder may show up imediately, or it may not occur until 6 months or more after the traumatic experience, in which case it is called delayed posttraumatic stress disorder. More than 400,000 Vietnam veterans were found to suffer from PTSD (Goldbers et al., 1990). The most serious cases have resulted from witnessing brutal atrocities, whether among Vietnam veterans (Yehuda et al., 1992), Cambodian refugees (Carlson & Rosser-Horgan, 1991), Holocaust survivors (Kuch & Cox, 1992), or victims of state-sanctioned terrorism and torture (Bloche & Eisenberg, 1993).

People with posttraumatic stress disorder often have flashbacks, nightmares, or intrusive memories in which they feel as though they are actually reexperiencing the traumatic event. They suffer increased anxiety and startle easily, particularly in response to anything that reminds them of the trauma (Green el al., 1985). Many survivors of war or catastrophic events experience survivor guilt because they lived while others died. Some feel that perhaps they could have done more to save others. Extreme combat-related guilt in Vietnam veterans is a risk factor for suicide or preoccupation with suicide (Hendin & Haas, 1991). 10

Research on 4,042 identical and fraternal twin pairs who were Vietnam veterans suggests a genetic susceptibility to posttraumatic stress symptoms. Identical twins were much more similar than fraternal twins in the posttraumatic stress symptoms they had in response to similar combat experiences (True et al., 1993). 11

Is there anything that can lessen the stress that follows a major trauma? According to Bloche and Eisenberg (1993), "Belief systems that give life a sense of purpose and meaning can prevent emotional damage" (p. 5). 12

Chapter Questions

1. How do approach-approach, avoidance-avoidance, and approach-avoidance conflicts differ? 13
2. How do the unpredictability of and lack of control over a stressor affect its impact?
3. How do people typically react to catastrophic events?
4. What is posttraumatic stress disorder?

—Samuel E. Wood and Ellen Green Wood

Purpose of Writer: _____

_____

Purpose of Reader: _____

_____

Assumptions: _____

_____

Support: _____

_____

Comparison and Contrast

As part of your course work, you will be asked to **compare and contrast** information and writers' ideas. Sometimes, you will be asked to do this on a test (see Appendix B) and, at other times, as part of a homework assignment or term paper. In any case, your ability to use a double-entry journal and your use of the P.A.S. strategy will enable you to make comparisons and contrasts efficiently.

To begin the process of comparison and contrast, set up a double-entry journal. Head your paper with the selections or ideas that you are going to compare and contrast, then head one column of your journal "Similarities" and the second "Differences." The exercise that follows will let you practice this process.

Note: Your course instructor does not expect a chart or double-entry journal as your response. You will set up the journal so that you can clearly see the similarities and differences. In class, however, you will need to write a paragraph or an essay showing your comparison and/or contrast.

Practice 4

Compare and contrast high school and college. We have set this one up for you. For practice purposes, try to list three to five similarities and/or differences. You do not need to have the same number of similarities and differences. First, take a look at the example below.

Example:

Comparison and Contrast of Men and Women

Similarities	*Differences*
In this column, you would list how men and women are similar. You might list that they are people, that they can be parents, or any other similarities that men and women have.	Here, you would list the ways that men and women are different. You might say that when a man becomes a parent, he is called a father, and when a woman becomes a parent, she is called a mother. You can probably think of many other differences.

1. Comparison of High School and College

Similarities	*Differences*

2. Use the information that you have listed to write a paragraph comparing and contrasting high school and college.

_____

_____

_____

_____

_____

_____

_____

_____

_____

_____

Practice 5

Read the following two poems about suicide. It might be interesting and helpful for you to know that "Richard Cory" was written in 1897 and "Barbie Doll" was first published in 1973. Think about the following as you read: (1) Why do you suppose the writer titled her poem, "Barbie Doll"? and (2) What kind of comparison/contrast can be made between poems written in such different times? After you have read both poems, **compare** and **contrast** the ideas that they represent.

Richard Cory

Whenever Richard Cory went down town,
We people on the pavement looked at him;
He was a gentleman from sole to crown,
Clean favored, and imperially slim.

And he was always quietly arrayed,   5
And he was always human when he talked;
But still he fluttered pulses when he said,

"Good-morning," and he glittered when he walked.
And he was rich—yes, richer than a king—
And admirably schooled in every grace: 10
In fine, we thought that he was everything
To make us wish that we were in his place.

So on we worked, and waited for the light,
And went without the meat, and cursed the bread;
And Richard Cory, one calm summer night,   15
Went home and put a bullet through his head.

—Edward A. Robinson

Barbie Doll

This girlchild was born as usual
and presented dolls that did pee-pee
and miniature GE stoves and irons
and wee lipsticks the color of cherry candy.
Then in the magic of puberty, a classmate said: 5
You have a great big nose and fat legs.

She was healthy, tested intelligent,
possessed strong arms and back,
abundant sexual drive and manual dexterity.
She went to and fro apologizing.   10
Everyone saw a fat nose on thick legs.

She was advised to play coy,
exhorted to come on hearty,
exercise, diet, smile and wheedle.
Her good nature wore out   15
like a fan belt.
So she cut off her nose and legs
and offered them up.

In the casket displayed on satin she lay
with the undertakers cosmetics painted on,   20
a turned-up putty nose,
Dressed in a pink and white nightie.
Doesn't she look pretty? everyone said.
Consummation at last.
To every woman a happy ending.   25

—Marge Piercy

Comparison and Contrast of "Richard Cory" and "Barbie Doll"

Similarities	Differences

Paragraph or essay comparing the two selections.

_____

_____

_____

_____

_____

_____

Practice 6

Read Selection 9 "The City of Brooklyn, July 13" (pages 378–381, Chapter 13). **Compare** *and* **contrast** *your lifestyle with that of the Lambert family.*

The City of Brooklyn

My Lifestyle	The Lamberts' Lifestyle

Read the following minibiographies about movie-makers Steven Spielberg and Spike Lee. Compare and contrast their successful careers.

Steven Spielberg

Imagine Steven Spielberg's excitement, at age 17, when a family visit to Los Angeles included a tour of the Universal studios. Imagine his disappointment when the tour bus bypassed the sound stages. At the next break, he gave the tour group the slip and headed straight back to the sound stages, somehow managed to get in, and ended up chatting for an hour with editorial head Chuck Silvers. The next day, with a pass signed by Silvers, Spielberg was back to show him four of his 8-millimeter home movies. Silvers liked what he saw but told the young Spielberg that he could not issue another pass for the next day. Undaunted, Spielberg put on a suit and tie the next day and carrying his father's briefcase, walked through the Universal gates, faking a familiar wave to the guard. It worked. Spielberg spent the whole summer in and out of Universal, hanging around as movies were being made.   1

Today, Spielberg is one of the world's best-known moviemakers. His 1993 movie, *Jurassic Park,* has earned more money than any other movie in history. The gross topped $900 million in less than a year and was heading toward $1 billion with home video and other after-market releases. That surpassed 1982's *E.T.: The Extra-Terrestrial,* another Spielberg film, which had been the top Hollywood moneymaker. Spielberg's *Indiana Jones and the Last Crusade* is fifth and *Jaws* eighth. His *Raiders of the Lost Ark, Indiana Jones and the Temple of Doom* and *Close Encounters of the Third Kind* all are in the top 20. In all, his 15 movies have grossed more than $4 billion.   2

Steven Spielberg's work embodies a whole range of qualities that tell us a lot about Hollywood and the role of movies in our culture. He is a wonderful, audience-oriented storyteller: "I want people to love my movies, and I'll be a whore to get them into theaters," he once said.   3

Spielberg's films also represent the glitz and glamour of Hollywood. Most are spectacularly filmed with dazzling special effects. And their box-office success has helped fuel the   4 extravagances that are part of the image Hollywood cultivates for itself.

But Spielberg is deeper than that. He entwines observations from his personal life into film commentary on fundamental human issues. The fantasy *E.T.* centers on a boy growing up alienated in a broken home who identifies with the alien E.T. Movie analysts see the boy as a metaphorical stand-in for Spielberg, who was taunted as a Jew when he transferred into a new high school and found himself alienated for something over which he had no control.

Moviegoers entranced by Spielberg's adventure stories sometimes forget his serious works. His 1985 *The Color Purple* adapted from Alice Walker's Pulitzer Prize-winning book, was a painful, insightful account of a southern African-American family during the first half of the century. *Schindler's List*, his acclaimed 1993 account of the Holocaust, flows from his own heritage. These movies, some say Spielberg's best, represent the potential of the medium to help us individually and collectively sort through the dilemmas of the human condition.

Schindler's List swept the Oscars in 1993, casting Spielberg in a whole new light as a director. Until then, Spielberg's critical success seemed to count against him at Oscar time, and even critics who liked his work for its seamless craft and visceral punch dismissed him as a serious director. Though he had tackled serious themes before, he always seemed uncomfortable with the material, as if he were trying too hard to make a point. All that changed with *Schindler's List*. The film, from the novel by Thomas Keneally, has been universally praised as one of the great films of the decade, and with it Spielberg has assured himself a place in film history not only as the highest-grossing director of all time, but as one of the great U.S. directors of the post-war period.

—John Vivian

Spike Lee

Spike Lee, a bright, clever young film director, was in deep trouble in 1992. He had persuaded Warner Brothers, the big Hollywood studio, to put up $20 million for a film biography of controversial black leader Malcolm X, one of his heroes. Lee insisted on expensive foreign shooting in Cairo and Soweto, and now, not only was the $20 million from Warner gone but so was $8 million from other investors. To finish the movie, Lee put up his own $3 million up-front salary to pay, he hoped, all the production bills.

The crisis was not the first for Lee, whose experience as a moviemaker illustrates several realities about the American movie industry, not all of them flattering:

- Hollywood is the heart of the American movie industry, and it is difficult if not impossible for feature filmmakers to succeed outside of the Hollywood establishment.
- Hollywood, with rare exception, favors movies that follow themes that already have proven successful rather than taking risks on innovative, controversial themes.
- Fortunes come and go in Hollywood, even studio fortunes. Although Warner is a major studio and often flush with money, it was on an austerity binge when Spike Lee came back for more money in 1992.
- The American movie industry has been taken over by conglomerates, which, as in the case of Warner Brothers, a subsidiary of Time Warner, was being pressured in 1992 to maximize profits to see the parent company through a difficult economic period.

To hear Spike Lee tell it, his problem also was symptomatic of racism in the movie industry. Addressing the Los Angeles Advertising Club during the *Malcolm X* crisis, Lee, who is black, was blunt: "I think there's a ceiling on how much money Hollywood's going to spend on black films or films with a black theme."

Although studio executives would deny Lee's charge, his perceptions were born of experience in making five movies, all critically acclaimed and all profitable but all filmed on shoestring budgets and with little or no studio promotion.

As a student at Morehouse College, Spike Lee had dabbled in film, and when he graduated he decided to commit himself fully to making movies. He enrolled in the film program at New York University. As his master's thesis he put together *Joe's Bed-Stuy Barbershop: We Cut Heads*. It won a 1982 student Academy Award and became the first student film ever shown in the Lincoln Center's new films series in New York.

That would seem to make a young filmmaker a sought-after talent in Hollywood, but such would not be Lee's experience. Despite the acclaim for *Joe's Bed-Stuy Barbershop*, which called for an awakening of American black consciousness, Lee could not interest Hollywood in financing any of his ideas for more black-oriented films. On his own, Lee raised $175,000 in 1986 to produce *She's Gotta Have It*, a sharp, witty movie that upset Hollywood's conventional wisdom by making $8 million.

Bristling with ideas for more films, Lee again went hat in hand to Hollywood; but the response was lukewarm. For lack of financing, he put his movie ideas on a back burner and kept busy as a filmmaker with an Anita Baker music video, the "Horn of Plenty" short for *Saturday Night Live*, and the "Hangtime" and "Cover" ads for Nike, with basketball star Michael Jordan and himself playing his Mars Blackmon streetwise hustler character from *She's Gotta Have It*. [7]

The videos won awards, and the Nike ads sold a lot of shoes, which finally enabled Lee to persuade Columbia Pictures to put up some money for a new movie, *School Daze*, although only one-third the studio's usual commitment for a movie. Columbia's hesitancy was understandable from a commerical perspective. The movie seemed risky. Not only did it delve into sensitive racial issues, including social stratification between light-skinned and dark-skinned blacks, but also, being a musical, it had complex production numbers that might confound a young director, even one as promising as Spike Lee. [8]

Columbia's hesitancy, it turned out, was misplaced. Despite weak studio publicity, *School Daze* turned out to be Columbia's top-grossing movie of 1988. Especially significant about *School Daze* was that Columbia had given Lee complete creative control, unusual even for many veteran filmmakers. That, of course, made the movie's success even a greater credit to Lee, and in 1989 *Newsweek* magazine proclaimed Lee one of the nation's 25 leading innovators. [9]

Lee followed *School Daze* with *Do the Right Thing, Mo' Better Blues* and *Jungle Fever*. None had strong studio financial backing. He remained an outsider. Not only was he a black person in a white-dominated business, but he also insisted on living in the New York neighborhood where he grew up—not California. [10]

When he proposed *Malcolm X*, Warner put up $20 million, unprecedented for a black film, but still short of the whole budget. Lee was sent out to raise the remainder of the $28 million budget from other sources, and then, when [11] the cost overruns came in, he found himself putting his own salary into the project to pay the bills and keep the project alive.

—John Vivian

Steven Spielberg and Spike Lee

Similarities | *Differences*

Comparison/Contrast Essay:

_____

_____

_____

_____

_____

_____

_____

_____

_____

_____

_____

_____

_____

_____

_____

_____

_____

_____

_____

_____

_____

Review: College Text Reading Strategies

P.A.S. Strategy Ask yourself:
- What is the writer's purpose?
- What are his or her assumptions?
- How is that information supported?

TIPS Strategy
- **T**—Read the chapter **Title**—Write it in your own words.
- **I**—Read the **Introduction**—Find the general topics, and chapter goals and objectives if they are covered. Write down the most important ideas.
- **P**—Read the headings and subheadings. Mark the main **Parts**.
- **S**—Find and read the study questions or questions for discussion. Rewrite the **Summary** in your own words.

Comparison/Contrast Remember to:
- Set up a double-entry journal.
- List all the similarities in one column and the differences in the other column.
- Write a paragraph or short essay using the information. Or put the information into the format that your instructor has specified.

CHAPTER

12

Applying Vocabulary Strategies

In this section, you practice the **vocabulary strategies** using college text materials. Application of the vocabulary strategies to college materials helps you learn new words more easily and better prepares you for additional course work.

Mathematics Vocabulary

Succeeding in the study of mathematics requires more than learning about numbers. You must read and learn words that may be familiar to you, such as *interest* and *table*, but have different meanings when they are used in mathematics. In addition, many mathematical terms have opposites, such as plus/minus or add/subtract. Knowing these opposites gives you a good understanding of several mathematical terms by helping you develop a connection between them. Last, but not least, there are many word parts that not only are used in mathematics but also are found in other college courses. Learning such word parts helps you in both mathematics and other courses.

This section introduces you to some basic math vocabulary and requires you to practice what you are learning. Specifically, you will work with **word parts** (prefixes, suffixes, and roots), **word opposites,** and words with **multiple meanings.** Learning more about the vocabulary of a subject can help you understand it better.

Practice 1

*Here is a chart of **word parts,** their meanings, and a mathematical vocabulary word for each word part. Memorize the word parts and their meanings. Use your dictionary or your mathematics textbook to find the definition of any word you do not know. Then list two other general words for each word part.*

Word Part	Meaning	Math Word	General Words
bi	two	binary	*bicycle*
			bisect
circum	around	circumference	_____
peri	around	perimeter	_____
deci	one tenth	decimal	_____
equi	the same, equal	equilateral	_____
meter	to measure	diameter	_____
semi	half	semicircle	_____
sub	below, under	subtract	_____
tion	act, state of	addition	_____
tri	three	triangle	_____

Practice 2

*For each of the words below, the **mathematical meaning** is given. Each word also has several other meanings. Write a second meaning in the space provided. If you cannot think of another meaning, use your dictionary.*

1. *base*—math: a number on which a mathematical system or calculation depends.

   another meaning: _____

2. *check*—math: to inspect a calculation for accuracy.

   another meaning: _____

3. *interest*—math: payment for the use of money as on a loan or an added charge on a credit card.

   another meaning: _____

4. *mean*—math: the sum of all the elements in a set divided by the number of elements.

   another meaning: _____

5. *notation*—math: any system of signs, figures, or abbreviations for convenience in mathematics, especially in algebra and arithmetic.

   another meaning: _____

6. *power*—math: the product of a number multiplied by itself a given number of times.

   another meaning: _____

7. *range*—math: the inclusive difference between extreme values of numbers; as a range of twenty from a value of zero to nineteen.

   another meaning: _____

8. *root*—math: a quantity taken a specified number of times as a factor will give another quantity called power.

   another meaning: _____

9. *scale*—math: a system of notation in which the successive places determine the value of figures; as the decimal system.

   another meaning: _____

10. *table*—math: a collection of related numbers, values, signs, or items of any kind arranged for ease of reference or comparison, often in parallel columns.

   another meaning: _____

Practice 3

*Working with **opposites** has a distinct advantage over learning words one at a time. When working with opposites, you get two for the price of one; that is, you learn two terms at the same time. Here are ten mathematical opposites and an exercise to help you understand them. Fill in the correct word in each sentence.*

1. *horizontal/vertical*

   He placed the bars across the windows in a _____ position.

2. *random/ordered*

   The numbers 1, 2, 3, 4, 5 are in _____ sequence.

3. *quotient/product*

   When 5 is multiplied by 12, the _____ is 60.

4. *sum/difference*

   The _____ between twenty and five is fifteen.

5. *numerator/denominator*

   In the fraction ¾, four is the _____ .

6. *increases/decreases*

   When ice melts, the temperature _____ .

7. *maximum/minimum*

   The _____ score on the test was 100%.

8. *even/odd*

   Any number that can be divided by two with no remainder is an _____ number.

9. *above/below*

In any fraction, the numerator is _____
the denominator.

10. *multiplied/divided*

One hundred _____ by twenty-five
equals four.

Practice 4

In the following selection from a mathematics textbook, you will find mathematical words and nonmathematical words or general words that you can learn by applying your vocabulary strategies. Words that may be unfamiliar to you have been underlined. You should underline any other words that are new to you. Use the **context** *and* **notations strategies** *to predict the meaning of the underlined words. Then complete the* **word chart** *by referring to the text. If necessary, use your dictionary.*

Installment Purchases

Martin was able to buy his new bicycle on credit. He   1
found a bicycle that would be perfect for his trip. The store
agreed to accept Martin's payment on <u>credit</u>. He paid some
money right away. He also signed an <u>agreement</u> stating that
he would pay a certain amount of money each month until
he had paid for the bike. There was an added charge for the
<u>privilege</u> of paying by credit, but Martin was happy. Credit
made his cross-country trip possible.

Some stores offer creditworthy customers the conve-   2
nience of credit through an <u>installment plan</u>. The customer
must pay *part* of the selling price at the time of purchase.
This part is called the <u>down payment</u>. The scheduled payments are usually made on a monthly basis and are called <u>in-
stallments</u>.

Installment buyers are charged a fee for the privilege   3
of using this "easy-payment" plan. This fee is called <u>interest</u>
or <u>finance charge</u>. It is added to the cost of the <u>merchandise</u>.
The consumer must decide if the convenience of install-
ment buying outweighs the extra cost. Installment buyers
sign an agreement that <u>specifies</u> the down payment, interest,
monthly payments, and payment schedule. Remember, before

you sign any agreement, be sure you understand all the terms used in the agreement.

—Robert K. Gerver and Richard J. Sgroi

Word	Definition
credit	*buy now, pay later*
agreement	
privilege	
installment plan	
down payment	
installments	
interest	
finance charge	
merchandise	
specifies	

Marketing Vocabulary

As in any college course, a marketing course introduces you to specialized meanings of words. Many of these words have other general meanings, such as *market* (a place to shop) and *product* (a direct result). Knowing the general meaning of a word may help you understand its specialized meaning. As you read a textbook, you will also come across nonspecialized words that you need to know the meaning of to understand the subject. As you read and study more, you will learn many new words. Increasing your general vocabulary will enable you to read more effectively and allow you to spend your study time working with new, specialized word meanings.

Practice 5

*Here is a chart of **word parts,** their meanings, and a marketing vocabulary word for each word part. Memorize the word parts and their meanings. Use your dictionary to find the meaning of any word that you do not know. Then list two other general words for each word part.*

Word Part	Meaning	Marketing Word	General Words
pro	for, in support of	product, promotion	*propose, proceed*
trans	across	transfer	_____ _____
con	together, with	consumer	_____ _____
ex	outside, away from	excess	_____ _____
sur	over, above, additional	surplus	_____ _____

Practice 6

*In the following list of "Important Points" taken from a marketing textbook, you will find specialized and general words that you can learn by applying your **vocabulary strategies.** Words that may be unfamiliar to you have been underlined. You should underline any other words that are new to you. Use the **context** and **notation strategies** to predict the meaning of the underlined words. Then complete the **word chart** by referring to the text. If necessary, use your dictionary.*

Important Points in the Chapter

1. As a society progresses economically, specialization of work occurs resulting in <u>surpluses</u>. Marketing becomes <u>indispensable</u>, since these surpluses must be exchanged for the necessities that are the surpluses of other workers.

2. There are many ways in which the word <u>market</u> is used. One of these is: a market is an area in which the <u>aggregate</u> of forces or conditions result in decisions that satisfy demand by the <u>transfer</u> of <u>goods</u> and <u>services</u>.

3. *Marketing* may be defined as the performance of business activities that direct the flow of goods and services from the producer to the consumer or user.

4. The marketing division is directly responsible for such activities as selling, advertising, transportation, and <u>promotion</u> and is indirectly involved in production and accounting.

5. The two basic elements of a marketing system are the surplus of a good or service in one sector of the economy (the producing sector) and a demand for such good or service in another sector of the economy (the <u>consuming</u> sector).

—Jay Diamond and Gerald Pintel

Word	Definition
surplus	*extra goods, services, supplies*
indispensable	
market	
aggregate	
transfer	
goods	
service	
marketing	
promotion	
consuming	

Practice 7

*For each of the following words, the **marketing meaning** is given. Think of another general meaning for the word or use your dictionary if necessary.*

1. *transfer*—marketing: to move goods or services from one place to another.

   another meaning:_____

2. *goods*—marketing: commodities or products.

   another meaning:_____

3. *services*—marketing: work done for others as an occupation or business.

   another meaning:_____

4. *promotion*—marketing: advertising or other publicity.

   another meaning:_____

5. *place*—marketing: transportation of goods to the customer.

   another meaning:_____

6. *form*—marketing: the extraction of goods from nature and changing them to satisfy human needs; manufacturing and production of goods.

   another meaning:_____

7. *time*—marketing: getting goods to the consumer when demanded.

   another meaning:_____

8. *target*—marketing: a particular group of consumers to whom managers want to sell their product.

   another meaning:_____

Practice 8

In the paragraph below, write the vocabulary word from the marketing exercises that correctly completes the meaning of the sentence. Be sure to change the ending of the word if needed.

One of the skills needed by a salesperson is the ability to convince the _____ that she needs the product. One way to attract the potential buyer to come to the store is to run a _____ advertisement in the newspaper. Another method that can be used to persuade the customer to buy a _____ is to offer a free _____ guarantee for at least the first year after the purchase is made. An enterprising salesperson who shows much initiative will convince the buyer that the product is essential to a happy life and therefore _____. Although there may be a large _____ of the item available, a successful salesperson will convince the buyer to _____ her money to the store in return for the _____. These sales skills are essential to the successful _____ of a product.

History Vocabulary

History, the branch of knowledge that records and analyzes past events, is probably more familiar to you than some of the other social science courses. In addition, some of the specialized vocabulary of history are also frequently used in the study of political science, another subject that you may choose to study.

Practice 9

*Here is a chart of **word parts**, their meanings, and a history vocabulary word for each word part. Memorize the word parts and their meanings. List two other general words for each word part.*

Word Part	Meaning	History Words	General Words
tion	action, process	legislation	*quotation, absorption*

archy	rule, government	anarchy	_____
			_____
con, com	together, with, joint	conservative	_____
			_____
ism	practice, theory	socialism	_____
			_____
ist	an advocate of a doctrine	anarchist	_____
			_____
mono, mon	one, alone	monarchy	_____

Practice 10

*Read the following selection, which describes some ideas that could be included in a college history course. Use the **vocabulary strategies** to predict the meaning of the underlined words. Also, underline any other words that are unfamiliar to you. Then complete the **word chart** by referring to the text. If necessary, use your dictionary.*

College History

In a college history course, you could learn about several different types of governments. For example, you may learn about countries where a king or queen still <u>reigns</u>. If the <u>monarch</u> has total control of the country, he or she is ruling the country through a <u>dictatorship</u>. If the citizens elect the people who govern the country, the form of government is called a <u>democracy</u>. You may also learn about countries where several groups are struggling to control the government. If no group or person can take charge of the government, the country is in a state of <u>anarchy</u>.   1

In the United States which has a written guide or <u>constitution</u> to organize the government, there is a president who heads the <u>executive</u> branch of government. The United States also has a <u>legislative</u> branch to make laws and a <u>judicial</u> branch to decide if laws have been broken.   2

People who are involved in the government are called <u>politicians</u> who may have different views about how the government should be run. Politicians who support little change in government policies are called <u>conservatives</u>. Other politicians who want to change government policies to meet changing social conditions are called <u>liberals</u>. The <u>policies</u>, or actions, of a government will also be determined by whether the people in charge of the government are <u>socialists</u> who support common ownership of the means of production, or are <u>capitalists</u> who support private ownership of the means of production.

3

—Sidney G. Becker

Word	Definition
monarch	*single ruler of a country*
reigns	
dictatorship	
democracy	
anarchy	
constitution	
executive	
legislative	
judicial	
politician	
conservative	
liberal	
policy	
socialist	
capitalist	

Practice 11

One method to remember the meaning of a word is to remember its **opposite.** *In the history* **word chart,** *there are several opposites. In each of the following sentences, write the correct opposite in the blank.*

1. *democratic/socialistic*

   In a _____ country, the government could own all property.

2. *monarchy/anarchy*

   When the king died without an heir, the country had no ruler and became a (an) _____.

3. *judicial/executive*

   The _____ branch of government decides if laws have been broken.

4. *capitalist/socialist*

   The new president, a _____, believed in private ownership of all utilities.

5. *dictatorial/democratic*

   King John, a _____ ruler, controlled the legislative, executive, and judicial branches of government.

Practice 12

Select the correct word from the history **word chart** *to complete each sentence. Be sure to change the word endings if needed.*

There are a number of similarities between a local school board and the national government in the United States. The school board is elected by citizens to make the _____ _____ that govern a school district. Therefore it is similar to the _____ branch of government. The superintendent of schools must implement these policies; she is the chief _____ of the school district. If the majority of school board members think that the school does a good job of providing educational services, they will want to maintain current policies and could be called

_____. When school board members disagree, they will try to convince the voters that their position is correct. The voters may, at the next election, end the _____ of the board member(s) with whom they disagree.

Psychology Vocabulary

Psychology is a course that many college students are interested in taking because they are curious about how the mind works and what causes people to behave in various ways. Sometimes students are overwhelmed by the new vocabulary that they must learn as they study psychology. For example, an introductory paragraph in a psychology textbook states:

> We can define <u>psychology</u> as the systematic, scientific study of behaviors and mental processes. The term <u>behavior</u> refers to observable actions or responses in both humans and animals. Behaviors might include eating, speaking, laughing, avoiding, sleeping, and hundreds of others. <u>Mental processes</u> which are not directly observable, include planning, thinking, imagining, coping, dreaming, and many others.
>
> —Rod K. Plotnik

In one paragraph, three new words—*psychology, behavior,* and *mental processes*—are explained. Remembering and using these words correctly might seem difficult, but by using the **vocabulary strategies** and keeping **word charts,** you would soon learn the words.

Practice 13

*Below is a chart of **word parts,** their meanings, and a psychology vocabulary word for each. Memorize the word parts and their meanings. List two other general words for each word part.*

Word Part	Meaning	Psychology Word	General Words
psycho	mental, mind	psychology	*psychodynamics*
			_____

en, em	to put into or onto	encode	_____
			_____
echo	repetition of sound	echoic	_____
			_____
ic	of, pertaining to	systematic	_____
			_____
dis	not, opposite of	distinctive	_____
		association	_____
ance	state or condition, action	maintenance	_____
			_____

Practice 14

*Read the following selection taken from a psychology chapter about memory. The reading is about strategies that people can use to encode or place information from short-term memory into long-term memory. As you read, use your **vocabulary strategies** to figure out the meaning of the underlined words. Also underline any other words that are unfamiliar to you. Then complete the psychology **word chart**. If necessary, use your dictionary but be sure to select a definition that fits the meaning of the word as used in the text. Write the meaning of the word in your own words.*

Strategies of Effortful Encoding

Maintenance Rehearsal

As you already know a common strategy to keep infor- 1
mation in short-term memory is to use <u>maintenance re-
hearsal</u>, which is simply repeating or rehearsing the
information. This method, which "maintains" or keeps information alive in short-term memory, is primarily for increasing the duration of short-term memory. However,
maintenance rehearsal is not very effective for <u>encoding</u> information into long-term memory, because it involves too

little thinking about, visualizing, or making new associations with this information.

Elaborative Rehearsal

A more effective way to encode information into long-term memory is a process called <u>elaborative rehearsal</u>, *which involves associating the new information with previous information that you already know.* The word <u>elaborative</u> refers to thinking about, elaborating on, or making new <u>associations</u> with the new, unfamiliar information and old, familiar information. For example, students who used elaborative rehearsal to remember a list of words (such as by associating words with cars) were significantly better at later recognizing the words than were students who just looked at the words (Fisk & Schneider, 1984). One reason elaborative rehearsal is more effective than maintenance rehearsal is that by "elaborating" you are actually thinking about, making associations with, and creating cues for the material that will help you remember it in the future.

You can use elaborative rehearsal to encode the definition of echoic memory. You might notice that this phrase contains the word echo, which you can associate with hearing. Further, you could associate an echo with lasting two seconds. By making these two associations, you have our definition of <u>echoic</u> memory as holding hearing information for several seconds. Because of the associations you are more likely to encode the definition of echoic memory in a way that you can easily *retrieve* for a future exam.

Imagery

Beside making associations with words or numbers, you can make associations with <u>images</u>. *Distinctive associations,* particularly those made with visual images, can serve as good memory aids. Researchers Mark McDaniel and Gilles Einstein (1986) asked students to remember three words—*dog, bicycle,* and *street*—using either <u>bizarre</u> associations, such as "The dog rode the bicycle down the street," or common associations, such as "The dog chased the bicycle down the street." They found that bizarre associations made the words more <u>distinctive</u> and thus easier to remember. Researchers suggest that it is the distinctiveness of association, rather than their bizarreness, that leads to better recall of information (Kroll, Schepler, & Angin, 1986).

—Rod K. Plotnik

Word	Definition
maintenance	*to keep in the memory*
rehearsal	
encode	
elaborative	
associations	
echoic	
retrieve	
images	
distinctive	
bizarre	

Practice 15

Learning just a few words and phrases can help you with a subject such as psychology. These self-test questions are taken from the same psychology textbook. First, try to answer them without using the **word charts.** *Then, if necessary, check your word chart to fill in the correct words. Be sure to change the endings of words when necessary.*

1. The study of memory, which is the ability to retain information over time, includes three separate processes. The first process, which is placing information in memory is called _____.

2. If you pay attention to information in sensory memory, this information is automatically transferred into a second kind of memory called _____ memory, which has a limited capacity and a short duration. If you rehearse or think about information in short-term memory, that information will usually be transferred or encoded into the third more permanent kind of memory called _____ memory.

3. Visual memory known as iconic memory may last about a quarter of a second. Auditory memory, known as _____ memory, may last as long as two seconds.

4. You can increase the length of time that information remains in short-term memory by intentionally repeating the information which is called _____.

5. If information in short-term memory is not _____, it will disappear in 2–30 seconds.

6. The transfer of information from short-term into long-term memory is controlled by a process called _____.

7. Much of semantic information is transferred from short-term to long-term memory by deliberate attempts to repeat, rehearse, or make associations. Together, these deliberate attempts are referred to as _____ encoding.

8. There are two kinds of effortful encoding that vary in their effectiveness. Encoding by simply repeating or rehearsing the information is called _____. This method is not very effective for encoding information into long-term memory because it involves too little thinking about, visualizing, or making new associations with the information. Encoding by thinking about and associating new information with previous information is called _____. Besides making associations with words or numbers, another method of elaborative rehearsal is to make associations with _____.

—Rod K. Plotnik

Practice 16

*Nearly all the words that you have learned from the psychology textbook have more than one, or **multiple meanings.** Carefully read the multiple meanings of each word, then read each sentence that contains the word and write the letter of the correct meaning in the blank next to the sentence.*

1. *effort*
   a. Conscious use of mental energy.

b. A difficult exertion of strength.

c. A sincere attempt.

d. An achievement produced through hard work.

_____ 1. The author's last book was his finest <u>effort</u>.

_____ 2. John's <u>effort</u> to learn sociology became more effective when he used visual imagery.

_____ 3. Tom's <u>effort</u> to arrive promptly was appreciated by the teacher.

_____ 4. Maria was so tired that it was an <u>effort</u> to close the door.

2. *maintenance*

a. The act of continuing.

b. The work of keeping something in proper condition.

c. A means of support.

_____ 1. When Elena repeats a telephone number again and again, she is trying to <u>maintain</u> it in her short-term memory.

_____ 2. Donna's former husband was late with his alimony or <u>maintenance</u> payments that she needed to pay the rent for her apartment.

_____ 3. Lem took his car to the same garage every six months for regular <u>maintenance</u>.

3. *association*

a. The act of mentally combining or linking.

b. An organized group of people who have a common interest.

c. A mental connection between sensations and ideas or events.

_____ 1. <u>Associating</u> words with pictures often helps students remember the meanings of the words.

_____ 2. My mother belongs to the American <u>Association</u> of Retired People.

_____ 3. When Joanne smells lilacs, she always <u>associates</u> the lovely odor with the arrival of spring.

4. *rehearsal*
   a. The act of practicing in preparation for a performance.
   b. A verbal repetition or recital.

   _____ 1. The children <u>rehearsed</u> their lines in the play many times.

   _____ 2. Carlo, the lead singer in the band, attended many <u>rehearsals</u> before the opening concert.

5. *retrieve*
   a. To regain what was lost.
   b. To remember.
   c. To discover and bring back.

   _____ 1. The dog located the dead bird and <u>retrieved</u> it for the hunter.

   _____ 2. The student was able to <u>retrieve</u> the names of all the elements when she took the chemistry test.

   _____ 3. The stockbroker <u>retrieved</u> his losses when he bought the new stocks.

Humanities Vocabulary

During your college career, you will enroll in one or more courses in the humanities. In these courses, such as philosophy, literature, art, or music, you will learn about the cultural arts as distinguished from the sciences. Scholars state that it is impossible to say when the humanities began, but the textbook passage you will read describes prehistoric human "records" that provide hints about very early human values.

Practice 17

*Below is a chart of **word parts,** their meanings, and a humanities word for each word part. Memorize the word parts and their meanings. Use your dictionary or the textbook selection that* *follows the chart to find the definition of any word that you do not know. Then list two other general words for each word part.*

Word Part	Meaning	Humanities Word	General Words
pre	before, in advance	prehistoric	*preview* _____
con, com	together, with	console	_____ _____
homo	same or alike	homo sapiens	_____ _____

Practice 18

*Read this selection taken from a humanities textbook. As you read, use your **vocabulary strategies** to predict the meaning of the underlined words. Also, underline any other words that are unfamiliar to you. Then complete the word chart by referring to the text. If necessary, use your dictionary.*

Valuing Life: Valuing Beauty

The study of the humanities is a study of values, begin- 1
ning with the special value of life and its concomitant, beauty.
The humanities <u>predate</u> our own species, *Homo sapiens sapiens*, which is no more than 50,000 years old. The oldest example of human <u>handiwork</u>, an architectural foundation of
rocks shaped into a circle, was created 2 million years ago in
Africa. Such shelters may still be in use somewhere today.
Terra Amata was found during excavations for apartments on
the Riviera, in Nice, France.

<u>Neanderthals</u> (*homo sapiens neandertalensis*) seem to 2
have been capable of an emotional life similar to ours. A carefully prepared burial site, discovered in Iraq at the mouth of
a cave, demonstrates their capacity to grieve and probably to
hope. The "Shanidar man" of approximately 40,000 B.C.—

almost certainly a Neanderthal—was buried with an arrangement of Saint Barnaby's thistle, cornflowers, and other medicinal plants; it is believed that this "flower burial" indicates the value of this man's life and the hope that the magic or medicinal qualities of the plants would ease him in death. That hope would imply a belief in an <u>afterlife</u>, which is important in most religions. The flower arrangement also suggests that the mourners valued balance and order—and that, in turn, implies a concern for art, which excites feeling. The <u>humanities</u> have to do with both the education of feeling and the establishment of a system of values.

Those who mourned the "Shanidar man" understood that life was different from death and must also have understood that they, too, would die. Because we are the only creatures who expect death, we have developed a special <u>reverence</u> for life, revealed in the care with which many prehistoric people were buried. Care in burial is also unique to humans, and it seems to have a special power to <u>console</u> the living.

Cornflowers have been found in the tombs of Egyptian pharaohs, and the "Shanidar man" may, like the pharaohs, have been a special figure in this society. Such flowers have long been thought to have special properties which ease the journey into death. The fact that the Neanderthals had a funeral ritual tells us that they must have already developed a system of communication to preserve it. Recent studies of Neanderthal anatomy—it is in some respects identical to that of newborn *Homo sapiens sapiens*—suggest that the Neanderthals may not have been able to speak as we do. (If this is true, we can understand why the Neanderthals, whose brain was as large as our own, disappeared 30,000 years ago.) However, <u>ocher</u> pencils have been found at Terra Amata, and it is possible that the Neanderthals had a form of <u>visual arts</u> to aid in communication.

If the Neanderthals had a sense of magic, they may also have had some form of religion. This view is supported by the care that is evident in the Shanidar burial. And if they had a religion, then it is also possible that they had music, dance, and other arts; in fact, dance is common in hunting-and-gathering societies. We have little evidence, beyond structure and occasional burial sites, of Neanderthal art; but that would be understandable if their creativity went mostly into dance and music.

—Lee A. Jacobus

Word	Definition
predate	*to exist before a certain date*
homo sapiens	
handiwork	
Neanderthals	
afterlife	
humanities	
reverence	
console	
ocher	
visual arts	

Practice 19

Use the words from the word charts in this section to correctly complete these summary paragraphs. Be sure to change the endings of the words when needed.

In _____ times, a now extinct species of people called the _____ buried their dead. This shows that they had some sense of not only preparing for death, but hoping for an _____ beyond the grave. Wildflowers placed in ancient graves demonstrate that the people had a sense of awe about life and death, _____ these mysteries as people do today. The flowers may also have been placed in the grave to _____ the dead person's family.

    Although these prehistoric people probably did not develop a language, they seem to have developed methods of communication, one of which was to draw with _____ _____ pencils. Drawings and dance may have been the _____ arts of these people.

Environmental Science Vocabulary

In addition to courses in the social sciences, humanities, and mathematics, you will be required to enroll in science courses when you are completing a college degree. You will probably have many courses to choose among. Because issues such as pollution control and depletion of natural resources are current topics, many students choose to study environmental science. In this section, you will read a passage from an environmental science textbook and apply your **vocabulary strategies** to words in the passage.

Practice 20

*Here is a chart of **word parts,** their meanings, and an environmental science vocabulary word for each word part. Memorize the word parts and their meanings. Use the text selection that follows or the dictionary to find the meaning of any word that you do not know. Then list two other general words for each word part.*

Word Part	Meaning	Environmental Science Word	General Words
ad, at	toward, to	atmosphere	*administer* _____
			_____
litho, lith	stone	lithosphere	_____
			_____
hydro	water	hydrosphere	_____
			_____
bio	life	biosphere	_____
			_____

Practice 21

*Read the passage from the environmental science textbook and use the **vocabulary strategies** to predict the meaning of the underlined words. Also, underline any other words that are unfamiliar to you. Then complete the environmental science word chart by referring to the text. If necessary, use the dictionary.*

Ecosystems: What Are They and How Do They Work?

What plants and animals live in a forest or a pond? How 1 do they get the underline{matter} and energy underline{resources} needed to stay alive? How do these plants and animals interact with one another and with their physical environment? What changes will this forest or pond undergo through time?

underline{Ecology} is the science that attempts to answer such 2 questions. In 1866 German biologist Ernst Haeckel coined the term *ecology* from two Greek words: *oikos*, meaning "house" or "place to live," and *logos*, meaning "study of." Literally, then ecology is the study of living things in their home. In more formal terms, **ecology** is the study of underline{interactions} among organisms and between organisms and the physical and chemical factors making up their environment. This study is usually carried out as the examination of **ecosystems**: forests, deserts, ponds, oceans, or any set of plants and animals interacting with one another and with their nonliving environment. This chapter will consider the major nonliving and living components of ecosystems and how they interact.

The Biosphere and Ecosystems

The Earth's Life-Support System What keeps plants 3 and animals alive on this tiny planet as it hurtles through space at a speed of 66,000 miles per hour? The general answer to this question is that life on earth depends on two fundamental processes: *matter cycling* and the *one-way flow of high-quality energy* from the sun, through materials and living things on or near the earth's surface and into space as low-quality heat.

All forms of life depend for their existence on the mul- 4 titude of materials that compose the (1) solid underline{lithosphere}, consisting of the upper surface or crest of the earth, containing soil and deposits of matter and energy resource, and the earth's upper mantle; (2) the gaseous underline{atmosphere} extending above the earth's surface, (3) the <u>hydrosphere</u>, containing all of the earth's moisture as liquid water, ice, and small amounts of water vapor found in the atmosphere; and (4) the <u>biosphere</u>, consisting of parts of the lithosphere, atmosphere, and hydrosphere in which living organisms can be found.

The biosphere contains all the water, minerals, oxygen, nitrogen, phosphorus, and other nutrients that living things need. For example, your body consists of about 70% water obtained from the hydrosphere, small amounts of nitrogen and oxygen gases continually breathed in from the atmosphere, and various chemicals whose building blocks come mostly from the lithosphere. If the earth were an apple, the biosphere would be no thicker than the apple's skin. Everything in the "skin of life" is <u>interdependent</u>: Air helps purify water and keeps plants and animals alive; water keeps plants and animals alive; plants keep animals alive and help renew the air and soil; and the soil keeps plants and many animals alive and helps purify water. *The goal of ecology is to find out how everything in the biosphere is related.*

—G. Tyler Miller, Jr.

Word	*Definition*
matter	*substance needed for life*
resource	
ecology	
interactions	
ecosystem	
lithosphere	
atmosphere	
hydrosphere	
biosphere	
interdependent	

Practice 22

For each of the words below, an environmental science meaning is given. Write another general meaning in the space provided.

1. *resource*—science: anything obtained from the physical environment to meet human needs.

   another meaning:_____

2. *sphere*—science: that which surrounds or encompasses.

   another meaning:_____

3. *matter*—science: anything that has mass and occupies space.

   another meaning:_____

4. *cycle*—science: a single complete execution of a periodically repeated phenomenon.

   another meaning:_____

5. *energy*—science: ability to do work or produce a change by pushing or pulling some form of matter or to cause a heat transfer between two objects at different temperatures.

   another meaning:_____

CHAPTER

13

Readings: Intergenerational Relationships

The reading selections that follow have been chosen to give you an opportunity to explore lifestyles and cultures that may be different from your own. They were selected around the theme of "Intergenerational Relationships" because they deal with interactions among different generations. This means that you will be reading about relationships between parents and children, and grandparents and grandchildren. In the readings, you will discover the way that family members interact with one another in different parts of the world. We hope that you will enjoy the reading selections, and learn about other people's lives as well.

Selection 1: Childhood

Most of us have heard about Mother Teresa. In this excerpt from her biography, we learn about her childhood and what motivated her to leave her family and become a nun and a missionary.

Before You Read

*Before reading the selection, do the **prereading activities**.*

1. Freewrite or list what comes to your mind about the topic of this selection.

_____

_____

_____

_____

2. Preview this selection. Write three questions that you think will be answered in the reading.

_____

_____

_____

_____

_____

_____

While You Read

1. Underline or highlight main ideas, details, and signal words.
2. Annotate the text.
3. Ten unfamiliar words have been underlined. Use the vocabulary strataegies to define them in context. You will practice using the words after the reading. Underline and define any other unfamiliar words as well.

Childhood

According to Mother Teresa's Indian Diplomatic passport, Mary Teresa Bojaxhiu was born on 26 August 1910 in Skopje, Yugoslavia. In 1910, Skopje was a small town with a population of about 25,000. It was then part of the kingdom of Albania, itself a part of the Ottoman Empire. Albania had experienced several centuries of Islamic rule under Turkish domination, and Catholics comprised only a small fraction of   1 the population. Albania, itself, was at that time at the cross-roads of <u>divergent</u> cultural and religious forces.

Her family were townsmen engaged in business. They were not of peasant stock, as is sometimes believed. Her father, Nicholas Bojaxhiu, was a building contractor. His firm was a well-known one and constructed the first Skopje Theatre. He was a member of the Town Council and spoke a number of languages, including, besides his native Albanian, Serbo-Croatian and Turkish. Father Celeste van Exem, Mother Teresa's spiritual director in the early days, was to tell me that she had described her father as a man with a charitable <u>disposition</u>, who never refused the poor. Her mother, Dranafile Bernai, came from nearby Venice. They lived in a large house set in a spacious garden with a number of fruit trees. There were two other children, Age, a sister born in 1904, and Lazar, a brother, in 1907.

Mother Teresa has said often that her family was a joyful one, and that, "We were very closely united, especially after my father's death." The children's early education was at the Sacred Heart Church. They moved on to non-Catholic state schools and were taught in the <u>compulsory</u> Serbo-Croatian language. However, their religious training continued to be strengthened, both at the parish as well as at home. In one of her few references to her family, Mother Teresa said, "I was very close to my mother," and described her as "very holy." Father van Exem believed that her mother had a far-reaching influence on young Agnes (as she was christened a day after her birth), particularly in her spiritual life, for her mother was not merely religious in the formal sense: her sense of commitment to her faith had its practical <u>aspects</u>, which caused her never to turn away those in need who reached her door, whether seeking food, shelter, clothing or even money. "She taught us to love God and to love our neighbour," said Mother Teresa.

A few fascinating glimpses of her early life were revealed to the world by her brother Lazar when he attended the Nobel Award ceremony in Oslo in December 1979, when Mother Teresa received the Nobel Peace Prize. As a child they called her not Agnes, but Gonxha, "flower bud" in Albanian, for she was pink and plump. She was neat and tidy and always helpful. Lazar confessed that as a child he had a great weakness for confectionery and desserts, and often made nocturnal visits to the kitchen cupboard. Gonxha was the only one who never stole the jam. She unfailingly reminded her brother that he should touch no food after midnight if they were to attend mass in the morning, but she never complained about these expeditions to their mother.

Gonxha's mother was <u>imbued</u> with a strong sense of values. The children called their mother *"Nana Loke,"* *"Nana"* meaning mother, *"Loke"* meaning the soul; "the mother of my soul." She disliked waste of any kind. Mother Teresa confirmed a tale I had once read about this sense of frugality. One evening the children were sitting around their mother, engaged in childish chatter. This went on for a considerable length of time, throughout which their mother remained silent. Finally she left the room, only to turn off the power switch, which plunged the house into darkness. It was of no use, she said, to waste electricity on foolish talk. 5

It could only have been her deep faith that helped her to overcome the tragedy if the untimely death of her husband in 1917, after which she lay in a <u>stupor</u> for several months. When eventually recovered, she turned resolutely to starting a small business of her own, that of selling embroidered cloth, turning <u>adversity</u> into enterprise. With her earnings she was able to bring up her three children; as Nicholas Bojaxhiu's business partner <u>misappropriated</u> the firm's assets, leaving the widow and her family with scarcely more than the roof over their heads, this was imperative. This self-sufficiency in the face of tragedy must have deeply influenced Agnes, who was seven when her father died. 6

The Church of the Sacred Heart, more than ever before, became an important part of the family's life. Agnes and her sister began to participate in a number of parish activities. Agnes was frequently in the Church library, as she loved books. 7

"I was only twelve years old and lived at home with my parents in Skopje when I first felt the desire to become a nun," recalled Mother Teresa. It was natural for her to turn to her mother, who at first opposed the idea, as Agnes was, after all, still a child. In due course Agnes forgot her first impulse, yet was moving <u>inexorably</u> on an almost preordained path. Mother and daughter spent many hours in church, their most fervent prayer the holy rosary recited at the feet of the Lady of Letnice in Skopje, or late at night in their own home. After school hours, Agnes was involved in parish activities. It was here that her family also came into contact with Father Jambrenkovic, who became the pastor in 1925. He started a branch of a society called the Sodality of the Blessed Virgin Mary. This was to have a far-reaching effect on Agnes, for it was the same Sodality that she was to join, years later, in the Entally Convent in Calcutta. 8

In the Sodality, they learned about the lives of saints and missionaries, and from Father Jambrenkovic about the Yu- 9 goslav Jesuits who went on a mission to the province of Bengal in India in 1924. The zeal of these early missionaries was recounted to members of the Sodality, and struck an especially strong chord in Agnes. "They used to give us the most beautiful descriptions about the experiences they had with the people, and especially the children in India," recalled Mother Teresa. She learned that there was an order of nuns serving in Bengal whose main work was in the field of education. These Loreto nuns were members of an international order, and Bengal was served by the Irish Province.

Now a young woman, Agnes had developed several 10 other important qualities. According to Lazar, she was a good student, meticulous in her appearance and well-organized. She started giving children religious instruction and grew to love teaching. A cousin also recalled that even in those early days, she was a girl who refused no-one help or assistance, who could be depended upon and who was friendly to all religious persuasions.

It was six years after those first stirrings that Mother 11 Teresa received a Call to leave her family and loved ones behind and become a missionary. In the face of her own doubts as to whether she had, indeed, received a Call, she turned to Father Jambrenkovic. It was he who explained to her that the Call of God had necessarily to be accompanied by a feeling of deep joy, especially where this was an indication of life's vocation.

Recently, sitting on a small bench outside the Chapel at 12 Motherhouse, Mother Teresa said to me, "At eighteen I decided to leave home to become a nun. By then I realized my vocation was towards the poor. From then on, I have never had the least doubt of my decision." Pointing a finger towards Heaven, she added, "He made the choice." Nor was there any doubt in her mother's mind this time. When Gonxha informed her, *Nana Loke* went to her room where she remained for twenty-four hours. When she emerged, both mother and daughter were aware of the chosen path, and she advised her young daughter, "Put your hand in His hand and walk all the way with Him."

In submission to what quite clearly was God's will, 13 Agnes applied to the Loreto order in Bengal. She was informed that the route to Bengal lay via Loreto Abbey in Rathfarman in Ireland, where she first must go to learn some English. On 26 September 1928, Agnes, accompanied by her mother and sister, left Skopje for Zagreb by train. At the Skopje railway station, she wished her relatives, friends and members of the Sodality, who had come to bid her goodbye, a tearful farewell. The few days in Zagreb with her beloved mother and sister went by in a flash. When finally she waved her mother goodbye at the Zagreb station, it was the last time she ever saw her.

—Navin Chawla

After You Read

Reading for Ideas

1. If you can, answer your preview questions here. Number your answers to match your questions.

_____

_____

_____

_____

_____

If you are unable to answer your preview questions, explain why here.

_____

_____

2. What is the topic of the selection?

_____

3. State the controlling idea of the selection in your own words.

_____

_____

4. List three or four major events in Mother Teresa's childhood that you think shaped her life as an adult.

a. _____

_____

b. _____

_____

c. _____

_____

d. _____

_____

5. Describe how your childhood was similar or different from Mother Teresa's.

_____

_____

_____

_____

_____

_____

Reading for Information

Circle the correct choice to complete each statement. Prove your answer by putting the number of the question next to the paragraph in the text where the correct information appears.

1. Father Celeste van Exem was Mother Teresa's
   a. father.
   b. uncle.
   c. spiritual director.
   d. teacher.

2. Mother Teresa was christened
   a. Mother Teresa.
   b. Agnes.
   c. Lazar.
   d. all of the above

3. Mother Teresa received the Nobel Prize for
   a. Science.
   b. Literature.
   c. Peace.
   d. Art.

4. "Nana Loke" means
   a. good friend.
   b. mother of my soul.
   c. political correctness.
   d. sister.

5. Mary Teresa Bojaxhiu became
   a. an actress.
   b. a priest.
   c. a novelist.
   d. a missionary.

Reading for Thinking

Answer the following questions in complete sentences. Support your responses with text information.

1. Why do you think that Mother Teresa described her own mother as "very holy"?

   _____

   _____

   _____

   _____

   _____

2. How did Lazar describe his sister?

_____

_____

_____

_____

_____

_____

_____

_____

3. What value did "Nana Loke" display in the selection? How is it described?

_____

_____

_____

_____

_____

_____

_____

_____

_____

4. What was Teresa's mother's reaction to the death of her husband? How did her actions finally keep the family together?

_____

_____

_____

_____

_____

_____

_____

_____

5. How did Agnes proceed toward fulfillment of her desire to be a nun?

_____

_____

_____

_____

_____

_____

_____

_____

_____

Group Activity

Find newspaper and magazine articles about Mother Teresa's later life. Discuss her philosophy, her accomplishments, and her uniqueness. Could you or your peers live a life such as hers was? Why? Why not? Discuss other unique individuals who are in the news. What do you think makes a person do "special" things as these individuals do or did?

Vocabulary

The words that were underlined in the text are underlined in the following sentences. **Define** *each word* **from the context.** *You may need to go back to the selection for additional help. Use your dictionary only if necessary. Write the meanings in your own words. Be sure that your meaning* **"makes sense"** *in the context of the sentence.*

1. Arthur's <u>domination</u> of the group's discussion did not give anyone else a chance to speak.

   _____

2. The thinking of the committee members was so <u>divergent</u> that their differences of opinion made it almost impossible to make a decision.

   _____

3. Her happy <u>disposition</u> made everyone want to be around her.

   _____

4. <u>Compulsory</u> education in the United States requires that all children must go to school until the age of sixteen.

   _____

5. One unusual <u>aspect</u> of his appearance was his extremely long neck, which was swan-like.

   _____

6. The little boy's mind was <u>imbued</u> with thoughts of what he might get for Christmas.

   _____

7. She was in a <u>stupor</u> until her child recovered from his terrible illness.

   _____

8. There is a saying that <u>adversity</u> is the mother of invention. This means that sometimes something negative can lead to something positive.

   _____

9. The executive <u>misappropriated</u> so much money that the company was forced to go out of business.

   _____

10. The <u>inexorable</u> movement of the clock brought Matthew closer and closer to his dreaded exam.

    _____

Selection 2: *Behind Closed Doors: Violence in the Family*

This selection, "The Changing Shape of Society," from a chapter in a sociology textbook, explores the myths Americans have developed about violence in the family. Information is also given about the causes of the violence and the recent decline in rates of family violence.

Before You Read

Before reading the selection, "Behind Closed Doors: Violence in the Family," be sure to do the **prereading activities**.

1. Freewrite or list what comes to your mind about the topic.

_____

_____

_____

_____

2. Preview the selection. Write three questions that you think will be answered in the reading.

_____

_____

_____

_____

_____

_____

While You Read

1. Underline or highlight main ideas, details, and signal words.
2. Annotate the text.
3. Note unfamiliar vocabulary. Ten unfamiliar words have been underlined. Use the vocabulary strategies to define the words in context. You will practice using the words after the reading. If you find other unfamiliar words, underline them.

Behind Closed Doors: Violence in the Family

"And they lived happily ever after." Hundreds of stories about marriages and families end with this line. Loved ones are reunited; obstacles to marriage overcome; problems with children resolved. Indeed, the very idea of living happily ever after is linked, in our minds, with the special warmth of the family. Yet if we look behind the closed doors of many

American households, we discover that all is not peace and harmony.

Myths and Realities

With the exception of the police and the military, the family is the most violent social group in American society. The home is a more dangerous place than a dark alley. A person is more likely to be murdered in his or her home, by a member of the family, than by anyone else, anywhere else, in society.

Fifteen or twenty years ago, few Americans would have believed these statements. Today most people recognize that family violence is a serious social problem. Yet myths abound.

Myth 1: Family violence is rare or <u>*epidemic*</u>. Public attention to family violence has skyrocketed in recent years. The growing number of books, articles, and TV reports on the problem has led some people to believe we are in the midst of an epidemic. Others have concluded that all this attention is "hype." Both are wrong. Family violence is not a modern phenomenon; it has existed in virtually all societies and times. Experts may disagree about whether family violence is increasing or decreasing. But all agree that it is a serious problem that will not go away by itself.

Myth 2: Abusers are mentally ill. When we read a description of family violence, we would like to believe that only someone who is sick could beat up a pregnant woman or torture a child. Health workers often find that abusers are disturbed. But whether they committed violent acts because they were disturbed or became disturbed after the act is impossible to say. Only about 10 percent of abusers are clinically diagnosed as mentally ill.

Myth 3: Abuse occurs only in poor, minority families. Rates of abuse are higher in poor and minority households, but violence occurs in families at all <u>socioeconomic</u> levels. One reason that poor and nonwhites are greatly overrepresented in official statistics is that they are more likely to be labeled as "abusers" or "victims." The sociologists Patrick Turbett and Richard O'Toole (1980) gave groups of physicians and nurses a file describing an injured child and the child's parents. These professionals were more likely to conclude the child was a victim of abuse when they were told the father was a janitor than when they were told he was a teacher, and when they were told the child was black as opposed to white. Except for these social markers, which were varied at random, the files were identical.

Myth 4: The real causes of family violence are alcohol 7
and drugs. A news report might highlight the fact that
a man who murdered his family was a "crack addict." Victims of family violence often say, "He only did it when he
was drunk." Does this mean drugs cause abuse? No. <u>Cross-
cultural</u> studies show that the effects of alcohol vary from
society to society. In some, people become quiet and withdrawn when they drink; in others, they become loud and aggressive. Our society is one of the latter. We define being
drunk as a "time out" from normal rules of behavior, when
a person can claim "I didn't know what I was doing." As a result, both abusers and victims often cite alcohol as the excuse for violence. In one study half the men arrested for
beating their wives claimed that they had been drunk, but
only 20 percent had enough alcohol in their blood to be considered legally intoxicated (Bard and Zacker, 1974). Frequent
drunks (and nondrinkers) are less likely than occasional
drinkers to become violent. Much less is known about the effects of illegal drugs on behavior. But the only one that has
been conclusively linked with increased aggression (in studies with monkeys) is amphetamine.

Myth 5: Children who are abused grow up to be 8
abusers. Children who are victims of family violence are
more likely to be abusive as adults than are children who experienced no family violence. But this does not mean that all
violent adults were abused as children, or that *all* abused
children grow up to be violent. Abuse makes children more
<u>vulnerable</u> to a host of social and emotional problems, but it
does not determine how they will behave as adults.

Myth 6: Battered wives like being hurt. Most people 9
are badly upset by reports of battered children but puzzled by
reports of battered wives. After all, the woman is an adult; if
her husband beats her, why doesn't she leave him? Abused
wives are often assumed to be masochists or, worse, to have
provoked their husbands to violence ("She asked for it . . .").
Anyone who has been through a divorce knows that there is
more to ending a marriage than simply walking out the door.
In most cases, violence isn't an everyday event. It may be easier to talk oneself into believing it won't happen again than to
face the world on one's own, with little money, credit, or experience, and perhaps children to care for as well. Where can
the battered wife go? Because our society has mixed feelings
about battered wives, we have been slow to build shelters.

If you reread this list of myths you will see a common 10
theme: Only people *other than us* assault their loved ones.
Assigning family abusers to <u>deviant</u> categories (mentally disturbed, poor, drunk) allows us to avoid thinking that it could

happen to us. These myths also blind us to the structural characteristics of the family that promote or at least allow violence.

Sociological Explanations

The potential for violence is built into the family. Many of the characteristics we cherish most about families also make us most vulnerable within the family. One is _intimacy_. Family members are intensely involved with one another. They know the private details of one another's lives, and what makes the others feel proud or ashamed. When quarrels break out or problems arise, the stakes are higher than in other social groups. For example, a man who is amused by the behavior of a female colleague who is drunk may become enraged if his wife has a little too much to drink. A politician who has been an active supporter of gay rights, at some risk to her career, may be appalled to discover that her own child is homosexual. Why? Because we perceive the behavior of a member of our family as a direct reflection on ourselves. The intensity of family relationships tends to magnify the most trivial things, such as a burned dinner or a whining child. When did you last hear of someone beating up the cook in a restaurant for preparing an unacceptable meal? But minor offenses and small oversights often spark violent family fights. 11

A second factor contributing to violence in the home is _privacy:_ because family affairs are regarded as private, there are few outside restraints on violence. When a family quarrel threatens to become a fight, there are no bystanders to break it up, as there might be on the street or in some other public place. The shift from extended to nuclear families, the move to detached single-family houses in the suburbs, and the trend toward having fewer children have all increased the potential for family violence, simply because there are fewer people around to observe (and try to stop) abuse. Children in isolated single-parent families are at high risk (Gelles, 1989). One reason the rates of family violence in black families are lower than one might expect (given high rates of single parenthood, poverty, and unemployment) is that blacks generally have more extensive social networks, and more frequent contacts with relatives and neighbors, than whites do. 12

A third factor is _inequality_. Few social groups routinely include members of both sexes and different ages. In school, for example, we are segregated by age; at work we are often segregated by sex—for example, men doing heavy labor, women doing clerical work. Because men are usually bigger and stronger than women, and women bigger and stronger 13 than children, they can get away with violent behavior that would provoke <u>retaliation</u> from someone their own size and strength. Moreover, the costs of leaving an abusive family—becoming a runaway child or a single mother—may seem higher to some family members than to others.

Fourth, and perhaps most disturbing, there is a good deal of *social and cultural support* for the use of physical force in the family. Parents are allowed—indeed, sometimes expected—to spank their children. "Spare the rod and spoil the child," the saying goes. Most people do not think of spanking a child as violence. Indeed, in a recent survey almost three out of four Americans said they saw slapping a twelve-year-old as often necessary, normal, and good. But suppose a teacher slapped the child, or a stranger slapped you for something you did or said in the supermarket? Either would constitute assault and battery in a court of law—but not in the family. In effect, a marriage license in our society is a license to hit. This applies not only to children, but also to spouses. In the same national survey one in four wives and one in three husbands said that slapping a spouse was sometimes necessary, normal, and good. 14

Finally, in the process of <u>socialization</u> we learn to associate violence with the family. Our first experience of force nearly always takes place at home. Most of our parents use physical punishment on occasion—for our own good, of course, and because they love us. (The child is told, "This hurts me more than it hurts you.") From here it is only a small step to the conclusion that the use of violence is legitimate whenever something is really important. And the things that are most important to us are often family matters. 15

An Update: Good News and Bad

The First National Family Violence Survey, conducted in 1975 to 1976 by the sociologists Murray Straus, Richard Gelles, and Suzanne Steinmetz (1980), found that physical abuse in the home was far more common than anyone suspected: 16

Three out of four parents had struck their child at least once, and nearly four in one hundred had used severe violence on a child. In all, 1.4 million children ages 3 to 17—roughly one child in every U.S. classroom—had been the victim of physical abuse. 17

One out of six wives had been struck by a husband; one in 22 had been victims of violent abuse; and the average battered wife was attacked three times a year. 18

More than four of every 100 husbands had been victims   19
of spousal violence. (In nearly all cases, however, the husband
initiated violence and the wife acted in self-defense.) (Steinmetz, 1978)

A second national survey was conducted in 1985, to de-   20
termine whether rates of family violence had changed (Straus
and Gelles, 1986; Gelles and Straus, 1988). To their surprise
the researchers found that the rate of child abuse had de-
clined by 47 percent, and the rate of spouse abuse had de-
clined by 27 percent. This does not mean that the problem of
family violence has disappeared; far from it. At today's
"lower" rates, more than a million children were abused and
1.6 million wives were battered in 1985. Nevertheless, the
change is substantial.

Gelles and Straus (1988) believe that a major reason for   21
this decline is changing public attitudes toward family violence. America seems to be undergoing a "moral passage"
(Gusfield, 1963), in which behavior that formerly was considered acceptable is now seen as abuse. An allegedly rare private problem has been redefined as a widespread social
problem. As a result, people may be less willing to quietly accept being hurt by their parents or spouse, and more willing
to <u>intervene</u> when they believe a friend, neighbor, or relative
is being abused. (The redefinition of family violence may also
make people less likely to admit to a pollster that they
slapped their spouse or punched their child.)

A number of structural changes in the family and society   22
as a whole may also have contributed to the decline in family
violence. First, many Americans are delaying the age at which
they get married and have their first child. Many more
women have entered the labor force. And today's couples
have a full range of family planning services at their disposal.
Late marriage, <u>egalitarian</u> marriage, and wanted children are
all associated with a lower risk of family violence. Second,
both child and wife abuse are linked to unemployment and
economic stress. By chance, the second survey was conducted
in the most prosperous year in a decade, at least for intact
families. Third, between 1975 and 1985 policies toward family violence have changed, and the number and variety of programs for treating abusers and victims have increased. All
states now have laws that make reporting child abuse or neglect mandatory. Police manuals used to recommend that officers summoned to the scene of domestic violence separate
the warring parties and leave; now most require that a man
who has beaten his wife be arrested. The number of shelters
for battered women and their children increased from a mere

four in 1975 to more than 1,000 in 1985. The number of family therapists tripled in the 1980s. Self-help groups for abusive parents and battered spouses have been formed. While these services do not begin to meet the need, they provide some troubled families with alternatives and may embolden victims of family violence to take steps on their own.
(2289 words)

—M. Bassis, R. Gelles, and A. Levine

After You Read

Reading for Ideas

1. If you can, answer your preview questions here. Number your answers to match your questions.

   _____

   _____

   _____

   _____

   _____

   _____

   If you are unable to answer your preview questions, explain why here.

   _____

   _____

2. What is the topic of the selection?

   _____

   _____

3. State the controlling idea of the reading in your own words.

   _____

   _____

4. List three or four major details that support or explain the controlling idea.

a. _____

_____

b. _____

_____

c. _____

_____

d. _____

_____

5. Make an outline or a map of the most important information from the selection.

6. Write a summary using your outline or map as a guide.

_____

_____

_____

_____

_____

_____

_____

_____

_____

_____

_____

_____

_____

Reading for Information

Circle the correct choice to complete each statement. Prove your answer by putting the number of the question next to the paragraph in the text where the correct information appears.

1. A person is most likely to be murdered
   a. in a dark alley.
   b. by a family member in the home.
   c. by a policeman.
   d. in a street fight.

2. All the following statements are myths about family violence except:
   a. Family violence is a recent epidemic.
   b. Most abusers are clinically diagnosed as mentally ill.
   c. Family violence occurs only in poor, minority homes.
   d. Twenty percent of men arrested for beating their wives were legally intoxicated.

3. Intimacy and privacy are structural characteristics of the family that
   a. decrease the risk of violence.
   b. increase the risk of violence.
   c. hinder men from hitting their wives and children.
   d. cause family members not to talk about any violence that occurs.

4. A national survey conducted in 1985 found that
   a. wife and child abuse had not decreased significantly.
   b. family violence was reported less frequently than in 1975.
   c. although there was a decrease in child and spouse abuse, more than a million children were abused and 1.6 million wives were beaten.
   d. more than 1.4 million children had been the victims of physical abuse.

5. All the following are causes of the decline in family violence except:
   a. The public is less willing to accept abusive behavior in the family.
   b. More Americans are marrying later and having their first child later.
   c. Police intervention has become more strict and there are more shelters for battered women and their children.
   d. Laws have been passed making the spanking of children illegal.

Reading for Thinking

Answer the following questions in complete sentences. Support your responses with text information.

1. Why do the myths about family violence allow people to think that family violence is not something that can happen to them?

_____

_____

_____

_____

_____

_____

2. Why are the rates of family violence lower than expected in African American families?

_____

_____

_____

_____

_____

3. Choose two of the structural characteristics of the family and explain how they contribute to family violence.

_____

_____

_____

_____

_____

_____

4. What structural changes in the family and society have contributed to the decline in family violence?

_____

_____

_____

_____

_____

5. Do you think that passing a law forbidding the use of corporal punishment by parents would further decrease child abuse? Why or why not?

_____

_____

_____

_____

_____

Group Activity

Work with a group of your classmates to make two lists: (1) write down the reasons that support a law against corporal punishment, and (2) list the reasons for legalizing corporal punishment. Which side are you on? Try to convince the opposing side to change their position.

Vocabulary

The words that were underlined in the text are underlined in the following sentences. **Define** *each word* **from the context.** *You* *may need to go back to the selection for additional help. Use your dictionary only if necessary. Write the meanings in your own words.*

1. One of the myths about family violence is that we are in the midst of an <u>epidemic</u> of such violence.

   _____

2. Although abuse is more likely to occur in poor and minority households, violence occurs in families at all <u>socioeconomic</u> levels.

   _____

3. <u>Cross-cultural</u> studies demonstrate that people respond differently to alcohol from society to society.

   _____

4. Children who are abused are more <u>vulnerable</u> to many social and emotional problems but do not all grow up to be violent.

   _____

5. By calling family abusers members of <u>deviant</u> categories, such as mentally disturbed, poor, or alcoholic, we allow ourselves to think that we could never be a part of this violence.

   _____

6. One structural characteristic of the family that supports abuse in the family is <u>intimacy</u>.

   _____

7. If family members were more equal in size and strength, there might be more <u>retaliation</u> from the abused wife or child.

   _____

8. <u>Socialization</u>, which begins at home, leads us to associate violence with the family.

   _____

9. Because family violence has become accepted as a major social problem, individuals are more willing to <u>intervene</u> when they think someone is being abused.

_____

10. Structural changes in the family, such as late marriage, <u>egalitarian</u> marriage, and wanted children, have helped decrease the risk of family violence.

_____

Selection 3: *Your Parents Must Be Very Proud*

The writer of the following selection, whose parents came to this country from Mexico, describes the difficulties he and his family experienced as he became more a part of the mainstream American culture and a famous author.

Before You Read

Do the **prereading exercises** *for "Your Parents Must Be Very Proud."*

1. Freewrite or list what comes to your mind about the topic of the reading.

_____

_____

_____

_____

2. Preview the selection. Write three questions that you think will be answered in the reading.

_____

_____

_____

_____

_____

_____

_____

While You Read

1. Underline or highlight main ideas, details, and signal words.
2. Annotate the text.
3. Ten unfamiliar words have been underlined. Use the vocabulary strategies to define the words in context. You will practice using the words after the reading. If you find other unfamiliar words, underline them.

Your Parents Must Be Very Proud

"Your parents must be very proud of you." People began   1
to say that to me about the time I was in sixth grade. To answer affirmatively, I'd smile. Shyly I'd smile, never betraying my sense of the irony: I was not proud of my mother and father. I was embarrassed by their lack of education. It was not that I ever thought they were stupid, though stupidly I took for granted their enormous native intelligence. Simply, what mattered to me was that they were not like my teachers.

But, "Why didn't you tell us about the award?" my   2
mother demanded, her frown weakened by pride. At the grammar school ceremony several weeks after, her eyes were brighter than the trophy I'd won. Pushing back the hair from my forehead, she whispered that I had "shown" the gringos. A few minutes later, I heard my father speak to my teacher and felt ashamed of his labored, accented words. Then guilty for the shame. I felt such contrary feelings. (There is no simple roadmap through the heart of the scholarship boy.) My teacher was so soft-spoken and her words were edged sharp and clean. I admired her until it seemed to me that she spoke too carefully. Sensing that she was condescending to them, I became nervous. Resentful. Protective. I tried to move my

parents away. "You both must be very proud of Richard," the nun said. They responded quickly. (They were proud.) "We are proud of all our children." Then this afterthought: "They sure didn't get their brains from us." They all laughed. I smiled. Tightening the irony into a knot was the knowledge that my parents were always behind me. They made success possible. They evened the path. They sent their children to parochial schools because the nuns "teach better." They paid a tuition they couldn't afford. They spoke English to us.

For their children my parents wanted chances they never had—an easier way. It saddened my mother to learn that some relatives forced their children to start working right after high school. To *her* children she would say, "Get all the education you can." In schooling she recognized the key to job advancement. And with the remark she remembered her past.

As a girl new to America my mother had been awarded a high school diploma by teachers too careless or busy to notice that she hardly spoke English. On her own, she determined to learn how to type. That skill got her jobs typing envelopes in letter shops, and it encouraged in her an optimism about the possibility of advancement. (Each morning when her sisters put on uniforms, she chose a bright-colored dress.) The years of young womanhood passed, and her typing speed increased. She also became an excellent speller of words she mispronounced. "And I've never been to college," she'd say, smiling, when her children asked her to spell words they were too lazy to look up in a dictionary.

Typing, however, was dead-end work. Finally frustrating. When her youngest child started high school, my mother got a full-time office job once again. (Her paycheck combined with my father's to make us—in fact—what we had already become in our imagination of ourselves—middle class.) She worked then for the (California) state government in numbered civil service positions secured by examinations. The old ambition of her youth was rekindled. During the lunch hour, she consulted bulletin boards for announcements of openings. One day she saw mention of something called an "anti-poverty agency." A typing job. A glamorous job, part of the governor's staff. "A knowledge of Spanish required." Without hesitation she applied and became nervous only when the job was suddenly hers.

"Everyone comes to work all dressed up," she reported at night. And didn't need to say more than that her co-workers wouldn't let her answer the phones. She was only a typist, after all, albeit a very fast typist. And an excellent speller.

One morning there was a letter to be sent to a Washington cabinet officer. On the dictating tape, a voice referred to urban guerrillas. My mother typed (the wrong word, correctly): "gorillas." The mistake horrified the anti-poverty bureaucrats who shortly after arranged to have her returned to her previous position. She would go no further. So she willed her ambition to her children. "Get all the education you can; with an education you can do anything." (With a good education *she* could have done anything.)

When I was in high school, I admitted to my mother   7
that I planned to become a teacher someday. That seemed to please her. But I never tried to explain that it was not the occupation of teaching I yearned for as much as it was something more <u>elusive</u>: I wanted to *be* like my teachers, to possess their knowledge, to assume their authority, their confidence, even to assume a teacher's <u>persona</u>.

In contrast to my mother, my father never verbally en-   8
couraged his children's academic success. Nor did he often praise us. My mother had to remind him to "say something" to one of his children who scored some academic success. But whereas my mother saw in education the opportunity for job advancement, my father recognized that education provided an even more startling possibility: it could enable a person to escape from a life of mere labor.

In Mexico, orphaned when he was eight, my father left   9
school to work as an "apprentice" for an uncle. Twelve years later, he left Mexico in frustration and arrived in America. He had great expectations then of becoming an engineer. ("Work for my hands and my head.") He knew a Catholic priest who promised to get him money enough to study full time for a high school diploma. But the promises came to nothing. Instead there was a dark succession of warehouse, cannery, and factory jobs. After work he went to night school along with my mother. A year, two passed. Nothing much changed, except that <u>fatigue</u> worked its way into the bone; then everything changed. He didn't talk anymore of becoming an engineer. He stayed outside on the steps of the school while my mother went inside to learn typing and shorthand.

By the time I was born, my father worked at "clean"   10
jobs. For a time he was a janitor at a fancy department store. ("Easy work; the machines do it all.") Later he became a dental technician. ("Simple.") But by then he was pessimistic about the ultimate meaning of work and the possibility of ever escaping its claims. In some of my earliest memories of him, my father already seems aged by fatigue. (He has never really grown old like my mother.) From boyhood to man-

hood, I have remembered him in a single image: seated, asleep on the sofa, his head thrown back in a hideous corpse-like grin, the evening newspaper spread out before him. "But look at all you've accomplished," his best friend said to him once. My father said nothing. Only smiled.

It was my father who laughed when I claimed to be tired 11 by reading and writing. It was he who teased me for having soft hands. (He seemed to sense that some great achievement of leisure was implied by my papers and books.) It was my father who became angry while watching on television some woman at the Miss America contest tell the announcer that she was going to college. ("Majoring in fine arts.") "College!" he snarled. He despised the <u>trivialization</u> of higher education, the inflated grades and cheapened diplomas, the half education that so often passed as mass education in my generation.

It was my father again who wondered why I didn't dis- 12 play my awards on the wall of my bedroom. He said he liked to go to doctors' offices and see their certificates and degrees on the wall. ("Nice.") My citations from school got left in closets at home. The gleaming figure <u>astride</u> one of my trophies was broken, wingless, after hitting the ground. My medals were placed in a jar of loose change. And when I lost my high school diploma, my father found it as it was about to be thrown out with the trash. Without telling me, he put it away with his own things for safekeeping.

These memories slammed together at the instant of 13 hearing that refrain familiar to all scholarship students: "Your parents must be very proud. . . ." Yes, my parents were proud. I knew it. But my parents regarded my progress with more than mere pride. They endured my early <u>precocious</u> behavior—but with what private anger and humiliation? As their children got older and would come home to challenge ideas both of them held, they argued before submitting to the force of logic or superior factual evidence with the <u>disclaimer</u>, "It's what we were taught in our time to believe." These discussions ended abruptly, though my mother remembered them on other occasions when she complained that our "big ideas" were going to our heads. More acute was her complaint that the family wasn't close anymore, like some others she knew. Why weren't we close, "more in the Mexican style"? Everyone is so private, she added. And she mimicked the yes and no answers she got in reply to her questions. Why didn't we talk more? (My father never asked.) I never said.

I was the first in my family who asked to leave home 14 when it came time to go to college. I had been admitted to Stanford, one hundred miles away. My departure would only make physically apparent the separation that had occurred long before. But it was going too far. In the months preceding my leaving, I heard the question my mother never asked except indirectly. In the hot kitchen, tired at the end of her workday, she demanded to know, "Why aren't the colleges here in Sacramento good enough for you? They are for your brother and sister." In the middle of a car ride, not turning to face me, she said with disgust, "Why do you have to put us through this big expense? You know your scholarship will never cover it all." But when September came there was a rush to get everything ready. In a bedroom that last night I packed the big brown valise, and my mother sat nearby sewing initials onto the clothes I would take. And she said no more about my leaving.

Months later, two weeks of Christmas vacation: The 15 first hours home were the hardest. (What's new?) My parents and I sat in the kitchen for a conversation. (But, lacking the same words to develop our sentences and to shape our interests, what was there to say? What could I tell them of the term paper I had just finished on the "universality of Shakespeare's appeal"?) I mentioned only small, obvious things: my dormitory life; weekend trips I had taken; random events. They responded with news of their own. (One was almost grateful for a family crisis about which there was much to discuss.) We tried to make our conversation seem like more than an interview.
(1849 words)

—Richard Rodriguez

After You Read

Reading for Ideas

1. If you can, answer your preview questions here. Number your answers to match your questions.

_____

_____

_____

_____

_____

If you are unable to answer your preview questions, explain why here.

_____

_____

2. What is the topic of the selection?

_____

3. State the controlling idea of the reading in your own words.

_____

_____

4. List three or four major details that support or explain the controlling idea.

a. _____

_____

b. _____

_____

c. _____

_____

d. _____

_____

5. Create a double-entry journal about the selection.

Writer's Ideas	My Ideas

6. Write a summary by using your double-entry journal as a guide.

_____

_____

_____

_____

_____

_____

_____

_____

_____

_____

_____

_____

_____

_____

Reading for Information

Circle the correct choice to complete each statement. Prove your answer by putting the number of the question next to the paragraph in the text where the correct information appears.

1. When Richard was in elementary school, he realized that he
   a. was very proud of his parents.
   b. did not understand why his parents were not as intelligent as he was.
   c. wanted his parents to be better educated and wanted to protect them from insults by his teachers.
   d. wanted to leave his immigrant culture to become more Americanized.

2. Richard's parents
   a. made him leave school when he completed eighth grade.
   b. sent him to parochial school to get a better education.
   c. spoke English to him.
   d. both b and c

3. Richard's mother was not successful in her job with the "anti-poverty agency" because she
   a. had not been sufficiently educated in English.
   b. could not spell.
   c. could not type rapidly.
   d. could not get along with her coworkers.

4. Richard's father believed that education
   a. did not require enough hard work from the students.
   b. was a waste of time.
   c. could not make people more successful in life.
   d. could free people from the bonds of hard labor.

5. Richard's success in college
   a. helped him become closer to his family.
   b. isolated him from his parents.
   c. made him wealthy.
   d. helped him to better understand his culture.

Reading for Thinking

Answer the following questions in complete sentences. Support your responses with text information.

1. In this selection, you read about several different views of the value of education. Identify these and explain whether you agree or disagree with each.

   _____

   _____

   _____

   _____

   _____

   _____

   _____

   _____

   _____

2. Have you, like Richard Rodriguez, experienced a conflict with your family that was caused by your desire to be different from

one of your parents or another family member? Explain the conflict and how it was or is being resolved.

_____

_____

_____

_____

_____

_____

_____

_____

3. Richard Rodriguez's parents wanted him to become more educated and successful than they were, but they also wanted him to keep the lifestyle and values of their generation and culture. This created a conflict in his family. If you were a parent, would you try to avoid this generational and cultural conflict? Why or why not?

_____

_____

_____

_____

_____

_____

_____

_____

_____

Group Activity

Meet with a small group of your classmates to create a list of the causes of conflict between Richard Rodriguez and his parents. Then make a list of causes of conflict between parents and children of today. Compare the two lists to determine which items are similar and which are different. Next, have a discussion to decide if the sources of parent and child conflict change from generation to generation. Support your decision with examples. Compare your group's answer with the work of other groups in the class.

Vocabulary

The words that were underlined in the text are underlined in the following sentences. **Define** *each word* **from the context.** *You may need to go back to the selection for additional help. Use your dictionary only if necessary. Write the meanings in your own words.*

1. Richard smiled <u>affirmatively</u> to show that he was proud of his parents.

   _____

2. The <u>irony</u> was that Richard was not proud of his parents.

   _____

3. When the teacher spoke English slowly to his parents, Richard thought she was being <u>condescending</u> to them.

   _____

4. Richard's <u>elusive</u> desire was to be like his teachers.

   _____

5. Richard wanted to assume his teacher's <u>persona</u>.

   _____

6. While Richard's father worked long hours in factory jobs, his <u>fatigue</u> became more serious.

   _____

7. Richard's father despised the <u>trivialization</u> of higher education caused by inflated grades and cheapened diplomas.

---

8. The shining figure <u>astride</u> one of Richard's trophies was broken when it fell to the ground.

---

9. Although Richard's parents endured his early <u>precocious</u> behavior, it must have caused them to be angry and to feel humiliated.

---

10. When Richard's parents could not win arguments with him because he had better logic or factual evidence, they argued with the <u>disclaimer</u>, "It's what we were taught in our time to believe."

Selection 4: Hail to Thee, Bankruptcy

In the following humorous article, the famous comedian Bill Cosby explains how fathers feel about the expense of a college education. He also uses humor to point out some very serious concerns that he has about what students learn in college.

Before You Read

*The following are **prereading activities** for "Hail to Thee, Bankruptcy." Read the title and the brief introduction before you begin.*

1. Freewrite or list what comes to your mind about parental concerns over the cost of a college education and the learning experiences their children will have in college.

---

2. Preview the selection. Write three questions that you think will be answered in the reading.

_____

_____

_____

_____

_____

_____

While You Read

1. Underline or highlight main ideas, details, and signal words.
2. Annotate the text.
3. Decide whether you will keep a double-entry journal or make an outline or a map about the selection.
4. Ten unfamiliar words have been underlined. Use the vocabulary strategies to define them in context. You will practice using the words after the reading. Underline and define any other unfamiliar words as well.

Hail to Thee, Bankruptcy

I was wrong when I said that the big expense for you 1 would be buying a car. Let us now discuss the cost of college—unless you would rather do something more pleasant, like have root canal work.

As you know, I have always put the highest value on ed- 2 ucation. However, one day last year, my eighteen-year-old daughter came in and told my wife and me that she had decided not to go to college because she was in love with a boy named Alan.

At first, my wife and I went crazy. 3

"What?" I cried. "You're standing there and telling your mother and me that you're *not* going to—" 4

And then a light went on in one of the <u>musty</u> corners of my mind: her decision would be saving me a hundred thousand dollars. 5

"—not going to college, which you have every *right* to tell us. Alan, you say? Well, he just happens to be the one I'm exceptionally fond of. I hope he's feeling well. Would you like me to send him to Palm Beach for a couple of weeks to get a little sun?" 6

A father like me with five children faces the terrifying <u>prospect</u> of sending five to college. When my oldest one went, the bill for her first year had already reached thirteen thousand dollars. I looked hard at this bill and then said to her, "Thirteen thousand dollars. Will you be the only student?" 7

I am lucky enough to make a lot of money, but to the average American father today, thirteen thousand dollars (which has now gone up to seventeen) is more than just a sum of money: it is the need for a winning lottery ticket. 8

When I saw my oldest daughter's first college bill, I multiplied thirteen thousand times four, added another thirty thousand for <u>incidentals</u> during these four years, and got the sum of eighty-two thousand dollars that I would be spending to see my daughter pick up a liberal arts degree, which would qualify her to come back home. 9

You think I'm <u>exaggerating</u> that extra expense for incidentals? For her freshman year, I had to spend another seventeen hundred for a tiny room just a quarter mile from a toilet. And then the college said that if my wife and I really cared for our child, we would pay another three hundred for the <u>gourmet</u> special. We wound up sending another five hundred to our daughter personally so that she would not have to eat the gourmet special but could get pizza instead. 10

"Dad, the food is terrible," she kept saying. 11

"But I <u>enrolled</u> you in *gourmet* food," I said. 12

"That's worse than the other. I want pizza." 13

And then, on top of the five hundred dollars a year that we sent for pizza, we also had to keep flying her home because her clothes kept getting dirty. She was studious, so she was unable to remember to wash her clothes. She simply flew them home every few weeks and put ten thousand dollars' worth of laundry into our washing machine. 14

At this college, my daughter did not major in mathe- 15
matics. *No* children learn mathematics at college, even when
they take the courses; I have never met a college student who
knows how to count. You give one of them a certain amount
of money and a budget <u>precisely</u> broken down to cover all her
expenses.

"This is for this," you say, "and this is for that." 16

The child listens carefully and calls you forty-eight 17
hours later to say she is broke.

"And, Dad, the telephone company is being really *un-* 18
reasonable."

"Did you pay the bill?" 19

"We're certainly *planning* to. And *still* they want to 20
turn it off."

"But I *gave* you enough—there's money in your *budget* 21
for the telephone bill."

"Oh, we used that money for important things." 22

In my daughter's sophomore year, one of these impor- 23
tant things was housing: she and her roommates decided that
they just had to have their own apartment. They no longer
could stand living in the dorm, where the shortsighted dean
had objected to their putting up pictures of naked people
playing guitars.

I discovered these pictures on a surprise visit, which I 24
had made to tell my daughter that her mother and I loved her,
wanted her to work hard, and were behind her all the way.
Upon entering her room, I expected to see pictures of little
kittens playing with thread, but instead I saw a young man
who looked as though he was making music at an Army
physical. My daughter, of course, was not supposed to be majoring in <u>anatomy</u>.

The eighty thousand dollars that you will be spending 25
for college might not leave you quite so depressed if you
knew that the school's curriculum were solid. I am afraid,
however, that the curriculum has turned to cottage cheese.

When I went to college, I sometimes cut classes to go to 26
the movies; but today the movies are the *class*—sorry, The
Film Experience. There are also such challenging courses as
The History of Western Belching, the Philosophy of Making
Applesauce, and Advanced Lawn Mower Maintenance. It is
not surprising to hear a college student say on his graduation
day, "Hopefully, I will be able to make an input. College was
a fun time, but hopefully now I'll have a viable <u>interface</u> with
software." The software is his *brain*. The degree he is truly
qualified to be given is one in Liberal Semi-Literacy.

I do not mean to sound stuffy or old-fashioned. I just feel 27
that for eighty thousand dollars a student should spend four
years in a school where English comes up from time to time.
I cannot stand to see it being scaled *down* to the students.
The students should be reaching up to *it* because success in
life demands the use of intellect under pressure. Also knowing how to spell.

A freshman today will change his schedule if he finds he 28
has signed up for a course that requires books. He wants
courses that will enable him to both sleep late and get rich,
so he will test his <u>intellect</u> with such things as The Origins
of the Sandbox, American National Holidays, and the Principles and Practices of Billing.

I have mentioned my feeling about grade school teach- 29
ers who keep saying, "He can do the work." My feeling is
that if only one of these teachers would call the boy a certi-
fied idiot, I would say, "Fine, we'll get someone to work with
him." Well, in college the teachers don't say, "He can do the
work." They say, "What kind of work would he like to do?"
And it is this new trend of letting students shape their own
curriculum that leads a student to tell his advisor, "I'd like
to study the number of times every day that the average light
at an intersection turns green. I want to major in Traffic."
(1155 words)

—Bill Cosby

After You Read

Reading for Ideas

1. If you can, answer your preview questions here. Number your
   answers to match your questions.

_____

_____

If you are unable to answer your preview questions, explain why here.

_____

_____

2. What is the topic of the selection?

_____

3. State the controlling idea of the reading in your words.

_____

_____

4. List three or four major details that support or explain the controlling idea.

a. _____

_____

b. _____

_____

c. _____

_____

d. _____

_____

5. Below, outline or map the selection.

6. Write a summary by using your map or outline as a guide.

_____

_____

_____

_____

_____

_____

_____

_____

_____

Reading for Information

Circle the correct choice to complete each statement. Prove your answer by putting the number of the question next to the paragraph in the text where the correct information appears.

1. According to Bill Cosby, the biggest expense in raising a child is
   a. a car for graduation.
   b. hospital expenses at birth.
   c. a college education.
   d. none of these

2. Bill Cosby estimates the cost of a four-year college degree to be
   a. $82,000.
   b. $52,000.
   c. $13,000 a year.
   d. $20,000 a year.

3. Mr. Cosby believes that
   a. college students love math.
   b. college students learn math.
   c. college students don't learn math.
   d. college students don't take math.

4. You can infer that Mr. Cosby is referring to the cost of a
   a. four-year degree at a private college.
   b. four-year degree at a public college.
   c. two-year degree at a private college.
   d. two-year degree at a public college.

5. You can infer that Bill Cosby thinks that
   a. colleges require students to take difficult courses.
   b. colleges don't care what courses students take.
   c. colleges should not let students shape their curriculum.
   d. colleges should tell students exactly what courses to take.

Reading for Thinking

Answer the following questions in complete sentences. Support your responses with text information.

1. Mr. Cosby states that a college education is very expensive. Discuss why you agree or disagree with his statement.

_____

_____

_____

_____

_____

2. Mr. Cosby also implies that college students are poor managers of money. Do you agree or disagree? Give specific examples to support your viewpoint.

_____

_____

_____

_____

_____

3. Do you think that many parents are surprised at the way that their children live when they go away to college or to live on their own? Why or why not?

_____

_____

_____

_____

_____

4. How does Mr. Cosby use exaggeration to prove that the college curriculum is not solid? Give examples.

_____

_____

_____

_____

_____

_____

5. Although Mr. Cosby thinks that college is too expensive and that the courses that students take are not as difficult or important as those he took in college, he is still willing to pay for his children's college education. Do you think that most parents who can afford to do this feel the same as he does? Why or why not?

_____

_____

_____

_____

_____

_____

Group Activity

Meet with your classmates in small groups to compare your answers to Question 5 in the above exercise.

Vocabulary

*The words that were underlined in the text are underlined in the following sentences. **Define** each word **from the context.** You may need to go back to the selection for additional help. Use* *your dictionary only if necessary. Write the meanings in your own words.*

1. The old books were hidden in a <u>musty</u> corner of the attic.

   _____

2. He was frightened by the <u>prospect</u> of losing his job.

   _____

3. He spent more on gifts and other <u>incidentals</u> than on airfare for his vacation.

   _____

4. The teacher was <u>exaggerating</u> the difficulty of her tests so that the students would study many hours.

   _____

5. We ordered the <u>gourmet</u> special in the French restaurant.

   _____

6. "But I <u>enrolled</u> in the American history course very early," I complained when it was canceled.

   _____

7. The new budget was <u>precisely</u> broken down into categories to cover all expenses.

   _____

8. Many art students take <u>anatomy</u> courses to better understand the structure of the body.

   _____

9. Most business persons know how to <u>interface</u> with many computer programs.

   _____

10. Success in business demands the use of the <u>intellect</u> under pressure.

_____

Selection 5: What Kind of Care Is Best for Your Child?

One of the issues facing working women today is what to do about child care for their preschoolers. Should they let parents or grandparents babysit, hire someone to come to the home, or use a child care agency? Grandparents and others sometimes disapprove of child care outside the home. This selection from a psychology textbook uses research to evaluate child care and to help parents choose the right day care for their child.

Before You Read

*Before reading this selection, do these **prereading activities.***

1. Freewrite about any opinions or experiences you have regarding child care.

_____

_____

_____

_____

2. Preview the reading. Write three questions that you predict will be answered in the reading.

_____

_____

_____

_____

_____

_____

1. Highlight main ideas, details, and signal words.
2. Annotate the text as you read.
3. Ten unfamiliar words have been underlined. Use the vocabulary strategies to figure out the meaning of the words. You will practice using the words after you read.

What Kind of Care Is Best for Your Child?

To work or not to work is not the question for well over half of all women with children in the United States. Seventy percent of women with young children, many of whom are single parents, must work to support their families (Hoffman, 1989). By comparison, in 1950 only 12 percent of mothers with young children were in the workforce.

Where do these millions of American preschool children go while their parents work? About 51 percent are cared for by grandparents or other relatives. Another 26 percent are enrolled in day care centers, 19 percent are in family day care homes, and 4 percent stay at home with a sitter (Hofferth, 1992).

Finding the best possible day care is a critical issue for many parents. Before exploring what parents should look for when searching for day care, let's try to answer a question that has perplexed both researchers and parents. How does day care affect children's development?

The Effects of Day Care on a Child's Development

It is difficult to make generalizations about the effect of day care, because there are many variables involved, including the quality of the care and the child's age, gender, temperament, and family background. Nevertheless, hundreds of studies have been undertaken to explore what effects, if any, day care has on children.

Belsky and Rovine (1988) found that infants exposed to more than 20 hours of nonmaternal care per week were at somewhat higher risk for insecure infant-mother attachment if they were male, had unresponsive mothers, and were considered by their mothers to have a difficult temperament. Clarke-Stewart (1989) found 47 percent of infants with extensive early nonmaternal care had secure attachments to their mothers, compared to 53 percent of infants who were cared for by their mothers. Curiously, almost all of the infants in day care who had insecure attachments were boys (Belsky & Rovine, 1988).

Despite these somewhat negative findings, a number of researchers have found that good-quality nonmaternal care has no <u>adverse</u> effects on children's development (Clarke-Stewart, 1989; Phillips et al., 1987). In fact, some researchers have reported that children in high-quality early day care were more competent socially in grade school than those who entered child care later (Andersson, 1989, 1992; Field, 1991; Howes, 1990). And children in early child care were found to be more assertive than those who enter later (Scarr & Eisenberg, 1993). 6

While good-quality care can have positive effects, low-quality care can negatively affect the adjustment of infants, with boys being more vulnerable than girls. Poor-quality care also poses a greater risk to children from highly stressed home environments or father-absent homes (Gamble & Zigler, 1986). 7

What can we conclude about the effects of day care on children's development? Scarr and Eisenberg (1993) reviewed research spanning some 20 years and came to the following conclusions: 8

1. In general, most children are not affected significantly by nonmaternal care when the care is of a reasonable quality.
2. If there are negative effects, they are more likely to be emotional.
3. If there are positive effects, they are more likely to be social.
4. In most cases, <u>cognitive</u> development is affected either positively or not at all.
5. Higher levels of aggression seem to be more common for children in day care, but these levels are within the normal range.

Although research on the effects of day care continues, two facts are <u>indisputable</u>: "Bad care is never good for any child, and good day care is all too hard to find" (Shell, 1988, p. 74). So how does one go about finding good day care for a preschool-age child? 9

Finding the Right Day Care Setting for Your Child

It seems clear that the ratio of children to caregivers in a day care setting should be low; that is, there should be enough adults so that each child gets the attention he or she needs. The National Association for the Education of Young Children recommends that each adult caregiver be responsible for 10 no more than four infants, eight 2- to 3-year-olds, or ten 4- to 5-year-olds. Others suggest ratios of one adult per three infants or one adult per four toddlers. In addition, the caregivers should be trained in early childhood education or developmental psychology. Try to find out how long the caregivers have been employed at the center. A high rate of staff turnover makes it difficult for children to develop stable, affectionate relationships with their caregivers.

If you are permitted to observe the center's operations 11 for an hour or two (and beware of a center that doesn't allow you to do so), you can find out a lot about the quality of care. As you watch, ask yourself these questions:

- Does the center provide a safe, clean environment? Are dangerous objects out of reach?
- Is there enough play space, both indoors and outdoors?
- Is the play equipment in good condition? Are all equipment and materials readily available and appropriate for children?
- How well are the children supervised when they use play equipment, go up and down stairs, or use sharp objects like scissors?
- Does the center promote good health habits? Do the children and caregivers wash their hands before eating? Is a first aid kit readily available?
- Is the food served to children nutritious and appetizing?
- Are there separate areas for meals and rest?

In addition to a safe, clean environment, the <u>interac-</u> 12 <u>tions</u> between caregivers and children are important. As you observe, ask yourself these questions:

- Do the caregivers stimulate children to ask questions and solve problems? Are curiosity and creativity encouraged?
- Do the caregivers attempt to improve children's language skills?
- Does the schedule provide time for active play, quiet play, naps, snacks, and meals? Is it flexible enough to meet each child's needs?
- Are children taught to respect both themselves and others?
- Are children encouraged to cooperate when working and playing together?
- Do the caregivers behave in a positive manner, giving praise and answering children's questions? Do they avoid commands, criticism, and <u>reprimands</u>?

You can find out a lot about a day care center just by   13
looking at the children's faces. Do they seem happy with
their activities? Do they smile at their caregivers? If the children look bored or unhappy, or if there is any evidence of
physical punishment, keep searching.
(1125 words)

—Samuel E. Wood and Ellen Green Wood

After You Read

Reading for Ideas

1. Answer your preview questions here. Number your answers to
   match your question numbers.

   _____

   _____

   _____

   _____

   _____

   _____

2. What is the topic of the selection?

   _____

   _____

3. Write the controlling idea of the selection in your own words.

   _____

   _____

4. List three or four details that explain the controlling idea.

   a. _____

   _____

b. _____

_____

c. _____

_____

d. _____

_____

5. Make a map or an outline of the most important information from the selection.

6. Write a summary by using your outline or map as a guide.

_____

_____

_____

_____

_____

_____

_____

_____

_____

_____

_____

_____

_____

_____

Reading for Information

Circle the correct choice to complete each statement. Prove your answer by putting the number of the question next to the paragraph in the text where the correct information appears.

1. Today the percentage of women working with young children to be cared for is
   a. twenty percent.
   b. sixty percent.
   c. fifty percent.
   d. seventy percent.

2. Most young children of working mothers are cared for by
   a. day care centers.
   b. grandparents or other relatives.
   c. family day care homes.
   d. sitters.

3. Infants in day care over twenty hours per week were found to have
   a. slightly more secure attachment to their mothers.
   b. slightly less secure attachment to their mothers.
   c. slightly more emotional problems.
   d. slightly less emotional problems.

4. Positive effects of day care are most likely to be
   a. health related.
   b. emotional.
   c. social.
   d. lost over time.

5. All the following are important things to look for when choosing a day care center except
   a. ratio of children to caregivers.
   b. a safe, clean environment.
   c. age and sex of caregivers.
   d. adequate supervision and positive manner of caregivers.

Reading for Thinking

Answer the following questions in complete sentences. Support your responses with text information.

1. Why do more mothers work when their children are very young today compared with mothers in 1950?

_____

_____

_____

_____

_____

_____

_____

2. What are some advantages of day care centers?

_____

_____

_____

_____

_____

_____

3. What are some disadvantages of day care centers?

_____

_____

_____

_____

_____

_____

4. Of the many questions to ask when you are observing a day care center, which do you think are most important and why?

_____

_____

_____

_____

_____

_____

5. Why do you think some grandparents and other relatives may not approve of day care centers for young children?

_____

_____

_____

_____

_____

_____

_____

Vocabulary

The words that were underlined in the text are underlined in the following sentences. Define each word from the context. You may need to go back to the selection for additional help. Use your dictionary only if necessary. Write the meanings in your own words.

1. A <u>generalization</u> that is not always accurate is that all babies are beautiful.

   _____

2. Most directions for driving a car are not <u>gender</u>-specific.

   _____

3. The boy's <u>temperament</u> was not suited to sitting still in a classroom all day.

   _____

4. My cat is very <u>unresponsive</u> even when I pet him.

   _____

5. Many <u>variables</u> influence men and women when they decide to get married.

   _____

6. The lawyer was not <u>adverse</u> to having his client testify on his own behalf.

   _____

7. The girl's <u>cognitive</u> skills were not as good as her motor skills.

_____

8. The fingerprints on the gun were <u>indisputable</u> evidence against the accused killer.

_____

9. The <u>interaction</u> between the teacher and the student sounded loud and angry.

_____

10. The teacher's <u>reprimand</u> made the child cry.

_____

Selection 6: In My Father's House

In the next essay, the writer describes his relationship with his elderly father. He also writes about his desire not to hurt his father, which prevents him from being honest about his lifestyle.

_____

Before You Read

*Before you read the following selection, do the **prereading activities** below.*

1. In the space below, freewrite or list what comes to your mind about the topic of sons and their relationships with their fathers.

_____

_____

_____

_____

2. Preview the selection. Write three questions that you think will be answered in the reading.

_____

_____

_____

_____

_____

_____

While You Read

1. Underline or highlight main ideas, details, and signal words.
2. Record what you read and your thoughts about the text in a double-entry journal.
3. Ten unfamiliar words have been underlined. Use the vocabulary strategies to define them in context. You will practice using the words after the reading. Underline and define any other unfamiliar words as well.

In My Father's House

Whenever I visit my father in Florida I surprise him. It means one less flight for him to worry about, and it also gives him a pure rush of joy that he rarely feels in days that can be filled with weather-channel reports, clipping coupons and driving to the convenience store for lottery tickets. 1

I am always near giddy with the anticipation of his surprise and often have to fight the impulse to let him know in advance that I am coming. This last trip I could hardly wait to drive up to the small town house he has shared for many years with his girlfriend (something of a <u>ludicrous</u> term, since they are both over 70) in a typical Florida development. I called him from the airport when I landed, having practiced my lines. As soon as he picked up the phone I asked, "So what do you want to do today—do we go to the beach or miniature golfing?" 2

"I hate to ask, but when do you have to leave?" my dad says within minutes of my arrival at his house, as he always does, and with a certain dread. His face registers a slight wince as he awaits my response. Already I could picture exactly how the final night of my stay would be. The three of us would be watching television, and at a certain point I would stand up to go back to the motel and pack for an early 3 morning flight. My dad would rise from his chair and retreat to the bathroom, where he would close the door and cry. His girlfriend would gently try to coax him out. As we walked to the car in the driveway he would slip me a $20 bill and begin to cry again, as would I. And so after days of constant activity and conversation, the final minutes of my visit would be in complete silence, neither of us able to <u>compose</u> ourselves sufficiently to utter any words.

Certain words, however, recited in a kind of <u>litany</u>, virtually always occur during each visit—the names of Civil War sites, with an occasional World War I battle thrown in. Since my dad's house is so small, I usually stay at a Howard Johnson motel on the beach. On the drive to the motel along a stretch of Florida gulf coastline with vintage 1950's motels, the names spelled out in neon, I begin the process of conversation that has become a routine with my father and me. Asking the <u>rhetorical</u> question, "You're still interested in the Civil War, right?" launches a topic he knows thoroughly and is eager to relate. "There's something about the names of the battle sites that haunts me," he says, as he has many times before. So we recite, in a kind of alternating joint <u>mantra</u>, the names—Shiloh, Chickamauga, Appomattox, the Wilderness, Gettysburg, Manassas. We say each name with a careful emphasis and clarity, even a poetic hush for full effect. In some ways it is our secret language, these battle site names.

From my motel balcony there was a view of a curving waterway that eventually led to the gulf and across which were small, appealing houses. Each was fitted with a tiny wooden dock at which a sailboat or a motorboat was <u>moored</u>. People could be seen hosing down their boats, sweeping patios or reclining in lawn chairs while reading newspapers. It was the kind of view that pleased my father. It was accessible, animated and reflected a certain rootedness that he has yet to feel in Florida; people lived in these houses, and <u>collectively</u> they became a neighborhood.

As I unpacked I put a Frank Sinatra tape into my Walkman and placed the earphones over my dad's ears. He moved a chair toward the view and began the newspaper crossword puzzle. For the first time in many months, I knew that my dad was content, that he wasn't worrying about the peculiar pain in his leg or about filling another blank day. On this visit especially, I realized how easy it was to give my father moments of real happiness.

It was also the first time in a long while that I, too, had come to Florida during a period of great happiness and change in my own life. I was beginning to fall in love with someone back in New York. It was a feeling that I must have had before. I had been in a relationship for eight years, but it had been unwinding for so long that it was difficult to recall the waves of affection and longing I now felt. A bouquet of flowers was on the dresser when I arrived in the motel room, sent by the person. So within minutes I managed to make my father exquisitely happy by simply being with him in the place where he lived. Realizing this, and knowing that I had secured love in New York where I lived, I, too, was happy.

My father has worried for years about my being alone. 8 "Everybody gets rejected sometimes," he often says to me. He thinks that's the reason why at 35 I still don't have a girlfriend or a wife or ever talk about one. "You know I'm just kidding when I say it," my dad began what I knew how to finish, "but you'd make me the happiest man in the world if you found a nice Italian girl." I wanted to tell him so badly, right there in the motel room, with the dull clang of boat lines hitting their masts just beyond, squawking sea gulls and the occasional plop of big silver fish leaping in the waterway below, that I was in love and happy. But I couldn't, because it was another man that I loved.

I don't fault my dad for the fact that this news would 9 trouble him deeply; there is no reason to try to radicalize him with this knowledge. The news, no matter how I presented it or whom I introduced as the man I love, would not be welcome. But I also won't lie and say that I am in love with a woman or that I'm sure I'll get married someday. I remain evasive only to the point of deceit. With the faintest strains of Sinatra's "Summer Wind" coming from the earphones my father has on and the quiet scrawl of his pencil filling in the crossword boxes, I read and reread the simple note of coded affection that came with the flowers. So much happiness was taking place in the motel room. As dusk approached, my dad and I remarked almost simultaneously of the oval shape silver fish that would fling themselves out of the water below, one eye, unlidded, wholly visible to us from our third-floor perch. I knew that detail would be a forever-memorable image that my dad and I would cite over and over again on each visit.

In the middle of my stay he overheard a phone conversa- 10 tion I was having in his kitchen and confronted me the next morning. Detecting a certain tenderness in my voice during the call, he asked with sudden rage, "What is there between you and that friend? Tell me, is he straight?" He began to form another question, but he was unable to complete the sentence.

In the trembling, awkward silence that followed, all had been asked and answered. My father's questions were, in fact, statements of his knowledge. We had played out our own peculiar battle and soon, while touring the sites we had mapped out that day, were back to reciting those of the Civil War. *(1281 words)*

—David Masello

After You Read

Reading for Ideas

1. If you can, answer your preview questions here. Number your answers to match your questions.

   _____

   _____

   _____

   _____

   _____

   If you are unable to answer your preview questions, explain why here.

   _____

   _____

2. What is the topic of the selection?

   _____

3. Write the controlling idea of the reading in your own words.

   _____

   _____

4. List three or four major details that support or explain the controlling idea.

a. _____

_____

b. _____

_____

c. _____

_____

d. _____

_____

5. Develop a double-entry journal about the selection here.

In My Father's House

Writer's Ideas	*My Ideas*

Summary: _____

_____

_____

_____

_____

_____

_____

_____

_____

_____

Reading for Thinking

Answer the following questions in complete sentences. Support your responses with text information.

1. Why does the author like to surprise his father when he comes to visit him?

_____

_____

_____

_____

_____

2. Why do visits so filled with conversation end in complete silence?

_____

_____

_____

_____

_____

_____

3. Why do father and son like to recite the names of the battle sites of the Civil War?

_____

_____

_____

_____

_____

4. Why does the son find it difficult to tell his father that he is in love with a man?

_____

_____

_____

_____

_____

5. How does the father respond when he discovers that his son is homosexual?

_____

_____

_____

_____

_____

_____

6. What do you think will happen between the father and son after this discovery?

_____

_____

_____

_____

_____

Group Activity

Meet with a small group of your classmates to share your responses to Question 6 above. Try to come to a consensus (general agreement) about your answers regarding the relationship between the father and son. Use material from the text to support your consensus statement.

Vocabulary

*The words that were underlined in the text are underlined in the following sentences. **Define** each word **from the context.** You may need to go back to the selection for additional help. Use your dictionary only if necessary. Write the meanings in your own words.*

1. The very large hat that the tiny woman was wearing looked <u>ludicrous</u> on her small head.

_____

2. The man was so upset about the car accident that he was not able to <u>compose</u> himself enough to answer the policeman's questions about what had happened.

_____

3. The young man practiced the <u>litany</u> that he would lead at his bar mitzvah over and over.

_____

4. Teachers frequently ask the <u>rhetorical</u> question, "Did you complete your homework?"

_____

5. My father recites a Buddhist <u>mantra</u> over and over to help him remain calm in stressful situations.

_____

6. The sailboats were <u>moored</u> in the beautiful Caribbean bay.

_____

7. <u>Collectively</u>, all the elephants seen traveling together form a herd.

_____

8. The new bride and groom look <u>exquisitely</u> happy in their wedding pictures.

_____

9. The salesman was <u>evasive</u> about the amount of the taxes and the cost of the delivery charge for the new appliances.

_____

10. The <u>scrawl</u> of the writers' pens was almost the only noise in the quiet reading room of the library.

_____

Selection 7: The Parrot's Beak

The writer of this essay came to the United States from India when she was a small child. She speaks of her relationship with her parents, particularly her mother, and how they influenced her attitudes about being a woman and a parent.

Before You Read

Before reading the selection "The Parrot's Beak," do the pre-reading activities below.

1. Freewrite any information that you might have about India and any Indians that you might know.

   _____

   _____

   _____

   _____

2. Preview the selection. Write three questions that you think will be answered in the reading.

   _____

   _____

   _____

   _____

While You Read

1. Underline or highlight main ideas, details, and signal words.
2. Annotate the text. Note in the margins your ideas about how your relationship with your own parents has influenced your own development as an adult. You will develop a double-entry journal after you read.
3. Ten unfamiliar words have been underlined. Use the vocabulary strategies to define the words in context. You will

practice using the words after the reading. If you find any other unfamiliar words, underline them.

The Parrot's Beak

My parents had five sons and three daughters, and it was the daughters who worried our mother the most. 1

Whatever we did that was different from the proper behavior of young girls in her village in India signified danger. And because most things in the United States were different, I was in constant trouble. 2

At a very early age, I became convinced that my mother hated me. It seemed to me that whatever I did, or didn't do, was wrong. She cursed and beat me so much that I automatically ducked if she lifted her hand. 3

When entering a room, I kept to the edges to stay out of her arm's reach. "Get up, you black-faced witch," was a usual eye-opener for me in the morning. And throughout the day, it was, "You parrot's beak," to remind me of my long, ugly nose. 4

Sometimes when I was no more than six or seven years old, I would wonder why she hated me so much. 5

Watching her nurse the newest baby, I would wonder what she felt about having carried me in her body. 6

She frequently talked to us about God. "He made parents to be as God over their children," she explained once. "If children do not obey their parents, they will surely go to hell after they die." Hell was a place, she said, where the disobedient would have to pass through walls set so close together it would be almost impossible to squeeze through them, and she would indicate a tiny space with her thumb and forefinger. I wasn't able to <u>envision</u> my soul, so I suffered endlessly imagining my body trying to squeeze through that tiny space. 7

Sometimes when she was particularly exasperated with me, she would say, "God must have given you to me to punish me for something I did in my previous life." 8

I went about feeling guilty most of the time, but I was never sure what I had done wrong. In time, I decided my crime was being a girl. 9

One day before she entered the hospital for surgery, she summoned me to her bedside, like a <u>sovereign</u> might summon a serf. I entered her room braced for a scolding. I knew she wouldn't hit me, because as I had grown older—I was sixteen then—she had given up on physical punishment, saying 10

"You are too old for whippings now. I can only appeal to your reason." The truth was, I had grown a head taller than my mother; I was too big.

I had learned long before not to speak when she scolded 11 me for something. If I ever dared to protest an unjust accusation, she shouted, "Do not speak back to your elders."

At first I did not speak back because of her order, later I 12 found not speaking to be a useful form of resistance. I would stand mute before her at times, even when being questioned, which added to her rage and frustration.

I went into her bedroom that day, tall and gangly, head 13 hanging, waiting for an outpouring of abuse. But it did not come. Instead she said, "You probably know that I don't expect to come out of the hospital alive. You will be alone now, with neither father nor mother to guide you."

She had never spoken to me in a confiding manner be- 14 fore. I felt a rush of sorrow for her, this frail woman lying before me out of whose body I had come, and I felt guiltier than ever. Two days earlier she had paid a doctor in Merced with chickens, eggs, and vegetables, to learn that the tumor, grown to the size of a melon, had to be surgically removed.

"Your father wanted to arrange marriages for you and 15 your sisters before he died," she continued, "but I absolutely refused. I told him "We came to this country to give our children an education. What good will it do them if they have to marry men they do not know and perhaps might not like? You were only eleven years old when he died, you know."

"Oh yes, Chachi," I wanted to cry out to her, "I know. 16 How well I know. But I thought it was only he who cared about me; it was only he who was kind to me. He would stop you from beating me, and when you pointed out my faults, he would say, she will learn better when she gets older, and you would reply, I doubt it. And yet it was you who saved me from a commitment I would have hated." I wanted to pour out words of gratitude, I wanted to comfort her, but I was too confused to say anything, and I remained silent.

"You will marry whom you please," she went on, "but 17 it is my duty to teach you how to conduct yourself in marriage.

"You must remember that a woman is <u>subservient</u> to a 18 man. When she is a child, she obeys her father; if he should die, then she must obey her oldest brother.

"When a woman marries, her husband is her master." 19

"If she becomes a widow, then she must defer to her 20 sons."

The year was 1932. My mother did die in the hospital, a few days after the surgery. Her youngest child, my brother, was not old enough for grade school yet, so we took him to high school with us for the remainder of my senior term. 21

I had dreams of becoming an artist; I planned to work actively for India's freedom from British rule. I looked upon marriage as a prison. But even though I abhorred the idea of marriage, that same year, right out of high school, I got married. 22

My oldest brother already had planned to send me to India to marry the "right person." But the man I married, a political activist, born and raised in India, warned me, "You will have no rights in India. Your brother can force you to marry anyone he chooses. Marry me, then he will have no power over you." 23

I idolized this man. I had been impressed from the start by his fiery speeches at meetings of the Gadar Party, an organization formed to fight British rule in India. He already had a degree in political science from the University of California in Berkeley. 24

"But I want to go to the university," I said. 25

"You can do both," he insisted. "I will help you." 26

We got married secretly so that I could go on caring for my younger brothers and sister. But I did not keep my secret for long, because soon I had morning sickness and was frequently running out of the house to throw up behind the trees and bushes. "No children," I had said to my husband. "Political activism and babies don't go together." Though he had agreed with me, I found myself pregnant nonetheless. 27

My oldest brother was so furious when he found out that he kicked me out of the house. "Go live off your husband," he said, though he had bragged to people earlier about how much I did for the family. 28

When I was in my eighth month of pregnancy, I had no medical care. A family friend took me to the director of the same county hospital where my mother had died. But she refused me admission, saying, "If these people can afford to farm, they can afford medical care." My friend pointed out that we did not have any money, that we could not even buy food. 29

"She can't have her baby on the street," my friend said. 30

The hospital official fixed her eyes on my friend and asked, "Then why do these people have babies?" 31

As we walked out the door, a nurse who had been in the room whispered to us, "The hospital can't turn you away in an emergency. Come in when you are in labor." 32

And that's what I did. My joy was great at learning my   33
baby was a girl. Because I was slipping in and out of the anes-
thesia, I asked three times to be assured I had heard right. I
had indeed. I was so happy it was a girl because I wanted to
prove to the world that she could be the equal of any boy ever
born.

Above that, I wanted a girl to give her the love and un-   34
derstanding that had been withheld from me.

In the hospital the nurses wouldn't believe that I was   35
married because I wore no wedding ring and I gave my own
last name instead of my husband's. I told them my mother
had not worn a wedding ring, that it was a cultural thing.
Also, I saw no reason for changing my name to someone
else's.

I eventually lost the battle to keep my identity when I   36
went to work in a war plant and was asked once too often
why, if I was really married, didn't I use my husband's name
and wear a wedding ring. I went to the dime store and bought
a "gold" ring which I wore until the day I decided not to be
married anymore.

My husband couldn't understand.   37

"What have I done wrong?" he begged to know.   38

I didn't have the courage to confront him, to tell him   39
how he cheated me out of an education. You see, the day I
was to sign up for classes at the university, he accused me of
wanting to be around other men.

I didn't confront him about how he put an end to my po-   40
litical work either. The day I was to cover a strike for the
workers' paper, he asked me, "And who will take care of the
children if you are arrested?"

I had been in the habit of keeping silent about my real   41
feelings for too many years and was unable to <u>articulate</u> all
my grievances. I decided at that moment that I was not going
to be a servant any longer—and an unpaid one at that.

Freedom from marriage at the age of twenty-seven with   42
no job skills and three children to support is not quite the
stuff of dreams, but I had finally taken my destiny into my
own hands. I could wait on tables, and my typing ability
could get me work in offices. Most important, I could live in
a city to avail myself of evening classes and guarantee a good
education for my children.

My <u>cardinal</u> rules for raising children were: no physical   43
punishment, no discrimination between boys and girls, and
no unfairness. When I was a child, my mother sometimes
punished me for someone else's misdeed because she thought
I looked guilty. I decided to believe my children.

We may have lived in the slums at times, but our apart- 44
ments were sunny with life. Our rooms were filled with
books and music, social activity, and intellectual endeavor.
No matter how shabby a place we moved into, I could make
it beautiful with paint and paintings. I sometimes think back
to the many homes I lived in as a child. I cannot recall a single house that had running water or a rug on the floor. But I
can recall vignettes of my mother and father seated at the
rough kitchen table. On one occasion my mother was draw-
ing a scroll of birds and flowers entwined with leafy vines
around the borders of a letter to her family written in Punjabi script. On another occasion my father sat at the table in
the light of a kerosene lamp writing poetry on a schoolchild's
lined tablet.

Was that where my interest in art and literature was 45
born? Was it their artistic creativity which sustained them in
the harsh reality of their barren existence? Sometimes, when
I look beyond my own hurts, I try to envision my mother's life
before I arrived. I marvel at her survival as the family trekked
around California and Oregon, living as they could wherever
my father found work. He had the company of other men,
friends and workers on the job. My mother had no one, no
other Indian women to keep her company, no sisters or relatives to give her a hand with the housework. She had to do it
all, that is, until her daughters grew old enough to help.

Both my father and mother were pioneers in those days 46
of the early West. My father arrived at the port of San Francisco in 1899 as a matter of choice, an economic choice. He
left his village in India of his own volition. Yet when my
mother came to California, it was not her choice, but her
husband's. My father had returned to India, and brought back
to the United States the wife selected for him by his father.
At the age of seventeen, she had been picked up virtually like
a piece of baggage and taken off to a foreign land by a man
who she never saw before her marriage.

It was her good fortune that he was a kind and generous 47
man who taught her to write in Punjabi so that she could
communicate with the family she left behind, the family she
would never see again. Neither of my parents went to school,
but my father had learned to read and write both Punjabi and
English in the course of his years of service in the British
army. His was the vision that motivated me to educate my
children.

With what wisdom I have gained, I now realize that 48
some of the bitterness my mother projected onto me, came
from her status as a woman in a world controlled by men.

I think my mother would agree, if she could, I consider   49
my greatest accomplishment summed up in a compliment
paid to one of my children: "She is not afraid to think."
(2322 words)

—Kartar Dhillon

After You Read

Reading for Ideas

1. If you can, answer your preview questions here. Number your
   answers to match your questions.

   _____

   _____

   _____

   _____

   _____

   _____

   If you are unable to answer your preview questions, explain
   why here.

   _____

   _____

2. What is the topic of the selection?

   _____

3. State the controlling idea of the reading in your own words.

   _____

   _____

4. List three or four major details that support or explain the controlling idea.

a. _____

_____

b. _____

_____

c. _____

_____

d. _____

_____

5. Develop your double-entry journal here.

Writer's Ideas	My Ideas

6. Summarize the events in the writer's childhood that you think shaped her life as an adult.

_____

_____

_____

_____

_____

_____

_____

_____

_____

_____

_____

Reading for Information

Circle the correct choice to complete each statement. Prove your answer by putting the number of the question next to the paragraph in the text where the correct information appears.

1. As a child, the writer was convinced
   a. that she was very smart.
   b. that her mother hated her.
   c. that she was a very good child.
   d. that she wanted to go back to India.

2. Kartar's most useful form of resistance to her mother was
   a. to ignore her.
   b. not going to school.
   c. not speaking.
   d. to answer her mother's questions.

3. According to the writer, marriage
   a. would be a prison.
   b. should be arranged by the groom's parents.
   c. would give her political power.
   d. meant wearing a wedding band.

4. Punjabi is
   a. slang.
   b. someone who lives in India.
   c. the Indian language.
   d. all of the above

5. According to the reading, we may infer
   a. that the writer hated her mother.
   b. that the writer realized that she learned a great deal from her parents.
   c. that the writer went to college.
   d. that the writer got remarried.

Reading for Thinking

Answer the following questions in complete sentences. Support your responses with text information.

1. What is the significance of the title "Parrot's Beak"?

   _____

   _____

   _____

   _____

   _____

   _____

2. The writer was a child in 1932. Do you think that her mother was an abusive parent by today's standards? Explain your answer.

   _____

   _____

_____

_____

_____

_____

3. How did the writer's mother contradict the Indian tradition of arranged marriages? Was her advice about how a married woman should act appropriate?

_____

_____

_____

_____

4. What kind of person was Kartar's husband?

_____

_____

_____

_____

5. How did the writer's parents influence her later life?

_____

_____

_____

_____

_____

_____

Group Activity

Use your double-entry journal to discuss the following:

1. What were the cultural factors that caused the writer's mother to act as she did toward her daughters? Are there similar factors that might influence your parents' behavior toward you?
2. Do you think that the writer was a feminist or rebelling against her cultural background?
3. Do you agree with the idea of arranged marriages? Of women being subservient to their husbands?

Vocabulary

*The words that were underlined in the text are underlined in the following sentences. **Define** each word **from the context.** You may need to go back to the selection for additional help. Use your dictionary only if necessary. Write the meanings in your own words.*

1. There is so much new technology that it is almost impossible to <u>envision</u> what the world will be like in a hundred years.

_____

2. The president of the country acted like a <u>sovereign</u>; he thought that he was elected king and ordered everybody around.

_____

3. Feminists believe that women are equal to, not <u>subservient</u> to, men.

_____

4. John <u>abhorred</u> the idea of ever getting a job. He hated the thought of working so much that he never left school.

_____

5. Learn to <u>articulate</u> your needs by speaking clearly.

_____

6. Some <u>cardinal</u> rules for being successful in college are come to class, do your homework, and pass your exams.

_____

7. Because his business <u>endeavor</u> was not successful, he went back to school for a law degree.

_____

8. She remembered many <u>vignettes</u> of her childhood when she lived with her grandparents in the country.

_____

9. The killer was hungry and cold. He walked into the police station and surrendered of his own <u>volition</u>.

_____

10. The <u>status</u> of women today is still sometimes controlled by men, especially in the workplace.

_____

_____

Selection 8: My Dear Camera

Arthur Ashe, a famous tennis player, died of pneumonia, as a complication of AIDS. He contracted AIDS through a blood transfusion during open heart surgery. In this letter to his daughter, Camera, he talks about their family history and the possibility of his not being with her as she grows up.

Before You Read

Before reading the letter, be sure to do the following **prereading activities.**

1. Freewrite anything that you know about AIDS, tennis, or Arthur Ashe.

_____

_____

While You Read

1. Underline or highlight main ideas, details, and signal words.
2. Annotate the text.
3. Eight unfamiliar words have been underlined. Use the vocabulary strategies to define the words in context. You will practice using the words after the reading. If you find other unfamiliar words, underline and define them.

My Dear Camera

By the time you read this letter from me to you for the first time, I may not be around to discuss with you what I have written here. Perhaps I will still be with you and your mother, sharing in your daily lives, in your joys and in your sorrows. However, I may be gone. You would doubtless be sad that I am gone, and remember me clearly for a while. Then I will exist only as a memory already beginning to fade in your mind. Although it is natural for memories to fade, I am writing this letter in the hope that your recollection of me will never fade completely. I would like to remain a part of your life, Camera, for as long as you live. 1

I was only a few months older than you are now when I lost my own mother. Eventually I had no memory of what she was actually like, how her voice sounded, how her touch felt. I wanted desperately to know these things, but she was gone and I could not recover that knowledge. For your sake, as well as mine, I hope that I am around for a long time. But we cannot always have what we want, and we must prepare for and accept those changes over which we have no control. 2

Some of my most important thoughts about you are in this book, only as far away as your bookshelf. And your mother will be with you, alive and well, for a long time, and she knows exactly how I feel about most matters. If you ever want to know what I would think or say, ask her. 3

Coincidentally, Camera, I am writing this letter to you on the same day as the inauguration in Washington, D.C.—January 20, 1993—just a few hours after William Jefferson Clinton became the new president of the United States of America. I have been watching much of the <u>pomp</u> and pageantry on the television in my study. I especially loved listening to Maya Angelou, tall and dignified and with a rich, melodious voice, read the poem that our new president asked her to write especially for this occasion.

4

Tears came to my eyes as I watched her <u>conjure</u> up symbols and <u>allusions</u> generations old in the African American world as she sought to describe the nature of life and to challenge humanity to do better. She spoke of "a rock, a river, a tree" as sites in and of the earth that over time have witnessed the sweep of recorded and unrecorded history. For me, the river and the tree hold special significance as symbols because they are so much a part of African American folklore and history, our religion and culture in the South, where I was born and grew up, and where so many other black folk have lived in slavery and freedom.

5

When I was a boy not much older than you, one of the most haunting spirituals I heard on many a Sunday morning in church spoke movingly of a "rest beyond the river." These words and music meant that no matter how harsh and <u>unrelenting</u> life on earth may have been for us as slaves or in what passed for our freedom, once we have crossed the river—that is, death—we will find on the other side God's promise of eternal peace. The river is death and yet it is also life. Rivers flow forever and are ever-changing. At no two moments in time is a river the same. The water in the river is always changing. Life is like that, Maya Angelou wisely reminded us today at the inauguration.

6

What is sure to be different for you will be the quickening pace of change as you grow older. Believe me, most people resist change, even when it promises to be for the better. But change will come, and if you acknowledge this simple but indisputable fact of life, and understand that you must adjust to all change, then you will have a head start. I want you to use that advantage, to become a leader among people, and never to lag behind and follow the selfish wishes and <u>snares</u> of others.

7

On the other hand, Camera, certain things do not change. They are <u>immutable</u>. Maya Angelou's tree stands for family, both immediate and extended. She had in mind, I imagine, some towering, leafy oak, with massive and deep roots that allow the tree to bend in the fiercest wind and yet

8

survive. The keys to the survival of this big tree are the strength and the depth of these roots, and especially of the taproot far down in the earth, sprung from the original seedling that long ago gave life to the tree. When you see a magnificent tree anywhere, you know it has had to fight and sway and bend in order to survive. Families that survive are like that tree. Even larger groups of people, such as those of an <u>ethnic</u> group, are also like that.

You must be like that, too, Camera, although your fighting must always be for <u>morally</u> justifiable ends. You are part of a tree. On Grandpa's—my father's—side of our family, we proudly display our family tree carefully painted by Grandpa's cousin Thelma, who lives in Maryland. On that side, we are descendants of the Blackwell clan. Your name, Camera Elizabeth Ashe, is one of the freshest leaves on this old tree. You are the daughter of a tenth-generation African American. You must never forget your place on that tree. 9

Mommy is a third-generation American. Like nearly all African Americans, Mommy is of mixed background. Her father's father was born in Saint François, Guadeloupe, of East Indian heritage. He came to America through Louisiana, where he married a black American woman who was herself born in St. James Parish. She was the daughter of a man born a slave in 1840. Then Mommy's grandparents moved to Chicago at the same time many other blacks in the South did, as part of what we now call "the Great Migration" that changed the North forever. They had children. One was Mommy's father, John Warren Moutoussamy ("Boompa" to you, as you are "Miss Camera" to him). He is an architect, so you can see where Mommy gets her talents as an artist. Everyone asks her about her last name, Moutoussamy, which puzzles them. It is only an English version of the Indian name "Moutou-swami." 10

... I saw my father lose his own father and his wife—my mother—in less than one year. Those were terrible blows, and ever since then, family has meant more to me than you can imagine. When I think of the many horrors of slavery, the destruction of the family strikes me as probably the worst. We are still facing the consequences of that destruction. What excitement there must have been in 1863 when word arrived that President Lincoln had freed the slaves. Historians tell us that thousands of black men then took off on journeys to find members of their family who had been traded away or sold like cattle. Can you imagine the depths of joy or of sorrow when these searches proved fruitful or fruitless? Suppose you and Mommy had been taken from me, and I had 11 tried to find you for ten years, only to discover in the end that you had died of typhoid fever and Mommy had simply disappeared.

Stories like this were true of many people. Maybe now you better understand why Grandmother Elizabeth and Granny Lorene send so many cards and presents to you. Or why Uncle Johnnie volunteered for a second tour of duty in the war in Vietnam, where many people died or were seriously wounded. He went again to Vietnam not simply because he was a brave and dedicated Marine but also so that I, his brother, would not have to go there as a soldier.

In all likelihood, you too will one day have your own family, which will enrich your life and bring you so much pleasure in knowing that the tree is still alive, still growing. Marriage will probably be the second most important decision of your life. The most important, I think, will be your decision about having a child. Today, about half of all marriages end in divorce, which is a sad and frightening thought. This means that you must choose a husband carefully, Camera. Two parents are usually better for a child. If you had children out of wedlock, as an increasing number of women have chosen to do, I would not be pleased, although I would still love you.

I only wish that you could be as fortunate in your choice of a spouse as your mother and I were when we chose each other. No marriage is without problems, as two individuals learn to adapt their ways for the sake of harmony. But your mother and I loved one another passionately; and we were never more in love than when you came into our lives to enrich and complete our sense of family.

I end, Camera, as I began, with family. In nearly every civilization of which I have heard, the family is the central social unit, the base and foundation of the culture. You are a member of the eleventh identifiable generation of a family on my side and the fourth generation on your mother's side. We have tried to prepare you as best we can to lead as happy and productive a life as possible. Along the way you will stumble, and perhaps even fall; but that, too, is normal and to be expected. Get up, get back on your feet, chastened but wiser, and continue on down the road.

I may not be walking with you all the way, or even much of the way, as I walk with you now. Don't be angry with me if I am not there in person, alive and well, when you need me. I would like nothing more than to be with you always. Do not feel sorry for me if I am gone. When we were together, I loved you deeply and you gave me so much happiness I can

never repay you. Camera, wherever I am when you feel sick at heart and weary of life, or when you stumble and fall and don't know if you can get up again, think of me. I will be watching and smiling and cheering you on.
(1630 words)

—Arthur Ashe and Arnold Rampersad

After You Read

Reading for Ideas

1. What is the topic of the selection?

2. State the most important or controlling idea of the reading in your own words.

3. List three main ideas that support or explain the controlling idea.

4. Write a summary of the selection.

Reading for Information

Circle the correct choice to complete each statement. Prove your answer by putting the number of the question next to the paragraph in the text where the correct information appears.

1. The writer tells his daughter that "we cannot always have what we want, and we must prepare for and accept those changes that
   a. we can control.
   b. we do not like.
   c. we want.
   d. we have no control over.

2. The letter was written
   a. while Maya Angelou read a poem.
   b. during the presidential inauguration.
   c. on January 20, 1993.
   d. a few hours after breakfast.

3. Maya Angelou reminded the writer that the river represents
   a. life.
   b. death.
   c. hope.
   d. life and death.

4. According to Arthur Ashe, most people
   a. resist change.
   b. like change.
   c. try to change.
   d. want to change.

5. Camera's father says that nearly all African Americans are
   a. rich.
   b. of mixed backgrounds.
   c. poor.
   d. successful.

Reading for Thinking

Answer the following questions in complete sentences. Support your responses with text information.

1. At the beginning, Arthur Ashe says that by the time Camera reads his letter for the first time, he might not be around to discuss what he has written. Why do you think that he expects her to read the letter more than once?

   _____

   _____

   _____

   _____

   _____

2. Why do you think that Camera will have an advantage in life if she understands that she must adjust to all change? If you do not think that she will have an advantage, explain why.

   _____

   _____

   _____

   _____

   _____

3. What do you think Arthur Ashe means when he says, "When I think of the many horrors of slavery, the destruction of the family strikes me as probably the worst"?

   _____

   _____

_____

_____

_____

_____

4. Family is obviously very important to the writer. Find three examples in the letter that support this feeling. Then explain what they mean to you.

_____

_____

_____

_____

_____

5. Why is Arthur Ashe so concerned about his daughter's future?

_____

_____

_____

_____

_____

Group Activity

Write a letter to a friend, classmate, or family member describing your own feelings about the importance of family. Discuss the responses as a group.

Vocabulary

*The words that were underlined in the text are underlined in the following sentences. **Define** each word **from the context.** You may need to go back to the selection for additional help. Use your dictionary only if necessary. Write the meanings in your own words. Be sure that your meaning **"makes sense"** in the context of the sentence.*

1. The coronation of the Queen was full of <u>pomp</u>. It was colorful and majestic.

   _____

2. The magician <u>conjured</u> a rabbit from an empty hat.

   _____

3. Her <u>allusion</u> (reference) to her grandfather showed how much she missed and loved him.

   _____

4. The roads were flooded for two days because of the <u>unrelenting</u> rain.

   _____

5. The man was <u>snared</u> by the salesman into buying a car that he could not afford.

   _____

6. The loss was <u>immutable</u>. The score was thirty to zero, and the team could never catch up.

   _____

7. Many <u>ethnic</u> foods are enjoyed in the United States. Pizza (Italian) and Chow Mein (Chinese) are among the most popular.

   _____

8. It was <u>morally</u> wrong of him to lie to his girlfriend about where he was on Saturday night.

   _____

Selection 9: City of Brooklyn, July 13

The following reading is about a day in the life of a typical Haitian family living in a slum. Haiti is a Caribbean country with much poverty and political unrest. This selection describes how poor the conditions are for this particular family and gives the reader an idea why many Haitians leave their country and emigrate to the United States in the hope of a better life.

Before You Read

*Before reading the selection "City of Brooklyn, July 13," do the **prereading activities** below.*

1. Freewrite any information that you might have about Haiti in the space below.

   _____

   _____

   _____

   _____

2. Preview the selection. Write three questions that you think will be answered in the reading.

   _____

   _____

   _____

   _____

   _____

While You Read

1. Underline or highlight main ideas, details, and signal words.
2. Annotate the text.

3. Ten unfamiliar words have been underlined. Use the vocabulary strategies to define the words in context. You will practice using the words after the reading. If you find other unfamiliar words, underline them.

City of Brooklyn, July 13

The fading moonlight shines on the sheet-metal shacks of the "City of Brooklyn," casting an <u>ethereal</u> glow that transforms the <u>squalor</u> of one of Haiti's poorest slums—a squalor that becomes harshly visible with the rising sun. The early-morning silence is broken by delirious chants coming from a makeshift chapel belonging to Haitian Baptists who practice Christianity laced liberally with voodoo and African <u>idolatry</u>. The starving slum dogs accompany the rising voices, filling the dawn air with an eerie otherworldly <u>lament</u>.

Gladys Lambert lies with her eyes closed, listening to the sounds of people in the alley hurrying to the morning market with their sorry baskets of goods perched on their heads. Her husband lies asleep beside her, and one-year-old Jesusla is curled against her right breast. Gladys waits for all the others to wake, holding on, it seems to the only peaceful time in her unfortunate life.

6:00. When Gladys and her family open their doors, they join the rest of their neighbors, squatting naked with their washbasins in front of their houses. People spit and urinate on the garbage-strewn ground. Children run to and fro carrying chamber pots on their heads; they empty them in the vacant field that leads to the slum. The <u>shantytown</u> has no running water or sewers, and as the children dump their pots, they must dodge people squatting on the ground relieving themselves in full view of their neighbors.

Gladys' oldest son goes to stand in line at the water tank in the neighboring shantytown. Water there costs only five centimes (one penny) a bucket instead of the ten centimes in the "City of Brooklyn." A man collects the money at each tap for its private owner.

Forty-five minutes later, Pierre Michelet comes struggling through the doorway, one bucket of water balanced on his head, the other dripping in his hands. He looks exhausted. Gladys is gambling everything on her oldest son. Every month she borrows 10 gourdes ($2 U.S.) at 50 percent interest to send Pierre to a private school. "He'll study," Gladys says hopefully, "and get a good job that will make enough money to repay my debt and give me money to help us live." Most Haitian students take an average of eleven years to complete the country's six-year primary school program. And seventeen-year-old Pierre is no exception. He still has two more years to go. Like many mothers, Gladys is blind to her son's lack of ability. In addition to the difficulties <u>inherent</u> in slum life, Pierre is sickly and does not have enough energy to realize his mother's ambition.

7:30. Gladys' husband, Vilbre, has already disappeared in the slum's <u>labyrinth</u>. Vilbre is a professional beggar. Every day, dressed neatly, his little purse tucked under his arm, he begs, centime by centime, for the 20 gourdes he needs to pay for his monthly medical attention. Vilbre has tuberculosis, probably contracted when he worked as a *faltra* (feces) collector, shoveling the slum's excrement from the vacant field. Vilbre always gets the money he needs. He has nine children by four different women, and one of his sons always helps him out. "Vilbre runs away," Gladys says. "He hates it when the children follow him around asking for a few centimes for something to eat." Gladys resents bearing all the responsibility for providing for her children. Vilbre's daughter Meprisa has come to live with them, and it's just one more mouth that Gladys must feed. She is a strong, compassionate woman and treats Meprisa as one of her own, but she cannot excuse her husband despite his illness. Both Lamberts, however, prefer their life in the shantytown to the one they led in the country.   6

8:00. Gladys spreads peanut butter on manioc biscuits, hands them to the four younger children, and shoos them out the door. They are on vacation. Gladys sweeps and washes the crude cement floor.   7

Their fifteen-square-meter shack has two rooms which she rents for 10 gourdes a month. The walls consist of a jumble of tin sheets nailed onto a frame made from small branches. Gladys has covered them with pieces of cardboard and pages from magazines. This is where her "customers" come. From the outside, no one would suspect that Gladys has a store, but word gets around quickly in shantytowns. Between the bed and the table, beside the door, she places a plank on a pile of cardboard. There she displays tiny packets of groceries—two centimes' worth of sugar, three centimes of salt, five centimes of detergent; that is all the poor can afford. Gladys serves everyone with Jesusla hanging at her breast.   8

9:00. Calling Rosis in to mind the store, Gladys goes to see her neighbors. She visits an old woman who lies naked and motionless on her bed, her body <u>devoured</u> by cancer. Gladys takes the emaciated woman in her arms and sets her   9 on a chair. She will return several times in the course of the day to change the dying woman's position. As Gladys leaves, a friend calls to her from the door of another shack. She is clutching her younger daughter who is delirious with fever. Malaria is a constant danger here, but before the mother can go to a doctor, she must find money to pay for the visit and the drugs. The friend turns to Gladys for sympathy and support. Gladys' attentiveness and her ability to listen quietly are invaluable to people who experience the indignity of death and starvation daily. Her final visit is to a shack where triplets were born a week earlier. One of them had diarrhea, and dehydration has set in. Again, no money, no doctor. Nothing to do but ask for God's mercy. Turning to God is often the only alternative for the majority of Haitians.

10:30. Children wait impatiently around Pierre Miche- 10 let, who squats in front of an outdoor brazier grilling peanuts. He sells *royales*, peanut butter spread on manioc biscuits. Those children who have scrounged up two centimes eagerly await their one treat of the day. Then they skip away in single file through the narrow passages around the houses. Some of the children are permanently on vacation, while others attend school every year. It's all a question of money. Watching their children go by, the women smile, forgetting their problems for a moment.

By early afternoon the sheet-metal houses have become 11 uninhabitable ovens. Gladys pours a little water into a plastic bowl and sits Jesusla in it. Somewhat refreshed, the baby dozes, and Gladys sits with her neighbors, their backs against the walls, in the filigree of shade. While they talk, they <u>plait</u> each other's hair. Other women weave baskets of straw to sell in the market. Two young women carrying buckets of water on their heads walk by, hoping that some of the mothers will pay twelve centimes for a bucket. No one moves in the intense heat.

5:00. Gladys prepares a puree of bananas and carrots for 12 her baby. The other children will have rice and kidney beans. The meals are not always as filling; sometimes there is nothing but bread and peanut butter.

A storm breaks over the mountain of Petionville, home 13 of the city's more fortunate citizens, whose gardens will benefit from the <u>precipitation</u>. The excess water rushes down the streets of Port-au-Prince to the slum. Children along the way bathe and play in the flood of muddy, but free, water. The slums of Port-au-Prince are built on a former swamp that lies a meter below sea level. When the rains are severe, the "City of Brooklyn" becomes a muddy pool and whole families must spend the night on tables and chairs.

6:45. It is cooler now. The merchants and beggars re- 14
turn, and the shantytown comes to life again. The air fills
with the aromas of spices and grilled fish. A noisy brawl
breaks out between two women weaving baskets, and a
crowd forms around them. Jesusla sits on the filthy ground
and is attacked by clouds of mosquitoes. Her skin is already
completely covered with sores. Gladys rinses her off in a tub,
and breast-feeds her before bed.

7:30. Meprisa lights the homemade kerosene lamp fash- 15
ioned from a jam jar. The slum is connected to the electricity grid, but the residents couldn't pay their bills, so the
power was cut off.

8:30. The afternoon storm didn't cause too much dam- 16
age, so the three girls spread their beds made out of cardboard
boxes on the ground near their parents' bed. Gladys lays rags
on top, and the girls pile onto them and fall asleep immediately. The boys sleep head to toe on a cot. Vilbre comes home
just in time to go to bed. Husband and wife have little to say
to each other, so Gladys puts out the lamp. "Until tomorrow," she mutters quietly. Another Haitian might add, "If
God in his mercy so wills."

(1485 words)

—Helene Tremblay

After You Read

Reading for Ideas

1. If you can, answer your preview questions here.

_____

_____

_____

_____

_____

_____

If you are unable to answer your preview questions, explain why here.

_____

_____

2. What is the topic of the selection?

_____

3. State the controlling idea of the reading in your own words.

_____

_____

4. List three or four major details that support or explain the controlling idea.

a. _____

_____

_____

b. _____

_____

_____

c. _____

_____

_____

d. _____

_____

_____

5. Make an outline or a map of the most important information from the reading.

6. Write a summary of the selection using your map or outline as a guide.

_____

_____

_____

_____

_____

_____

_____

_____

_____

_____

_____

Reading for Information

Circle the correct choice to complete each statement. Prove your answer by putting the number of the question next to the paragraph in the text where the correct information appears.

1. According to the writer, Gladys Lambert's only peaceful time is
   a. when her children go to school.
   b. when her husband goes to work.
   c. while her family is asleep.
   d. when she is working.

2. Gladys borrows money to send her son to a private school so that he
   a. will be able to leave Haiti.
   b. will earn money to help the family live better.
   c. will attend an American university.
   d. will be able to get medical attention.

3. Vilbre Lambert
   a. is responsible for providing for the children.
   b. helps his wife whenever he can.
   c. is a strong, compassionate man.
   d. hates when the children ask him for money.

4. The only alternative for the majority of Haitians is to
   a. turn to God.
   b. move to another country.
   c. get better jobs.
   d. see a physician.

5. The storm
   a. was good for the Lambert's garden.
   b. provided clean, free water.
   c. washed away the "City of Brooklyn."
   d. made the "City of Brooklyn" a muddy pool.

Reading for Thinking

Answer the following questions in complete sentences. Support your responses with text information.

1. What does the writer mean when she states that Gladys Lambert's life is unfortunate?

   _____

   _____

   _____

   _____

2. Which details about Pierre might lead you to conclude that Gladys's hopes for her son might not be realized?

   _____

   _____

   _____

   _____

   _____

   _____

3. Describe Gladys's relationship with her husband.

   _____

   _____

   _____

   _____

   _____

4. Consider the information given about Vilbre Lambert. What does this information indicate about his character?

_____

_____

_____

_____

_____

5. When the Lambert children grow up, how do you think they will look back on the relationship that they had with their parents when they were children?

_____

_____

_____

_____

_____

_____

_____

Group Activity

Discuss the differences between life in the United States and life in Haiti. Find information about Haiti from newspapers and magazines with respect to Haitian religion, politics, and history. Compare your information. What points about human nature or human experience come to light as a result of your information?

Vocabulary

The words that were underlined in the text are underlined in the following sentences. **Define** *each word* **from the context.** *You may need to go back to the selection for additional help. Use your dictionary only if necessary. Write the meanings in your own words.*

1. The moon cast an <u>ethereal</u> glow, which made the shantytown look like something from another world. It seemed clean and peaceful.

   _____

2. The <u>squalor</u> of the "City of Brooklyn" was visible when you saw garbage strewn all over and the children covered with sores.

   _____

3. The chapel was filled with African <u>idolatry</u>, which included masks representing gods and animal figures.

   _____

4. Gladys's neighbor <u>lamented</u> the death of her husband.

   _____

5. The shabbiness of the houses in the <u>shantytown</u> contrasted the beautiful houses of Port-au-Prince.

   _____

6. Although poverty is one of the <u>inherent</u> difficulties in slum life, it is not <u>inherent</u> in the life of the middle class.

   _____

7. The twisting streets became a <u>labryinth</u> that caused many strangers to lose their way in the town.

   _____

8. The child was so hungry that she <u>devoured</u> her dinner.

   _____

9. Her hair was <u>plaited</u> down to her waist. A ribbon was woven into the braid.

   _____

10. Snow fell in the mountains. Hail fell in the suburbs, and it rained in the city. The type of <u>precipitation</u> depended on the temperature of the air in different places.

_____

_____

Selection 10: Diversity in U.S. Families

The author of this selection, from a sociology textbook, states that there is no such thing as *the* American family. Rather, family life and intergenerational relations within the family vary widely throughout the United States. The author also points out that social class (standing in society based on income, power, background, and prestige) is a very significant aspect of diversity in U.S. families.

Before You Read

*Before you read this selection, do the **prereading activities** below.*

1. Freewrite a description of your family. What social class do you think you and your family belong to? What do you think is typical about your family? What do you think makes your family unique?

_____

_____

_____

_____

_____

_____

_____

2. Preview the selection. Write three questions that you think will be answered in the reading.

_____

_____

_____

_____

While You Read

1. Underline or highlight main ideas and number important details.
2. Make annotations in the margins. That is, write definitions of new words, note your reactions and questions, and identify the main idea of the charts. This will prepare you to make a map or outline of the material.
3. Use your vocabulary strategies to define the ten unfamiliar words that have been underlined. This will help you with the vocabulary practice at the end of the selection.

Diversity in U.S. Families

African-American Families

Note the heading is African-American *families*, not *the* African-American family. There is no such thing as *the* African-American family. There is no such thing as *the* white family or *the* Latino family (Taylor 1994). The primary distinction is not between African Americans and other groups but among social classes. Because African Americans who are members of the upper class follow their class interests—preservation of privilege and family fortune—they are especially concerned about the family background of those whom their children marry (Gatewood 1990). To them, marriage is viewed as a merger of family lines. Children of this class marry later than children of other classes.

Middle-class African-American families focus on achievement and respectability. Both husband and wife are likely to work outside the home. Their concerns are that the family stay intact and that their children go to college, get good jobs, and marry well—that is, marry people like themselves, respectable and hardworking, who want to get ahead in school and <u>pursue</u> a successful career.

African-American families in poverty face all the prob- 3
lems that cluster around poverty (Franklin 1994). Because the men are likely to have few skills and to be unemployed, it is difficult for them to fulfill the cultural roles of husband and father. Consequently, these families are likely to be headed by a woman and to have a high rate of unwed motherhood. Divorce and desertion are also more common than among other classes. Sharing <u>scarce</u> resources and stretching <u>kinship</u> are primary survival mechanisms. That is, people who have helped out in hard times are considered brothers, sisters, or cousins, to whom one owes obligations as though they were blood relatives (Stack 1974). Sociologists use the term *fictive kin* to refer to this stretching of *kinship*.

From Figure 13.1, you can see that African-American 4
families are the least likely to be headed by married couples and the most likely to be headed by women. Because of a **marriage squeeze**—an imbalance in the sex ratio, in this instance fewer unmarried men per 100 unmarried women—

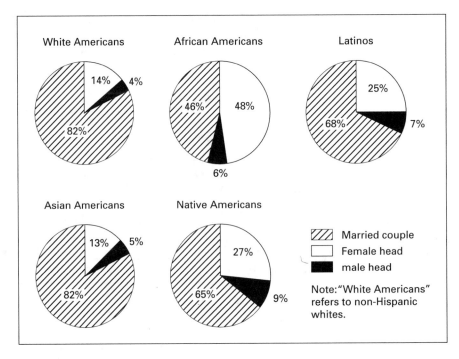

Figure 13.1 Family Structure: The Percentage of U.S. Households Headed by Men, Women, and Married Couples

Source: Statistical Abstract 1995: Table 70; except O'Hare 1992 for Native Americans.

African-American women are more likely than other racial groups to marry men who are less educated than themselves, who are unemployed, or who are divorced (South 1991).

Latino Families

As Figure 13.1 shows, the proportion of Latino families headed by married couples and women falls in between whites and African Americans. The effects of social class on families also apply to Latinos. In addition, families differ by country of origin. Families from Cuba, for example, are more likely to be headed by a married couple than are families from Puerto Rico (Statistical Abstract 1995: Table 53).

What really distinguishes Latino families, however, is culture—especially the Spanish language, the Roman Catholic religion, and a strong family orientation with a disapproval of divorce. Although there is some debate among the experts, another characteristic seems to be <u>machismo</u>— an emphasis on male strength and dominance. In Chicano families (those originating from Mexico), the husband-father plays a stronger role than in either white or African-American families (Vega 1990). Machismo apparently decreases with each generation in the United States (Hurtado et al. 1992). In general, however, the wife-mother makes most of the day-to-day decisions for the family and does the routine disciplining of the children. She is usually more family centered than her husband, displaying more warmth and affection for her children.

Generalizations have limits, of course, and as with other ethnic groups individual Latino families vary considerably from one another (Baca Zinn 1994; Carrasquillo 1994).

Asian-American Families

As you can see from Figure 13.1, the structure of Asian-American families is almost identical to that of white families. Apart from this broad characteristic, because Asian Americans come from twenty countries, their family life varies considerably, reflecting their many cultures. In addition, as with Latino families, the more recent the immigration, the closer that family life reflects the family life of the country of origin (Kibria 1993; Glenn 1994).

In spite of such differences, however, sociologist Bob Suzuki (1985), who studied Chinese-American and Japanese-American families, identified several distinctive characteristics. Although Asian Americans have adopted the nuclear family common in the United States, they have retained Confucian values that provide a distinct framework for family life:

humanism, <u>collectivity</u>, self-discipline, hierarchy, respect for the elderly, moderation, and <u>obligation</u>. Obligation means that each individual owes respect to other family members and carries the responsibility never to bring shame on the family. Asian Americans tend to be more permissive than Anglos in child rearing and more likely to use shame and guilt rather than physical punishment to control their children's behavior.

Native-American Families

Perhaps the single most significant issue that Native-American families face is whether to follow traditional values or to <u>assimilate</u> (Yellowbird and Snipp 1994). This primary distinction makes for vast differences in families. The traditionals speak native languages and emphasize distinctive Native-American values and beliefs. Those that have assimilated into the broader culture do not. 10

Figure 13.1 <u>depicts</u> the structure of Native-American families. You can see how it is almost identical to that of Latinos. In general, Native-American parents are permissive with their children and avoid physical punishment. Elders play a much more active role in their children's families than is true of most U.S. families: they not only provide childcare, but they teach and discipline children. Like others, Native-American families differ by social class. 11

In Sum Social class and culture hold the keys to understanding family life. Race by itself signifies little, if anything. The more resources a family has, the more it assumes the middle-class characteristics of a nuclear family. Compared with the poor, middle-class families have fewer children and fewer unmarried mothers, and place greater emphasis on educational achievement and <u>deferred</u> gratification. 12

One-Parent Families

From TV talk shows to government officials, one-parent families have become a matter of general concern. The increase is no myth. Since 1970, the number of one-parent families has tripled, while the number of two-parent families has actually decreased by 250,000 (Statistical Abstract 1995: Table 71). Two primary reasons underlie this change: The first is the high divorce rate, which each year forces a million children from two-parent homes to one-parent homes (Statistical Abstract 1995: Table 146). The second is the sharp increase in unwed motherhood. Overall, 30 percent of U.S. children are born to women who are not married, a 50 percent increase in just ten years. This is three times higher than in 1970 (Statistical Abstract 1995: Table 94). 13

The primary reason for the concern, however, may have 14
less to do with children being reared by one parent than the
fact that most of these families are poor. The poverty is primarily due to most one-parent families being headed by
women. Although 90 percent of children of divorce live with
their mothers, most divorced women earn less than their former husbands. In the case of unwed mothers, most have little education and few marketable skills, which condemns
them to bouncing from one minimum-wage job to another,
with welfare sandwiched in between.

To understand the typical one-parent family, then, we 15
need to view it through the lens of poverty, for that is its primary source of strain. The results are serious, not just for these
parents and their children, but for society as a whole. Children
from single-parent families are twice as likely to drop out of
high school and, if a female, to have a child while still a
teenager (McLanahan and Sandefur 1994). They also are more
likely to get arrested, to have emotional problems, to bear
children outside marriage, and to get divorced (Wallerstein and
Blakeslee 1992; Whitehead 1993; O'Neill 1993). The cycle of
poverty is so powerful that *nearly half* of all recipients of welfare are current or former teenage parents (Corbett 1995).

Families Without Children

Overall, about 11 percent of U.S. married couples never 16
have children (Statistical Abstract 1995: Table 102), but the
actual percentage changes by education and race-ethnicity.
The more education a woman has, the more likely she is to
expect to bear no children. Latinas are much more likely to remain childless than are white and African-American women.

Why do some couples choose not to have children? Soci- 17
ologist Kathleen Gerson (1985) found that some women see
their marriage as unstable and either do not believe their relationship can withstand the strains a child would bring or think
it may break up before the child is grown. Some women look
on children as binding them to the home, and believe that as
mothers they would be bored and lonely and would lose career
opportunities. Other couples simply see a child as too expensive. With trends firmly in place—more education and careers
for women, technological advances in contraception, abortion,
the high cost of rearing children—it appears that the proportion of women who never bear children will increase.

Blended Families

An increasingly significant type of family formation 18
found in the United States is the blended family, one whose

members were once part of other families. Two divorced person who marry and each bring their children into a new family unit become a blended family. With divorce common, many children spend some of their childhood in blended families.

Gay Families

In 1989, Denmark was the first country to legalize marriage between people of the same sex. Since then, two neighbors, Norway and Sweden, have also made same-sex marriages legal (Ingrassia 1996). Although such marriages remain illegal in the United States, same-sex couples in San Francisco can register as "domestic partners," publicly agreeing to be jointly responsible for their basic living expenses. The city offers health benefits to the domestic partners of its employees, and the employee can take paid bereavement leave if the partner dies. New York, Seattle, and a scattering of other cities have made similar arrangements for their employees (Hartinger 1992), as have more than seventy major corporations such as Ben & Jerry's, Lotus, and Apple (Jefferson 1994). 19

What are gay marriages like? As with everything else in life, same-sex couples cannot be painted with a single brush stroke (Allen and Demo 1995). As with opposite-sex couples, social class is highly significant, and orientations to life differ according to education, occupation, and income. Sociologists Blumstein and Schwartz (1985) interviewed same-sex couples and found their main struggles to be housework, money, careers, problems with relatives, and sexual adjustment—the same as heterosexual couples. Same-sex couples are much more likely to break up, however, probably because of a combination of higher levels of sexual infidelity and a lack of legal and broad social support. 20
(1832 words)

—James M. Henslin

After You Read

Reading for Ideas

1. If you can, answer your preview question here.

_____

_____

_____

_____

_____

_____

2. What is the topic of this selection?

_____

3. What does the writer stress as the main factor in creating diversity in American families?

_____

4. In addition to ethnic background, what categories of families does the author describe?

_____

_____

_____

5. Using your marking of the selection, make a map or outline of the most important information from this reading.

Reading for Information

Circle the correct choice to complete each statement. Prove your answer by putting the number of the question next to the paragraph in the text where the correct answer appears.

1. According to the pie graphs,
   a. Native-American and African-American families have the most female heads.
   b. Asian-American families have the fewest male heads.
   c. Latino families have the most married couple heads.
   d. white American families have the least female heads.

2. Middle-class African-American families focus on
   a. preservation of privilege.
   b. avoiding marriage with white Americans.
   c. religion and education.
   d. achievement and respectability.

3. Latino families are distinguished from other families by their emphasis on
   a. religion and education.
   b. Spanish language and educational achievement.
   c. Spanish language, religion, and family orientation.
   d. Spanish language, religion, and assimilation.

4. Asian-American families with their emphasis on a nuclear family are most like
   a. African-American families.
   b. Latino families.
   c. Native-American families.
   d. white families.

5. Since 1970, the number of one-parent families in the United States has
   a. tripled.
   b. doubled.
   c. decreased.
   d. quadrupled.

Reading for Thinking

Answer the following questions in complete sentences. Support your responses with text information.

1. After reading this selection, what do you think are the major problems that American families face? Use information from the text to support your answer.

_____

_____

_____

_____

_____

2. How does the author show or demonstrate that there is no such thing as *the* American family?

_____

_____

_____

_____

_____

3. Reread the reasons that some couples do not have children and explain why you agree or disagree with their reasons for that decision.

_____

_____

_____

_____

_____

_____

4. What do you think could be some of the problems of blended families and what could be some of the benefits of these families?

_____

_____

_____

_____

_____

5. Explain how this selection has changed your thinking about the concept of American families.

_____

_____

_____

_____

_____

Vocabulary

*The words that were underlined in the text are underlined in the following sentences. **Define** each word **from the context.** You may need to go back to the selection for additional help. Use your dictionary only if necessary.*

1. The <u>preservation</u> of old homes is expensive but is considered a worthwhile project.

   _____

2. The college football player did not want to <u>pursue</u> a career in professional football.

   _____

3. Because of the drought, food was <u>scarce</u>.

   _____

4. Although they may have different fathers or mothers, children in an extended family have a close <u>kinship</u> with each other.

   _____

5. <u>Machismo</u> is very important to many adolescent boys.

   _____

6. The union's decision to strike was made <u>collectively</u> by the members.

   _____

7. The young man felt a strong <u>obligation</u> to go into the family business.

   _____

8. People who do not speak English have a difficult time <u>assimilating</u> in America.

   _____

9. Cartoonists often <u>depict</u> the worst features of famous people.

   _____

10. The young girl <u>deferred</u> to the older woman as they entered the building.

   _____

Five Methods to Learn New Words

You probably have been repeatedly encouraged to learn new words to expand your vocabulary. However, you may find vocabulary assignments and exercises uninteresting or difficult. The **vocabulary game plan** in this chapter teaches you effective strategies that you can use in all your college courses. When you learn and apply the **vocabulary strategies** to words in a particular subject, you will find the course content easier to learn and to remember.

In the first part of this chapter, you will learn five methods to help you master unfamiliar words. They are:

1. Context Strategies
2. Print Symbol Strategy
3. Word Parts Strategy
4. Dictionary Strategies
5. Memory Strategies

When you have mastered these strategies, you will be better able to discover and remember the meaning of new words in all your reading.

In the second part of this chapter, you will practice using these five strategies on college reading material. Applying the strategies will enable you to better remember difficult vocabulary and to learn how strategy use can increase your understanding of what you read.

Context Strategies

You learn the meaning of nearly all the words that you speak and write by hearing or reading them in the **context** (as part of the text) of a sentence, a paragraph, or a passage. For example, if you read, "The thief was caught because he sold the stolen jewelry to the neighborhood <u>fence</u>," you might wonder why a thief would sell the stolen jewelry to a wooden or metal structure designed to show property lines. However, you could reread the sentence and figure out that *fence* can also mean a person who buys stolen goods because you know that jewelry is sold to people. The meaning of *fence* is explained, in part, in the sentence in which it is written. When a word is totally or partially explained in the sentence in which it is written or in a nearby sentence, you can learn the meaning from the context. In fact, because many words have more than one meaning, the only way to define a word is from the context in which it is used.

There are several **context specific strategies** that you can use when you are not sure of the meaning of a word. They are explained in the following section.

Explanations

When you see an unfamiliar word, it is important to carefully read and reread the sentence in which the word occurs and the sentences that come immediately before and after. You do this because the writer may tell you the meaning of the word in any of these sentences. For example, consider the sentence, "John found reading very <u>tedious</u>; in fact, he frequently fell asleep while reading long chapters." You can figure out that *tedious* means tiresome or uninteresting due to length because the sentence explains that John falls asleep when reading long chapters.

Sometimes the **explanation** of a word is found in the sentence before or after the word is used. Suppose you read these sentences: "Mary enjoyed bungee jumping. She felt <u>elated</u> after each jump. She always left the jump site feeling proud and joyous." Because you read that Mary enjoyed bungee jumping, you can safely assume that *elated* has a meaning similar to joy. By continuing to read, you learn that your guess is correct and that *elated* also means feeling proud.

In the sentence or groups of sentences below, use the **explanation** clues to state the meaning of the underlined word.

1. My roommate was much more <u>garrulous</u> than I was; she talked more than she studied.

   Garrulous means _____

2. <u>Vivid</u> colors of red, yellow, and orange were used to decorate the room.

   Vivid means _____

3. When the boy was killed, the family experienced deep <u>anguish</u>. His mother mourned for years.

   Anguish means _____

4. The cook had an <u>eclectic</u> method of cooking. He made dishes from Italy, China, and the United States.

   Eclectic means _____

5. Sam worked very hard in school, but he always had trouble with <u>phonetics</u>. He could not remember the sounds of the letters of the alphabet.

   Phonetics means _____

Signal Words

Many times writers use certain words to signal you that they are going to tell you the meaning of a more difficult word. The common **signal words** are *that is, means* or *meaning, such as, for example, is called, or.* Consider the sentence, "Shoppers frequently make <u>impulsive</u> purchases; that is, they buy items that are attractively displayed that they did not intend to buy when they came into the store." The word *impulsive* is clearly explained after the signal words *that is.*

Practice 2

*In the sentences below, circle the **signal word** or words and write a definition of the underlined word.*

1. A house that is constructed in standard sections that can be easily shipped to and assembled on your property is called a <u>prefabricated</u> house.

   Prefabricated means _____

2. Wanda was considered <u>egocentric</u> or self-centered and selfish by her classmates.

   Egocentric means _____

3. Some diseases are <u>contagious</u>, such as measles and chicken pox, which are transmitted by direct or indirect contact with an infected person.

   Contagious means _____

4. Mothers usually want their children to practice proper <u>etiquette</u>. For example, they want them to be polite to teachers, to chew with their mouths closed, and to show respect to older people.

   Etiquette means _____

5. The word *race* is a <u>homonym</u>, which means that it is one of two words that have the same spelling and pronunciation but different meanings.

   Homonym means _____

Contrast

You will find that writers often let you know what a word means by describing behaviors, actions, or thoughts that are different from or in direct contrast to the meaning of the unfamiliar word. Suppose you come across this sentence, "The teacher was an <u>optimistic</u> person; he rarely expected the students' work to turn out badly." When you read the last part of this sentence, you can figure out that an optimistic person is the opposite of one who expects events to go wrong. You could then define *optimistic* as describing someone who expects events in life to turn out well.

Practice 3

For the sentences below, write the meaning of the underlined word using the contrast clues.

1. The female basketball player was quite tall; she could not shop in the petite clothing department.

   Petite means _____

2. The older brother thought his little sister was a pest, unlike his little brother who never annoyed him.

   Pest means _____

3. Marvin was apprehensive about flying, whereas his friend Juan had no anxiety about getting on the plane.

   Apprehensive means _____

4. Elliott was respectful to his grandparents, unlike his brother who was contemptuous of them.

   Contemptuous means _____

5. The national test in mathematics was developed by a panel rather than by one person.

   Panel means _____

Print Symbol Strategy

In the preceding section, you began to learn to use **context strategies** to learn the meaning of new words. Sometimes writers make it easier for you to learn the meaning of words by actually marking the meaning of a word for you. That is, they use punctuation such as dashes (—), brackets ([]), parentheses, or commas to set off the meaning of the difficult word. If you recognize what the writer is doing and can identify the meaning of a word within the punctuation, then you have learned the **print symbol strategy.**

Consider the sentence, "The man lost all of his <u>investments</u>, the money he had paid in premiums, when the insurance company went bankrupt." In this sentence the commas set off or mark the words that explain *investment*. In this context, *investment* means an amount of money.

Practice 4

*In the following sentences, use the **text punctuations** (parentheses, dashes, or commas) to guide you to the meaning of the underlined word. Then, write the meaning of the underlined word.*

1. Adolph Hitler became a <u>tyrant</u>—a ruler who exercised power in a cruel, harsh manner.

   Tyrant means _____

2. The value of the house had <u>depreciated</u> (decreased in value because of age and wear).

   Depreciated means _____

3. When signing a contract, the most important facts to <u>verify</u>, to check the truth of, are those that might lead to legal difficulties.

   Verify means _____

4. During the war, military <u>recruitment</u> (enrollment of men in the armed forces) decreased the labor supply for manufacturing jobs.

   Recruitment means _____

5. The <u>rabble</u>, that angry mob, threatened the policemen who were guarding the stores.

   Rabble means _____

Word Parts Strategy

You have probably heard the terms *prefix, suffix,* and *root* many times. You may remember that a **prefix** is a group of letters before the **root** or main part of a word and that a **suffix** is a group of letters at the end of the **root** word. Prefixes, suffixes, and roots are useful because they have definitions that can help you figure out the meaning of the entire word. If you see the word *uninteresting,* and you know that "interesting" means holding your attention and that "un" means not, you will quickly realize that "uninteresting" refers to something that does not hold your attention.

To use **word parts** to figure out the meaning of words, you must memorize their meanings. In this chapter, you have to memorize several word part lists. Once you have done that, you can combine their meaning with other **context clues** to help you learn the meaning of many new words.

Prefixes

Read and memorize the following list of word parts. Then, in the practice that follows, use their meanings and the other strategies you have learned to find the meanings of the underlined words.

Prefix	Meaning	Sample
mono	alone, one	monotone
re	again, back	review
de	remove, reverse	declassify
intra	within	intramural
in	into	inside
inter	between	intervene
pre	before	precede
post	after	postscript
anti	opposite, against	antiwar
un	not, to do the opposite	untrue
dis	not, no	distrust
super	above	superstar
uni	one	unicycle

Practice 5

*Using the previous list of **prefixes** that you memorized, find the meaning of the underlined word in each sentence. Write the meaning in the space provided.*

1. The teacher <u>dismissed</u> the class early yesterday.

   _____

2. Greek gods and goddesses are seen as <u>superhuman</u>.

   _____

3. A <u>unicycle</u> is more difficult to ride than a bicycle.

   _____

4. Traffic moves at high speeds on <u>interstate</u> highways.

   _____

5. Most Americans, because they are married to only one person at a time, are <u>monogamous</u>.

   _____

6. The garbage that had been outside the house for two weeks began to <u>decompose</u>.

   _____

7. The researcher discovered the <u>antidote</u> for the poisonous snake bite.

   _____

8. Today <u>postsurgical</u> treatment can be given at home.

   _____

9. The <u>pregame</u> show begins at noon.

   _____

10. There was serious <u>unrest</u> among the prisoners.

   _____

Practice 6

*Use the **prefixes** you have memorized and the **context** of the sentence to write the meaning of the underlined word in each sentence.*

1. Marcus took the <u>antibiotic</u> drug to prevent an infection from the tick bite.

   _____

2. The new governor, who barely won the election, headed a very <u>unstable</u> government.

   _____

3. Hopes for world peace were high as the <u>disarmament</u> conference began.

   _____

4. A major company finds it harder to become a <u>monopoly</u> today than it would have 50 years ago because there are government regulations against exclusive manufacture of a product.

   _____

5. Anna thought that her beauty <u>detracted</u> from her intelligence.

   _____

6. The delivery man placed the package at the <u>posterior</u> door instead of the front door.

   _____

7. The patient needs an <u>intravenous</u> blood transfusion.

   _____

8. David acquired new <u>insight</u> about various religions in the philosophy course.

   _____

9. The <u>postmortem</u> examination of the body proved that a stroke was the cause of death.

   _____

10. The <u>preliminary</u> meetings did not begin on time. The heavy rains caused many individuals to arrive late.

_____

_____

Suffixes

Read and memorize the following list. Then use these **suffixes,** the previously learned prefixes, and your other vocabulary strategies to write the meaning of the underlined words in the practice that follows.

Suffix	*Meaning*	*Sample*
able, ible	capable or worthy of a specific action, inclined to a specific action	debatable responsible blamable
al	of or pertaining to	parental
ance, ence	state or condition	dependence variance
er	one that performs action	swimmer
ly	like, resembling recurring at specified time	sisterly hourly
hood	condition, state group sharing a quality	manhood sisterhood
ic	of or pertaining to	problematic
ify	to make	beautify
ion	action or process	nutrition
ious, ous	state or condition, full of	joyous conscious
ite	resident of, follower of rock, mineral	Israelite graphite
ment	action, process, result of an action	argument
or	state, quality, activity	behavior
y	characterized by, like, to some degree, tending	sleepy

Practice 7

*Use the **suffixes** you have memorized; find the meaning of the underlined word in each sentence and write it below.*

1. Looking back at his life, the old man realized that his teenage behavior was <u>objectionable</u> to his parents.

   _____

2. The young actor gave a <u>masterly</u> performance in his first appearance in a Shakespearean play.

   _____

3. Jon worked as a <u>choreographer</u> for the American Ballet Company.

   _____

4. Even though Hitler's demands were met, the policy of <u>appeasement</u> did not prevent World War II.

   _____

5. After the breakup of the Soviet Union, <u>nationhood</u> became very important to various groups formerly under the USSR's control.

   _____

6. The enormous <u>meteorite</u> made a large hole in the ground when it fell from the sky to earth.

   _____

7. The <u>approachable</u> teacher made the students feel so comfortable that they were not at all hesitant to express their ideas.

   _____

8. When Jessica learned that she graduated first in her class, her graduation day, already important, became a <u>momentous</u> occasion.

   _____

9. The lawyer will <u>notify</u> the family when the case against the robber will begin in court.

_____

10. The <u>emergence</u> of buds on the trees is often one of the first signs of spring.

_____

Practice 8

Use the preceding list of **suffixes** and the **context** to write the meaning of the underlined word in each of the following sentences. Write the meaning in the space provided after each sentence.

1. Most adolescents go through a struggle for <u>independence</u> from their parents.

_____

2. The student's performance was so <u>commendable</u> that his teacher praised him frequently.

_____

3. Historians often present events in a <u>chronological</u> order.

_____

4. Today's college students are often said to <u>embody</u> the "me first" generation.

_____

5. The sorority's coat of arms is <u>emblematic</u> of its ideal.

_____

6. The <u>navigator</u> tells the driver when and where to turn in a road car race.

_____

7. The state of New York was late in approving the new constitution; it was the last state to <u>ratify</u> it.

_____

8. <u>Verification</u> of your age is necessary to obtain your first driver's license.

_____

9. The painter's work was of the <u>classic</u> school; he did not paint modern designs.

_____

10. The <u>immensity</u> of the new apartment complex was overwhelming.

_____

Root Words

Read and memorize the following list. Then use the other **word parts** that you have learned, as well as the **context,** to write the meanings of the underlined words in the following practice exercises.

Root Word	Meaning	Sample
aud	hear	auditory
capit	head	capital
cur	to run	concurrent
cycle	circle	motorcycle
equ	equal	equation
ethno	race	ethnology
flu	flow	influence
geo	earth	geography
patho	disease, suffering	pathology
pend	hang	appendix
sens, sent	feel, think	sensual, resentment
temp	time	contemporary

Practice 9

*Use the **root words** you have memorized to find the meaning of the underlined word in each sentence. Then write it below each sentence.*

1. Our end of the year dinner consisted of <u>ethnic</u> foods such as kielbasa and pasta.

   _____

2. Under <u>equitable</u> distribution laws, a divorcing couple must share all their assets equally.

   _____

3. Her infection kept <u>recurring</u> until the appropriate antibiotic was found.

   _____

4. The high school boy took a <u>circuitous</u> route home because he did not want his parents to see his report card.

   _____

5. Even after serving a long prison term, the <u>psychopath</u> could not be released. The prison psychiatrist thought that he could not be trusted within society because he was still mentally ill.

   _____

6. Mary spoke French so <u>fluently</u> that many Parisians thought that she was born in France.

   _____

7. The <u>caption</u> of the photograph explained what the ceremony was about.

   _____

8. <u>Cognitive</u> ability depends on how much you are able to learn. Some people know much more than others.

   _____

9. When the club unexpectedly honored Mr. Morgan, he was forced to speak <u>extemporaneously</u> because he did not have time to prepare a formal statement.

_____

10. One part of town was reserved for people who could not pay their bills. It was called the debtors' <u>sector</u>.

_____

Practice 10

*Use all your **vocabulary strategies** to figure out the meaning of the underlined word in each sentence. Write the meaning in the space provided.*

1. Her date gave the dinner bill such a <u>cursory</u> glance that he did not realize the waiter had made a mistake in the restaurant's favor.

_____

2. It is unfortunate that in today's world, there are still people who are so <u>ethnocentric</u> that they believe they belong to a master race.

_____

3. Witnesses were asked to <u>recapitulate</u> the events that led to the accident. The police hoped that by going over what happened before the crash, they would be able to determine who was at fault.

_____

4. Mary was <u>cognizant</u> of the fact that she was a victim of sexual harassment, and she told her supervisor about it.

_____

5. The <u>cyclical</u> weather patterns of the past seemed to indicate that the approaching winter would be very cold and snowy.

_____

6. You should keep all your expense records for seven years be-cause the Internal Revenue Service can <u>audit</u> your tax returns over that period of time.

_____

7. A <u>geocyclic</u> diagram of the Earth's movement around the Sun is very helpful to astronomers who want to keep track of how the Earth revolves.

_____

8. Poor Jim worked for his father-in-law for five years before his wife could <u>influence</u> her father to give him a raise.

_____

9. When putting together ingredients for a recipe, the chef was careful to use <u>equivalent</u> wet and dry measures.

_____

10. The homeless men were so <u>pathetic</u>. They had to sleep in the cold streets during the winter. You could sense their suffering.

_____

_____

Dictionary Strategies

Dictionaries can be very useful tools because there are in-stances when using **context** and **word part strategies** are not suf-ficient to learn the meaning of a new word. However, your **vocabulary game plan** should not be to look up every unfamiliar word in the dictionary. If you do this, you will lose the meaning of your text. When you cannot figure out the meaning of a word and you realize that its meaning is essential to understanding what you are reading, check for a **glossary** in your textbook. If there is none, _then_ use the dictionary.

It is important to own a dictionary published within the last ten years because new words are placed in the dictionary periodi-cally. Also, it is a good idea to own two dictionaries. One should be a hardcover standard dictionary to use in the dorm or at home, and the other should be a paperback dictionary to use in class.

In this section, you will learn or review the typical dictionary entry so that you can use your dictionary strategies quickly and efficiently.

Information in a Short Dictionary Entry

Each word in the dictionary has an entry, which is presented in the same sequence and tells you the answer to many questions about the word. But each dictionary may present information in a slightly different sequence, so be sure to check the front of your dictionary for an explanation of its order of entries. Consider the following short dictionary entry from *The American Heritage College Dictionary, Third Edition*:

> **fear less** (fîr′lĭs) *adj.* Having no fear; brave. — fear′less-ly *adv.* — fear′less-ness *n.*

This entry or any entry tells you at least five important facts about the word:

1. The number of **syllables** in the word. The division of a word into syllables can help you pronounce and spell a word, as well as know where to divide a word when typing or writing.

2. The **spelling** of the word. In this case, there is only one correct spelling. If there were other acceptable spellings, they would follow the entry word.

3. The **pronunciation** of the word. The letters and symbols found inside the parentheses tell you how to pronounce the word. There is a key at the bottom of each dictionary page that tells you how each letter or group of letters sounds. For example, in *fearless,* the "ear" is pronounced as "ir" as in *pier,* and the "e" in *less* is pronounced as in *pit.* The heavy black mark (′) is called an accent. The accent mark tells you which syllable to stress or emphasize when saying the word.

4. The **part of speech** that the word can be used as is shown by the abbreviation in italics. *Fearless* can only be used as an adjective (describes a noun or pronoun), abbreviated as "adj." If you want to use it as an adverb (modifies a verb, an adjective, or another adjective), abbreviated as "adv.," you must change the form to *fearlessly.* If you want to use it as a noun (name of a person, place, or thing), abbreviated as "n.," you must change the form to *fearlessness.* It is important to use the correct form of a word to insure that a sentence makes sense.

5. The **meaning** of the word. The definition of the word is written after the part of speech. In this entry, there is only one meaning. Meanings are numbered. The first entry is usually the most common, or preferred meaning.

Practice 11

*Find the following words in your **dictionary** and answer the questions about them.*

1. horselaugh

   a. As what part of speech can this word be used?

   _____

   b. Is this entry spelled as one word or two?

   _____

   c. What kind of laugh is a horselaugh?

   _____

2. bucktooth

   a. What two parts of speech can this word be used as?

   _____

   b. What does it mean to say that a person has a bucktooth?

   _____

   c. In this sentence, write the correct form of the entry word:

   The _____ boy had a lisp.

Information in a Long Dictionary Entry

If you wanted to know the meaning of *buoyant* and looked it up in the dictionary, you would find an entry that said:

buoy ant (boi'ənt, boo'yənt) *adj.* 1. Capable of floating or keeping things afloat. 2. Animated; sprightly; cheerful. [Sp. *boyante,* pr. part. of *boyar,* to refloat a boat OFr. *boie*] **buoy'ant ly** *adv.* (from *The American Heritage College Dictionary, Third Edition*)

This longer entry, in addition to the five facts found in the preceding main entry, tells you:

1. The acceptable **pronunciations** of the word.

2. The **multiple meanings** of the word. Many words in the dictionary have more than one meaning. In this dictionary, as in most dictionaries, the most common meaning is given first.

3. A **brief history** of the word from one language to another. Abbreviations may be used to refer to the languages. For example, in this entry, "Sp." refers to Spanish, and "OFr." refers to Old French.

Additional Dictionary Information

There are several other dictionary terms that you should be familiar with so that you can quickly understand any dictionary entry. Additional terms that are frequently included in a dictionary entry are:

- *Archaic,* which means that the word or the meaning was used in a much earlier time but is not used today. For example, "Where wilt thou go?" would be a question you might find in a Shakespearean play, but today you would not hear or write "wilt" or "thou."
- *Informal, Colloquial,* or *Slang,* which indicates that a word is used in casual conversation or in a particular region but it is inappropriate in formal speech or writing. For example, when the word *bad* is used to mean "very good" or "great," it is considered slang, as is the word *goes* when used to mean "say" or "said."
- Subject terms, such as *Biology, Mathematics,* or *Music,* which tell you that the particular meaning is correct when used in an area of study. For example, only when studying music does *harmony* mean the study of the structure, progression, and relation of chords.
- *Nonstandard,* which refers to the fact that the use of the particular word is not acceptable by most speakers of the

English language. *Ain't,* meaning am not, is a common example of a nonstandard word.

- *Synonyms,* which precede a word or words that have similar meanings to the entry word. The word *beautiful* usually has a list of synonyms such as lovely, pretty, handsome, comely, fair. The entry will also tell you how each contrasts with the entry word. Each of the synonyms has a slightly different meaning than the entry word and cannot be used interchangeably.
- *Vulgar,* which signals that this word or expression is considered insulting or crude and should not be used in speaking or writing.

Practice 12

*Six words are listed below. Look each word up in your **dictionary** and use the information you find to answer the questions about the entry for each word.*

1. *angling*
2. *angry*
3. *angular*
4. *anhydrous*
5. *animal*
6. *animalcule*

1. Questions about the entry *angling:*

   a. What part of speech is the word *angling?*

   _____

   b. What equipment is used when angling?

   _____

   c. "The boy was angling for a new car from his father." What is the meaning of *angling* in this sentence?

   _____

2. Questions about the entry *angry:*

   a. What is the most common meaning of the word *angry?*

   _____

b. What does "angry sore" mean?

_____

c. Write a sentence using the word *angriest.*

_____

_____

3. Questions about the entry *angular:*

a. What part of speech is the word *angular?*

_____

b. Use the word *angular* in a sentence.

_____

_____

c. What ending must be added when you use the word *angular* as an adverb? _____ As a noun? _____

d. What other meanings does this word have in addition to angles (when used in mathematics and buildings)?

_____

e. What is the origin of this word?

_____

4. Questions about the entry *anhydrous:*

a. What is the meaning of the word *anhydrous?*

_____

b. What does the prefix "an" mean?

_____

c. What does the root "hydrous" mean?

_____

d. What is the origin of the word?

_____

5. Questions about the word *animal:*

   a. What does the Latin word *animal* mean?

   _____

   b. What are two characteristics of an organism classified as animal?

   _____

   _____

   c. What is another meaning of *animal?*

   _____

6. Questions about the entry *animalcule:*

   a. How is the "cule" pronounced?

   _____

   b. What is an example of an animalcule?

   _____

Multiple Meanings

You have probably noticed that many of the words in the dictionary entries have more than one meaning. In fact, many words have **multiple meanings.** An example is the word *context*, which has two meanings.

1. The sentence or passage in which a word occurs, which often specifies its meaning.
2. The situation in which a particular event takes place.

When you read this carefully, you understand that the first meaning refers to the use of the word in the **context strategies** that you have learned in this chapter. However, in the sentence "Jake's screaming and fighting was inappropriate in the context of the classroom," the meaning of the word is found in the second definition.

As helpful as a dictionary is, it cannot tell you which meaning is correct for the word in a particular sentence or paragraph. You must read all the definitions and decide which fits the context of your reading. In many cases, you can make this decision by substituting the various definitions for the word in the context.

Consider the word *wave* in the sentence, "Maria's hair fell down her back in long waves." Three meanings for *wave* are:

1. To move the air up and down
2. To make a motion with an up-and-down or back-and-forth movement of the hand
3. To curl

If you insert each meaning for the word *wave* into the context, you will quickly decide that the third one is the correct meaning in this sentence. You could also make this choice by thinking carefully about which meaning most closely matches the context of the sentence. You would quickly discard the second meaning because the sentence describes Maria's hair, not her hands. The first meaning is a possibility because hair can move in the air, but the third meaning is a better choice because hair frequently curves or curls.

Practice 13

*Carefully read the **multiple meanings** of each word. Then read each sentence that contains the word and write the letter of the correct meaning in the blank next to it.*

1. *wear*
   a. To have on or put on clothes
   b. To carry on one's body
   c. To exhibit
   d. To display (colors), as a ship
   e. To use up by long or hard use
   f. To fatigue or tire

   _____ 1. The opposition's constant guarding <u>wore</u> down the home team player's energy.

   _____ 2. The cowboy always <u>wears</u> his gun.

_____ 3. The little boy <u>wore</u> holes in his blanket because he carried it everywhere he went.

_____ 4. Amanda <u>wore</u> a beautiful smile on her birthday.

_____ 5. The hockey team proudly <u>wears</u> the school colors of red and black.

2. *cry*
   a. To make sobbing sounds expressing sorrow or pain
   b. To call loudly
   c. To make a sound or call of an animal (i.e., cry like a wolf)
   d. To demand action or solution for a problem

   _____ 1. The coyote's <u>cry</u> reverberated across the desert.

   _____ 2. The widow <u>cried</u> for hours after her husband's death.

   _____ 3. The people in the protest parade <u>cried</u> out for justice.

   _____ 4. Mother's <u>cry</u> for us to come to dinner could be heard for several blocks.

3. *rule*
   a. Authority giving power to govern
   b. A regulation for conduct
   c. A usual or customary behavior
   d. A statement telling what is true most of the time
   e. A standard procedure for solving mathematical problems

   _____ 1. The <u>rule</u> of the president is established by the Constitution.

   _____ 2. The <u>rule</u> for changing a word to past tense is to add "ed."

   _____ 3. Until recently, the <u>rule</u> seemed to be that boys called girls for dates.

   _____ 4. The <u>rule</u> in our college is that there is no smoking in any building.

   _____ 5. The Pythagorean theorem or <u>rule</u> is hard to learn.

4. *shock*
   a. A violent collision or impact

b. A sudden emotional disturbance

c. A severe insult to one's sense of decency

d. A massive physiologic reaction to bodily trauma

e. The muscular spasm caused by an electric current passing through the body

f. A thick, bushy mass

_____ 1. The young boy's sudden death <u>shocked</u> his friend.

_____ 2. When John stuck his metal knife into the outlet, he received a <u>shock</u>.

_____ 3. The elderly man still had a <u>shock</u> of white hair.

_____ 4. The man's cursing <u>shocked</u> the store owner.

_____ 5. When the two freight trains collided, the <u>shock</u> could be felt several miles away.

5. *peak*

a. A tapering, projecting point

b. The pointed summit of a mountain

c. The part of a hat that sticks out

d. The narrow portion of a ship's hull at the bow or stern

e. To become sickly or pale

_____ 1. After the roller coaster ride, the boy looked very <u>peaked</u>.

_____ 2. The climbers reached the <u>peak</u> of Mount Everest.

_____ 3. The <u>peak</u> of the boy's cap was in the back instead of the front.

_____ 4. The women jumped from the <u>peak</u> of the cruise liner.

_____ 5. The <u>peak</u> of the church seemed to blow about in the breeze.

Practice 14

*Below are several words that have **multiple meanings.** Write as many definitions as you can think of for each word. Then check your dictionary for additional meanings.*

1. *plane*

   Meanings I know: _____

   _____

   Meanings I learned from the dictionary: _____

   _____

   _____

2. *part*

   Meanings I know: _____

   _____

   Meanings I learned from the dictionary: _____

   _____

   _____

3. *burn*

   Meanings I know: _____

   _____

   Meanings I learned from the dictionary: _____

   _____

   _____

4. *passage*

   Meanings I know: _____

   _____

   Meanings I learned from the dictionary: _____

   _____

   _____

5. *golden*

Meanings I know: _____

_____

Meanings I learned from the dictionary: _____

_____

_____

_____

Review: Vocabulary Strategies

To find the meaning of unfamiliar words, use:

1. Context Strategies
   - Look for **explanations** or **examples** of the meaning of the word in the sentence or nearby sentences.
   - Look for **signal words** that let you know that a word is to be defined. Some signal words are *such as, is called,* and *for example.*
   - Look for **contrast** words that describe ideas or actions that are different from the word.

2. Print Symbols
   - Find the **punctuation marks** that set off the definition of the word.

3. Word Parts
   - Learn common **prefixes, suffixes, roots,** and their meanings. Use them to help figure out new words.

4. The Dictionary
   - Know how the dictionary is organized.
   - Use it when other strategies do not work.

*Remember: Many words have **multiple meanings.** Be sure to define a word as it is used in the context.*

*Write the answer to the following questions based on what you have learned about how to use the **vocabulary strategies** to figure out the meaning of words.*

1. Why is it important to use vocabulary strategies before looking words up in the dictionary?

_____

_____

2. How can knowing the meaning of prefixes and suffixes help you learn the meaning of new words?

_____

_____

3. Why is it important to define a word within the context in which it is used?

_____

_____

4. How can you choose a correct meaning of a word when multiple meanings are given in the dictionary?

_____

_____

Remembering New Words

It can be difficult to remember new words and their meanings because you may not use them frequently. Yet most of your college courses will require that you **remember and use many new vocabulary words** accurately. Thus, you need to develop a game plan for remembering new words. In this section, you learn several strategies that can help you build a large memory bank of new vocabulary words. These strategies are more effective than saying or writing a word and its definition(s) many times because they require you to think about the word. The more you think about and use a word, the more likely you are to remember it.

Predict, Verify, and Record

When you see an unfamiliar word, use the strategies you have learned to **predict** the meaning of the word. When you are reading quickly and for pleasure, this game plan is usually sufficient. However, if you are reading material for a college course or are learning a new skill at work, you may need to **verify** or determine the accuracy of your prediction of the word's meaning by using the textbook glossary or your dictionary.

You should set up a vocabulary section in your notebook for each of your college courses. In this section, you need to **record** the word and the textbook or dictionary definition paraphrased, or written in your own words. It is much easier to remember the definition of a new word when you translate or paraphrase it into words that you clearly understand.

To help you learn and remember new words, you could make a chart such as the one below, which a student used for a European history course. You will notice that rather than just writing the word, she copied the sentence in which the word was used. This helped her explore the meaning of the word in context and to decide which meaning of several in the dictionary was correct for the particular textbook usage. She also thought about the strategies she used to help her predict the meaning of the word. Then she verified her prediction in the dictionary and recorded a paraphrased version of that meaning in her own words.

Course: European History—Chapter 2

Sentence	Definition
One reason the people of France were so unified was their strong feeling of nationalism.	devotion to the interests or culture of a particular country

Practice 15

Use your knowledge of vocabulary and dictionary strategies to **predict, verify,** *and* **record** *the meaning of the underlined words from a European history course.*

Sentence	Definition
1. Charles II was <u>restored</u> to the throne after his family's long absence.	
2. People bought clothing in their country because of the expensive <u>tariff</u> they had to pay on imported clothing.	
3. Louis XIV <u>persecuted</u> Protestants instead of allowing them the same freedom as Catholic church members.	
4. There was a struggle toward a new political <u>synthesis</u>, in the form of alliances between nations.	
5. The seventeenth century inherited the advances in thought made possible by science, humanism, and the <u>Reformation</u>, the loosening of religious restraints.	

Practice 16

Recording or writing about new words in the **predict, verify, and record strategy** will help you remember the meaning of new words because you will be writing and thinking about the words. You can then use your vocabulary charts to review and study for tests. Simply cover all but the sentence section of the chart and say the meaning of the word; then check or verify the correctness of your answer.

Associate and Visualize

Sometimes new words are so unfamiliar that students have a very difficult time recalling their meaning or remembering the word when given the definition. If you are having difficulty with new words, you should practice the use of **association** and **visualization.**

Association means choosing another common word to go with or associate with a new vocabulary word. For example, if you needed to remember the word *oxalis,* you could associate it with the similar sounding word *ox. Ox* would be the **key word.**

Visualization means to see a picture of the word. In this case, you could visualize or picture the ox and then visualize the ox eating clover-like plants. Clover-like plants are the meaning of **oxalis.**

The three steps to remembering or recalling the meaning of any word are:

1. Think of the keyword.

2. Think of the picture of the keyword.

3. Think of what is happening in the picture.

Use Word Cards and Practice

Another way to help you remember difficult words is by using a **word card strategy.** On the front of an index card, write the word and a **pronunciation guide** if you need it. In parentheses below the word, write your **keyword.** On the bottom of the card, write a sentence that describes your **visualization** of the word. On the back of the card, write the **definition** of the word. The front and back of a word card for *oxalis* might look like this:

Front   *Back*

oxalis   äk'sal-əs
(ox)
The ox is eating the clover-like plants.

Oxalis are a variety of clover-like plants that have pink, yellow, or white flowers.

Word cards will be most helpful if you use them on a daily basis until you can easily and quickly recall the meaning of the new word. Use these words in class discussions and study sessions as well.

You should try this **association** and **visualization strategy** on many new words so that you will begin to use it easily. You may or may not need to make word cards, but try the technique several times before you accept or reject it. It is important to use the new strategies that you learn in this book several times to decide if they work for you.

Practice 17

*By working individually or in groups, develop a **keyword** and **visual image** for each of these words from an American history textbook. The first two words have been started as examples for you.*

Word	Key Word	Picture Key Word	What Else?
embargo	bar	a metal bar	big metal bar keeping products out of the country
emancipation	man	a man	a man leaving or being freed from a plantation
charisma			
inauguration			
elite			

Word	Key Word	Picture Key Word	What Else?
oppression			
nullification			
coalition			
tariff			
aligned			

Practice 18

*Select a reading assignment from one of your courses and, on a separate piece of paper, make a **predict, verify,** and **record chart** of new words and word practice cards for those words that are difficult for you to remember.*

Review: Remembering New Words

1. Predict, Verify, and Record

   - **Predict** the meaning of a new word by using context, print notations, and word parts strategies.

   - **Verify,** if necessary, your prediction by checking in the glossary or dictionary.

   - **Record** the meaning of the new word in your own words in your notebook dictionary.

2. Associate and Visualize

   - **Associate** a common word that sounds similar to the new word with the new word.

   - **Visualize** or see a picture of the key word interacting with the definition.

3. Use Word Cards and Practice

   - **Make a Word Card** for any word that you find difficult. Put the word and sentence describing your visual image on the front of the card and the definition on the back of the card.

   - **Practice** by testing yourself using the word card on a daily basis.

Questions about Remembering Vocabulary Strategies

*Write the answer to the following questions based on what you have learned about the strategies that can help you **remember the meanings** of unfamiliar words.*

1. How can you verify your prediction of the meaning of an unfamiliar word?

   _____

   _____

2. Why does writing the meaning of a word in your own words help you remember the meaning of the word?

   _____

   _____

3. Which do you find more helpful: (1) associating and visualizing or (2) keeping notebook dictionaries?

   _____

   Why?_____

   _____

B

Game Plan Review: The Main Idea

In this appendix, you find a summary of all the strategies that you learned in the text. By now you should be comfortable using each of them. We hope that you use this chapter as a handy reference when you want to apply the strategies to the material you are expected to read, understand, and evaluate in your classes.

Previewing a College Textbook

- Read the **title:** What do I think this book is about?
- Check **copyright date:** Am I reading the most recent edition? When was it first published?
- Read the **foreword** and/or **preface:** What is most important about this book?
- Read the **introduction:** How is this book organized?
- Check the **table of contents:** What topics and subtopics are covered in the book? Will this be mostly new to me?
- Look for an **index, glossary,** or **appendix.**

Previewing a Textbook Chapter

Use **TIPS** to preview a textbook chapter or part of a chapter.

T. Read the **T**itle and say or write it in your own words.

I. Read the Introduction and find out the general topics to be covered and the chapter goals and objectives if they are included.

P. Mark the main **P**arts and the subheadings to see how they relate to each other.

S. Read the **S**ummary if there is one. Read the **S**tudy questions. Paraphrase (rewrite) the summary and/or questions in your own words.

Previewing a Reading Selection

Read:

- Title
- Headings, if any
- Introduction, or first paragraph
- First sentence of each paragraph
- Last paragraph
- Visual aids

Developing Questions Before You Read

To develop prereading questions from a textbook chapter:

- When there are main headings, turn the headings into questions.
- When there are no main headings, turn the first sentence of each paragraph into a question.

To develop prereading questions from a textbook chapter:

- Use the TIPS strategy.
- Turn the headings into questions.
- Read the questions at the end of the chapter.

Finding the Main Idea

To find the main idea, ask yourself three questions:

1. What is this text mainly about? (What is the **topic**?)

2. What is the most important point about the topic? (What is the **main,** or **controlling, idea?**)
3. How is the main idea supported or explained? (What are the **details,** or facts?)

Remember: Writers do not always state the main idea. If it is not stated clearly, look at the details and make an inference about the main idea, based on the information given.

State the main, or controlling, idea in your own words so that you will remember it more easily. In longer selections, you will have to look at the main idea of the paragraphs to determine the controlling idea of the entire reading.

Writing to Read and Remember

- Underline or highlight *only* main ideas, supporting details, and signal words.
- Annotate in the margins. Jot down comments, questions, and additional information about the reading.
- Answer your preview questions.

Outlining

- Use the **preview** and **main idea strategies.**
- Use the **underlining** and **annotating strategies.**
- Think and decide which main ideas and details to include in the **outline.**
- Show the **relationship** of the important details to the main ideas and the main ideas to the controlling idea.

Mapping

- Use the **preview** and **main idea strategies.**
- Use the **underlining** and **annotating strategies.**
- Make a **map** by connecting the main ideas and important details related to the topic in a short selection or the controlling idea in a long selection.

Summarizing

- Use the **preview** and **main idea strategies.**
- Use the **underlining** and **annotating strategies.**
- Make a **map** or an **outline.**
- Begin the **summary** with the **controlling idea.**
- Write the main ideas and important details **in your own words.** Keep the sequence of ideas the same as they are in the text.

Game Plan for Before, While, and After You Read

1. **Preview.**
2. Develop three **preview questions.**
3. Find the **main ideas** and **details.** Underline them. Underline signal words.
4. **Annotate** in the margin.
5. Answer your preview questions.
6. Make a **map** or an **outline** of the selection.
7. Write a **summary** of the selection.

Critical Reading

Make Sense of Information

Ask yourself:

- What is this about? (**topic**)
- What is the most important point? (**main idea**)
- What is the issue? (**question to be argued**)
- What is the writer's **point of view?**

Evaluate Information

- Be alert to a writer's argument and reasoning. Decide whether the writer's evidence is truthful, logical, and really supports the information.

Make Informed Decisions about Information

- Separate fact from opinion.

- Make inferences.
- Make notes and take notes.
- Write informed opinions about what you read.

P.A.S. Strategy

Ask yourself:

1. What is the writer's **purpose?**
2. What are his or her **assumptions?**
3. How is the information **supported?**

Comparison/Contrast

1. Set up a double-entry journal.
2. List all the similarities in one column and the differences in the second column.
3. Write a paragraph or short essay using the information. Or put the information into the format that your instructor has specified.

Finding the Meaning of New Vocabulary

Context Strategies

- Look for **explanations** or **examples** of the meaning of the word in the sentence or nearby sentences.
- Look for the **signal words**—*means, meaning, such as, is called, for example*—that let you know that a word is to be defined.
- Look for **contrast words** that describe behaviors, thoughts, or actions that are different from the word.

Print Symbol Strategies

- Find the punctuation marks that set off the definition of the word.

Word Parts

- Learn common prefixes and suffixes and their meanings.
- Use the word parts to help figure out the meaning of a word.

The Dictionary

- Know how the dictionary is organized.
- Use it when other strategies do not work.

Remember: Many words have **multiple meanings.** *Be sure to define a word so that the definition fits the context in which the word is used.*

Remembering New Words

Predict, Verify, and Record

- **Predict** the meaning of a new word by using context, print notations, and word parts strategies.
- **Verify,** if necessary, your prediction by checking in the glossary or dictionary.
- **Record** (write) the meaning of the new word in your own words in your notebook dictionary.

Associate and Visualize

- **Associate** (pair) a common word that sounds similar to the new word with the new word.
- **Visualize** or see a picture of the key word (common word) interacting with the definition.

Use Word Cards and Practice

- Make a **word card** for any word that you find difficult. Put the word and sentence describing your visual image on the front of the card and the definition on the back of the card.
- **Practice** by testing yourself using the word cards on a daily basis.

C

Test-Taking Strategies

The purpose of testing is to see how well you have learned information that was taught during a semester. The reading strategies that you have mastered will help you learn that information. The strategies in this appendix will help you develop test-taking skills; that is, these strategies will help you *show* that you already knew or have learned what you were expected to learn.

Just reading a textbook chapter does not mean that you have learned it. Many students think that by reading something over and over, they will come to know it. This is not true. Reading something over many times will probably make you familiar with information, but if you are asked specific questions about it, you may not be able to give the correct answer.

Consider a test as an opportunity to show what you know. Try not to treat a test as a "do or die" situation. Try to remember that grades are not a measure of your intelligence. They do not indicate your value as a person. Do not give any test power over you. The first effective test-taking strategy is to determine who is the boss—you or the test. Do not exaggerate the importance of any test. Put things in perspective. Many students put tremendous pressure on themselves at exam time. Sometimes they do this because they are not prepared. At other times, they think that if they are not nervous, they will not do well. You *can* become a proficient test taker if you learn how to deal with test material.

The Best General Test Preparation

Test preparation begins with your course outline. On it, your instructor has indicated important topics and material that you will be required to learn about. Read your course outline to get a preview of the information that you will learn during the semester. Then follow the guidelines below:

1. Do your work all semester. This means both classwork and homework.
2. Pay attention to what your instructor says in class. If there is anything that you do not understand, ask for clarification immediately.
3. Get to know your instructor. Take advantage of office hours.
4. Participate in class discussions. Ask questions.
5. Take notes.
6. Develop outlines, maps, and/or summaries of important information, so that when exam time comes, you know what to study. The material will already be familiar to you, and you will know important facts and ideas.

Tip

a. Review material periodically—it will become more and more familiar. There is nothing so frustrating as being faced with what you think is "new" material on a test.

b. Relate new information to information that you already know. When you make connections, you learn the material more easily.

c. When you are assigned a chapter to read, read the study questions first. This will focus your reading.

d. Think about whether your test anxiety is "real"—you know more than you think you do.

Types of Tests

Tests usually fall into two (2) categories:

1. Objective tests
2. Essay tests

Objective Tests

These tests usually require a short, or one word, answer, or they are multiple-choice. To do well on objective tests, you need to know the facts about what you have read. Objective tests do not require you to give an opinion. Here are some strategies to help you do well on objective tests, *provided you have studied.*

Multiple Choice

These kinds of questions begin with a statement and are usually followed by four choices. You need to choose the answer that will correctly complete the statement. Consider the following example:

1. Previewing means
   a. to go over what you have read.
   b. to reread a selection.
   c. to look over a selection before reading.
   d. to annotate the selection.

You probably know what previewing is. However, you might be surprised at how many students get this type of question wrong.

The statement that you are required to complete in multiple-choice tests is called the *stem.* The answers that you need to choose from are called *distractors.* Very often, two or more of the distractors, or choices, might be very close to the correct answer, or the language might be similar enough to confuse you. In the previous example about previewing, students usually get confused between answers "a" and "c"—can you explain why? (The correct answer is "c.")

To do well on multiple-choice tests, you need to read the statement carefully and focus on the choices given. Many of the choices will seem familiar. But only one is correct. Be careful to choose the answer that *best* or *most accurately* completes the statement.

You might think of multiple-choice questions as being true or false. Ask yourself if each choice makes the statement true or false. If more than one seems true, ask yourself which one is the *most* true.

Be careful of choices that state "all of the above." Although this is sometimes a correct choice, you should not choose it without going over the other choices carefully. Too often, students mark this answer without careful consideration of the other choices.

True or False

These can be tricky. Look for clue words like *all, some, most, always, sometimes, usually, many,* and *never.* Remember that very few things are always true or untrue. Consider the following example.

1. All women are feminists. True or False?

Do you know for sure that *all* women are feminists? To know this, you would have to ask every woman in the world if she was a feminist. The answer is false. The clue words should make you think about the truth of the statement.

Fill-In

The best strategy to use when answering this type of question is to make sure that your answer makes sense. Sometimes, you will be given choices. To do really well on fill-in questions, you should know your material backward and forward. If the fill-in requires more than a one-word answer, be brief. State only the fact that completes the answer.

Machine Graded

If your test is going to be graded by machine, use a ruler or index card to make sure that you have answered the question in the correct space. Try not to erase; the machine might pick up your mark. Avoid any stray marks.

Tip

a. Do what you really know first.

b. Try not to change answers unless you are absolutely sure. Your first answer is usually correct.

c. Answer all the questions. Guess if you must. On multiple-choice tests, you have a 25 percent chance of guessing a correct answer if nothing is familiar. On True/False, you have a 50 percent chance of getting an answer right. Remember: Guessing is no substitute for studying!

Essay Exams

Essays need to be organized, whether they are written in class or taken home, and whether they are with or without the help of the textbook. Your instructor is looking for your understanding of the material. How you present your information can be as important as the information itself. You need to organize your answer so that you have a topic sentence, use examples, include important details about the topic, and finish with a logical conclusion.

Essay questions may have more than one part. Students often fail to answer all parts of a question and lose points because of this.

First, you must try to understand the question. Ask yourself, *What information is given?* Then, ask yourself, *What information do I need to supply?* To answer essay questions, you need to know *both* facts and ideas about a topic. Here are some words that signal or tell what the instructors expects you to do in your essay.

1. *Compare/Contrast:* Show both similarities and differences between items.
2. *Describe:* Tell about something. Use question words. Tell what, when, how, and why.
3. *Discuss:* Show the main points about something.
4. *Define:* Give the meaning of a word or phrase.
5. *Explain:* Make something understandable. Give details.
6. *Summarize:* Briefly tell the most important ideas.
7. *Prove:* Show how and why something is correct or incorrect by using facts and details.
8. *Evaluate:* Look at an issue or event from a critical point of view. Discuss strengths and weaknesses and how and why they are important. Examine the writer's point of view. Discuss whether or not you agree with his or her line of reasoning. Double-entry journals are helpful when you need to answer this type of exam question.

Tip

a. After you read the entire question, map or outline the points you wish to include in your answer.

b. Do not try to include all the information that you know about the topic. Use only the information that will answer the question.

c. If you are asked to give your opinion or take a position about an issue, be sure to give facts and examples to back up what you have stated in your answer.

d. Use signal words to clarify your answer. Words such as *therefore* and *because* help to create a smooth, flowing essay.

e. Do not erase. It makes your paper look sloppy. Use a single stroke to cross out anything that you want to omit.

f. If you run out of time, outline or map the rest of your information. You might not get full credit, but sometimes an instructor will give you partial credit.

When the Test Is Announced

Ask your instructor what kind of test it will be so that you can plan your strategy.

Tip

a. Try to predict what questions will be on the test. Make up questions in the test format.

b. It might be a good idea to form study groups—two or more minds are often better than one!

c. Check if the instructor has any old exams available for you to look at. Be careful though. Sometimes there is new information. Do not get lazy if you are able to look at old tests.

At the Test

Be sure that you come on time—a little early is best. Be sure to bring all the supplies that you will need. These might include pens, pencils, a ruler, etc. Listen carefully to any verbal instructions that might be given.

Tip

a. Read the directions *very* carefully.

b. Preread the entire exam. This will help you focus on what you can easily answer.

c. Budget your time according to which questions are worth the most points. Give the most time to the most important parts of the exam.

d. Check your answers. Correct any errors you find. Sometimes you find answers in other questions.

e. Ignore students who finish quickly. Do not allow their quick finish to cause you to lose confidence and rush through the test.

Credits *(continued)*

Page 73. Charles P. Pierce, excerpt from "Soul on Ice" from *Gentlemen's Quarterly*, March 1993. Reprinted with permission of the author. Charles P. Pierce is a writer-at-large for *Gentlemen's Quarterly*. Page 109.

Page 76. Anita E. Woolfolk, "American Families Today," from *Educational Psychology*. Copyright © 1995 by Allyn and Bacon. Reprinted/Adapted by permission. Pages 87–88.

Page 76. Richard H. Beatty, excerpt from "The Purpose of a Resume," from *The Complete Jobs Search Book*. Copyright © 1988. Reprinted by permission of John Wiley & Sons, Inc. Page 11.

Page 79. Excerpt from *Open Water Diver's Manual*. Copyright © 1989 by Concept Systems, Inc. Reprinted with permission. Page 11.

Page 81. William Kephart and William Zellner, "Gypsies," from *Extraordinary Groups*, 5th ed. Copyright © 1994. Reprinted with permission of St. Martin's Press, Inc. Page 88.

Page 83. Claudia Bowe, "Are You Sick of Those Phony Sweepstakes?" from *New Woman*, April 1993.

Page 86. Beth Hess, Elizabeth W. Markson, and Peter J. Stein, "Latinos," excerpt from *Sociology*, 4th ed. Copyright © 1991 by Allyn and Bacon. Reprinted/Adapted by permission. Page 89.

Page 93. Excerpt from *Open Water Diver's Manual*. Copyright © 1989, Concept Systems, Inc. Reprinted with permission. Page 88.

Page 93. Richard Lederer, excerpt from *Crazy English—The Ultimate Joy Ride through Our Language*. Copyright © 1989, Richard Lederer. Published by Pocket Books division of Simon and Schuster. Pages 22 & 23.

Page 95. Theo Haimann, William G. Scott, and Patrick E. Connor, excerpt from *Management*, 5th ed. Copyright © 1985, Houghton Mifflin. Page 5.

Page 95. Paul Leedy, excerpt from *Practical Research Planning 5th ed.* Copyright © 1989, Macmillan Publishing Company. Page 341.

Page 97. M. Bassis, R. Gelles, and A. Levine, "American Democracy," excerpt from *Sociology: An Introduction*, 4th ed. Copyright © 1991 by McGraw-Hill, Inc. Reprinted with permission. Pages 478–479.

Page 99. Robert K. Gerver and Richard J. Sgroi, excerpt reproduced from *Dollars and Sense: Problem Solving Strategies in Consumer Mathematics*, with the permission of South-Western Educational Publishing, a division of International Thomson Publishing Inc. Copyright © 1989 by South-Western Educational Publishing. All rights reserved. Pages 2 & 3.

Page 100. M. Bassis, R. Gelles, and A. Levine, "Illiterate? Who, U.S.?" excerpt from *Sociology: An Introduction*, 4th ed. Copyright © 1991 by McGraw-Hill, Inc. Reprinted with permission. Pages 428–429.

Page 105. Harold H. Eibling, Carlton L. Jackson, and Vito Perrone, *Two Centuries of Progress*, 2nd ed. Copyright © 1977 by Macmillan/McGraw-Hill. Reprinted by permission of Glencoe/McGraw-Hill. Pages 13 & 16.

Page 108. Charles B. Simone, "Smoking—A Slow Suicide," from *Cancer and Nutrition*. Copyright © 1992. Published by Avery Publishing Group, Inc., Garden City Park, N. Y. Reprinted by permission. Pages 151–153.

Page 113. Mirta Ojito, "Culture Clash: Foreign Parents, American Child Rearing," from *New York Times*, page 3, June 29, 1997. Copyright © 1997 by The New York Times Company. Reprinted by permission.

Page 120. Samuel E. Wood and Ellen Green Wood, excerpt from "Gender Differences in Aggression," from *The World of Psychology*. Copyright © 1996 by Allyn and Bacon. Reprinted/Adapted by permission. Pages 405–406.

Page 123. "A Nation of Beepers," from *Kiplinger's Personal Finance Magazine*, November 1993. Copyright © 1993 by the Kiplinger Washington Editors, Inc. Page 17.

Page 124. Samuel E. Wood and Ellen Green Wood, excerpt from "Gender Stereotyping—Who Wins? Who Loses?" from *The World of Psychology*. Copyright © 1996 by Allyn and Bacon. Reprinted/Adapted by permission. Page 408.

Page 125. Rod K. Plotnik, "Risk Factors for Becoming an Alcoholic," from *Introduction to Psychology*, by R. Plotnik. Copyright © 1996, 1993 Brooks/Cole Publishing Company, Pacific Grove, CA 93950, a division of International Thomson Publishing Inc. By permission of the publisher. Page 195.

Page 127. John R. Conklin, "A Function of Education: Socialization," from *Sociology: An Introduction*. Copyright © 1984 by Macmillan Publishing Co. Pages 273–274.

Page 128. Karen O'Connor and Larry J. Sabato, "Frederick Douglass," from *American Government*. Copyright © 1997 by Allyn and Bacon. Reprinted/Adapted by permission. Page 187.

Page 132. C. J. Vimont, "Heartening Health News," from *First for Women*, November 1993. Copyright © 1993. Page 20.

Page 134. "Alternative Medicine," in *NEA TODAY*, November 1993. Copyright © 1993, The National Education Association of the United States. Reprinted by permission. Page 34.

Page 135. Norman K. Risjord, "Mayan Culture," from *America: A History of the United States, 2nd ed. Vol. I: To 1877*. Copyright © 1988. Reprinted by permission of Prentice-Hall, Englewood Cliffs, NJ. Page 3.

Page 136. Manuel J. Smith, "Depression," from *When I Say No, I Feel Guilty*. Copyright © 1975, Manuel J. Smith, Bantam Doubleday Dell, The Dial Press. Pages 10–11.

Page 137. William Ebenstein and Edwin Fogelman, excerpt from "Profit" from *Today's Isms: Communism, Fascism, Capitalism, Socialism*. Copyright © 1985 by Prentice-Hall. Pages 131–132.

Page 145. Norman K. Risjord, "Amelia Bloomer and Women's Dress Reform," from *America: A History of the United States, 2nd ed. Vol. I: To 1877*. Copyright © 1988. Reprinted by permission of Prentice-Hall, Englewood Cliffs, NJ. Pages 319–320.

Page 147. "Drowsiness and Driving," from *Defensive Driving Course Guide*. Copyright © 1992 National Safety Council. Page 16.

Page 149. Gary S. Green, "The Concept of Occupational Crime," from *Occupational Crime*. (Chicago: Nelson-Hall, 1990) Copyright © 1990. Reprinted with permission. Page 3.

Page 154. Samuel E. Wood and Ellen Green Wood, "Lifestyle Patterns in Adulthood," from *The World of Psychology*. Copyright © 1996 by Allyn and Bacon. Reprinted/Adapted by permission. Pages 340–341.

Page 159. Jay Diamond and Gerald Pintel, "Packaging," from *Principles of Marketing, 4th ed.* by Diamond/Pintel, © 1994. Reprinted by permission of Prentice-Hall, Inc., Upper Saddle River, NJ. Pages 220–222 & 237.

Page 166. Samuel E. Wood and Ellen Green Wood, "Eating Disorders—The Tyranny of the Scale," from *The World of Psychology*. Copyright © 1996 by Allyn and Bacon. Reprinted/Adapted by permission. Pages 393–394.

Page 171. Jane Stern, "The Big Fat Lie." Originally appeared in *Allure*, September 1993. Copyright © 1993 Jane Stern. Reprinted with permission of Jane Stern.

Page 183. Exercise excerpt adapted from "Lifeline," in *USA TODAY*, November 8, 1993. Copyright © 1993, USA TODAY. Reprinted with permission.

Page 192. Lead poisoning excerpt adapted from "Get the Lead Out," editorial in *USA TODAY*, May 12, 1993. Copyright © 1993, USA TODAY. Reprinted with permission. Sec. A, Page 12.

Page 193. "Tougher Standards for College Athletes," from an editorial, *New York Post*, November 8, 1993. Reprinted by permission. Page 16.

Page 195. René J. Francillon, "Air Safety Need Not Be Pie in the Sky." Reprinted with permission of the author. This editorial first appeared in *Newsday*, June 16, 1997. Page A27.

Page 201. Excerpt based on information in "Don't Rage over Steroids," by Jeff Riggenbach, which first appeared in *USA TODAY*, July 29, 1992. Reprinted by permission. Page 6A.

Page 202. Personal money excerpt based on information in *Newsday*, November 30, 1993, editorial, "Canada's Health-Care System Isn't for Us" by Leonard J. Morse.

Page 203. Julianne Malveaux, "Blacks Need Uncle Sam." Reprinted with permission. This article first appeared in *USA TODAY* on March 11, 1992. Page 10A.

Page 206. Rating code excerpt based on information in "Night Trap," *Newsday*, January 15, 1994, editorial.

Page 207. Income tax excerpt based on information in *Newsday*, January 15, 1994, *Viewpoints*.

Page 207. Panhandling excerpt based on information from "Subway Supplicants," in *Newsday*, January 15, 1994, *Viewpoints*. Page 18.

Page 207. Anna Quindlan, excerpt from "The Smoke Bomb" *New York Times*, January 14, 1994. Copyright © 1994 by The New York Times Company. Reprinted by permission.

Page 208. AIDS excerpt from "Relief for the AIDS Disaster," from *New York Times*, April 4, 1990. Copyright © 1990 by The New York Times Company. Reprinted by permission.

Page 208. Steven A. Beebe and Susan Beebe, "Delivering Your Speech," from *Public Speaking: An Audience-Centered Approach, 3rd. ed.* Copyright © 1997 by Allyn and Bacon. Reprinted/Adapted by permission. Pages 298–299.

Page 336. Samuel E. Wood and Ellen Green Wood, "What Kind of Care Is Best for Your Child?" from *The World of Psychology, 2nd ed.* Copyright © 1996 by Allyn and Bacon. Reprinted/Adapted by permission. Pages 317–318.

Page 346. David Masello, "About Men: In My Father's House," from *The New York Times Magazine*, January 2, 1994. Copyright © 1994 by The New York Times Company. Reprinted by permission. Page 13.

Page 356. Kartar Dhillon, "The Parrot's Beak," from *Making Waves* by Asian Women United of California. © 1989 by Asian Women United of California. Used by permission of Beacon Press, Boston.

Page 368. Arthur Ashe, excerpt from *Days of Grace* by Arthur Ashe and Arnold Rampersad. Copyright © 1993 by Jeanne Moutoussamy-Ashe and Arnold Rampersad. Reprinted by permission of Alfred A. Knopf, Inc.

Page 378. "The Lambert Family: 'City of Brooklyn' (Haiti)," from *Families of the World: Family Life at the Close of the Twentieth Century: The Americas and the Caribbean* by Helene Tremblay and translated by Hilary and Paul Childs-Adams. Copyright © 1988 by Famo Limited and translation copyright © 1988 by Hilary and Paul Childs-Adams. Reprinted by permission of Farrar, Straus & Giroux, Inc.

Page 389. James M. Henslin, "Diversity in U.S. Families," from *Sociology, 3rd ed.* Copyright © 1997 by Allyn and Bacon. Reprinted/Adapted by permission. Pages 317–318.

Pages 417, 419. Dictionary entries from *The American Heritage College Dictionary, Third College Edition.* Copyright © 1997 by Houghton Mifflin Company. Reprinted by permission from *The American Heritage Dictionary, Third College Edition.*